The Silk Road Gourmet

VOLUME ONE:
Western and Southern Asia

A Journey through the Cuisines of Georgia,
Armenia, Azerbaijan, Iran, Afghanistan,
Pakistan, Bangladesh, India, and Sri Lanka

Laura Kelley

iUniverse, Inc.
New York   Bloomington

The Silk Road Gourmet
Volume One: Western and Southern Asia

iUniverse books may be ordered through booksellers or by contacting:

iUniverse
1663 Liberty Drive
Bloomington, IN 47403
www.iuniverse.com
1-800-Authors (1-800-288-4677)

ISBN: 978-1-4401-4305-2 (pbk)
ISBN: 978-1-4401-4307-6 (cloth)
ISBN: 978-1-4401-4306-9 (ebk)

Library of Congress Control Number: 2009904674

Printed in the United States of America

iUniverse rev. date: 7/10/2009

For my husband, Stephen,
and my children, Miranda and Liam

Table of Contents

Introduction

About *The Silk Road Gourmet*

If asked, most people in the West would define Asian food as Chinese, Indian, or Thai food, with the more adventurous diners citing Indonesian, Japanese, or Korean food. Very few would say Uzbek or Burmese; and I bet that no one would mention Georgian food at all. But in fact all these cuisines are part of the great continuum of Asian food that sweeps and swirls in regional patterns across the continent. From the Caucasus and Caspian states of Georgia, Armenia, and Azerbaijan to the far reaches of Indonesia there are connections between the types of foods eaten and how they are prepared. If there is a purpose to this book, it is to introduce or in some cases to reintroduce these foods and flavors to the West in the hope that they will be incorporated into Western diets in a more regular way than they currently are.

To share my love of Asian food with readers, I have selected a handful of my favorite recipes from each country that I feel are a combination of the most delicious dishes I have encountered and those that help to illustrate the similarities and differences between the cuisines. This book is not intended to provide an exhaustive compendium of national cuisines, but rather to offer a first exploration of the abundant foods and flavors of

I

each regional or national cooking style. It is a toe in the water, if you will, not a headlong plunge into deep waters of Asian food.

Because of the expansive breadth of the subject, I have had to keep the depth of recipes relatively shallow—only a few recipes in each category are offered. Certainly for the larger, better known cuisines, such as Indian and Chinese, it would be possible to write an entire volume and still not plumb the depths of their food. In these pages, recipes are selected that were representative of the types of food—Meat Dishes; Vegetables and Salads; Sauces, Spice Mixtures, and Condiments; Rice and Grain Dishes and Breads; and Appetizers, Desserts, and Beverages—and styles of preparation used. To that end, and hopefully to the delight of the vegetarians amongst us, I have tried to place vegetable dishes on the same footing as recipes featuring meat by highlighting strongly flavored dishes that will easily sing solo on any vegetarian or omnivore table. The focus of most meat recipes are curries, stews, and stir-fried dishes—and to a lesser extent, roasted, grilled, or baked meats. Vegetable dishes are usually single vegetables sautéed or stir fried in thick, flavorful sauces, but there are some recipes for baked vegetables and fruits along with a few curries.

All of the dishes have also been selected with Western cooking styles and habits in mind. Where possible, without sacrificing authenticity of flavor, I have simplified preparation methods to fit the needs of Western cooks. Most recipes should take no more than one hour to prepare, and many should fall within the 15–30 minute range—providing cooks have a basic familiarity with the ingredients. Each recipe has not only been test-cooked by me but also by at least two friends or colleagues of varying cooking experience. Based on their feedback, I have often modified recipes or preparation methods to make them easier to understand for curious cooks with only moderate experience.

A word (or perhaps a warning) about measurement: I've never been much for real precision, and certainly that is not the way people cook in most of the world, where dishes vary by cook and even by different days that something is prepared by the same cook. For example, in much of

Southwest and Central Asia, recipes are given with ingredients such as "greens" in them, with no specific mention of whether the cook means dill, cilantro, or tarragon. This allows for a certain amount of creativity and individual variation on the part of the chefs and also allows them to use what they have on hand. By comparison, Western cookery has imposed something of an artificial uniformity on the art of the kitchen by demanding that all food adhere rigorously to prescribed recipes. All that aside, I have done my best to reconstruct the recipes according to how they tasted at the time and in the place that I had them in Asia. Any Asian cook worth bumming a recipe off of will have several variations of the dish, depending on her mood and the contents of her refrigerator or cellar. Most measurements provided are meant to be generous or heaping portions and not carefully leveled off. In the few cases where I felt that it was important to be precise, I have indicated for cooks to be exact.

Lastly, I hope that the recipes will be tasty enough and accessible enough to get Western cooks to use them in creative ways on an everyday basis. These delicious foods and unique flavor combinations no longer need to be confined to an occasional exploration of "ethnic" food. In our globalized world, a rich and delicately flavored Azeri pilaf should feel at home on the same table with a Western baked lamb chop, just as spicy Afghan potatoes should complement a hearty grilled steak. Likewise, mixing and matching recipes within Asian cuisines can also lead to unusual, flavorful combinations that may reveal connections between the cultures that created and nurtured them. May this book be a helpful guide to your own Asian food journey. Enjoy!

Cooking and Culture

As a young woman I studied anthropology. At the time, I was interested in physical anthropology, which, very roughly speaking, is the rocks, bones, and bodies side of the field. To complete my degrees, I had to take a great deal of cultural anthropology as well, which I suffered through. I was lucky enough to go to some fine schools that had some of the best professors in the field, and even though I squirmed or watched the clock through the lectures, I've found over the years that I learned a great deal about cultural anthropology despite my bad attitude. All around the world, people love their food and express their nationalism or ethnicity through the preparation of specific dishes that they identify as *belonging* to them. Dietary habits are so much an ingrained part of human cultures that some groups with strict habits inadvertently undernourish their children and put them at risk for poor growth, disease, and even death rather than change the foods they eat.

As my lifelong cooking hobby became a more consuming interest, I began to realize that food and preparation styles are an incredibly important aspect of a nation's or people's material culture and that these foods and preparation styles can often reveal links between cultures that people would rather not acknowledge or that have passed out of living memory. Food can help us reconstruct political histories of who ruled over whom and relationships of diplomacy and trade between people. Similarities between foods eaten can even reveal the belief in a common creed or system of worship and show how that belief has spread over time.

Above all, food and cuisines are not ideal forms fixed in time and space. Since man (or, for the most part when it comes to the preparation of food, woman) is the great experimenter, cuisines are always evolving. Each period of ingenuity and prosperity that links cultures for purposes of business, diplomacy, and trade also brings changes to the cuisines of those participating. For example, the Great Silk Road, which arose from the Afghan-Chinese trade in lapis lazuli and jade over four thousand years ago, eventually became a land and sea route that stretched thousands of miles and linked China with such faraway places as Roman Europe, North Africa, and the Levant states of the Middle East. As a result, Chinese foods and preparation methods such as stir frying spread west with the silks, gems, and spices, and flavors enjoyed in the west such as sesame, tamarind, and cardamom came east and were eagerly adopted by the Chinese people.

The modern era of globalization is also bringing about a global food revolution. The unprecedented rise in per capita incomes throughout the twentieth and into the twenty-first century coupled with the significant technological advances in agricultural practices has radically changed what most people eat. For starters, ecological disasters aside, most people have enough food that is nutritious enough to sustain them throughout their lives. For the mass of people living above subsistence level, this new wave of ingenuity and prosperity has increased food choices from those produced only locally to those brought in from elsewhere in the region or even from halfway around the world. Just as the global age of exploration brought New World foods such as peppers, tomatoes, and corn to the East or Pacific spices such as cloves and nutmeg to the rest of the world, so the current wave of globalization is bringing a whole world of food to the markets in the Caucasus and central Asian states that were dominated by the Soviet Union for most of the twentieth century. The markets that were once regulated and sometimes all but bare by ten in the morning are now teeming with delectable delicacies from the other side of the planet that can be had by anyone—for a price.

The modern era has also brought about global migrations of people the likes of which have never been seen before. As people move temporarily or permanently to different regions or countries, they are exposed to cultural and culinary influences that their more settled parents and grandparents could never have imagined. So as Georgians and Sri Lankans move around their regions and around the world, they begin to eat new foods and to prepare them in new ways. Because it is easier to communicate with people at a distance these days, the new cuisines and cooking methods that these migrants and diaspora populations have adopted can be shared with those left behind. This means that the spread of dietary habits has become faster and more abstract than ever before. Likewise, as the global market in cooking books and ethnic restaurants brings faraway foods to us in the comfort of our own communities, the ability to mix and blend dietary practices has been accelerated to warp-speeds in recent years.

Although all this change is interesting to ethnic food detectives like me, it sometimes also makes it difficult to determine which ingredients are new but bona fide parts of a cuisine and which may have been added by a nonindigenous cook simply to make the recipe more familiar to his or her palate. Where I have been fairly sure of the transgression by Western cooks, I have excised incongruous ingredients from ethnic recipes that just don't feel right to me. I've done my best to offer delicious authentic recipes for interested readers.

Patterns, Patterns Everywhere

Over the years, I began to notice distinct patterns in the use of ingredients by Asian peoples sometimes separated by thousands of miles. For example, pomegranates—the use of which began in Iran in antiquity—are now common ingredients from Georgia in the far northwest to Uzbekistan and Kazakhstan in the northeast. Examining the political history of the area, we see that successive Persian Empires ruled all of these areas at one time or another—often dominating the cultural landscape for hundreds or thousands of years at a time. Another example can be found in the distinctly Southeast Asian elements present in Sri Lankan cooking. In this case, lemongrass and roasted rice reveal strong connections between the island nation and countries of that region. Consulting the histories of trade and diplomacy for the countries, we find out that there was a vibrant maritime trade along the Silk Road in centuries past that Sri Lanka had with Burma, Thailand, and Malaysia.

If I could draw a line that separated western Asia from eastern Asia by taste, it would run diagonally through Lhasa and the western half of Burma or Myanmar, zigzag through Nepal, and continue on up through eastern Kazakhstan. On the south side it would separate Malaysia and Indonesia from other Southeast Asian and Pacific cuisines. Most food to the east of that line is influenced in some way by Chinese cuisine, and most food to the west of that line has strong elements of Indian or Persian cuisine. These "fusion" cuisines are fascinating and are explored in depth in volume two of this series.

One of the big themes of this series is that everyone's "national" cuisine that they feel defines them as a people has been influenced by someone else—sometimes extensively. All cuisines have the peaceful imprint on them of regional or global trade or of the more violent tides of war and conquest. This speaks volumes to the human need for social contact and to our ability to learn and adapt new ideas in ways that are both useful and comfortable for us. No nation's cuisine—not even that of the great, monolithic China—has remained untouched by others over the millennia.

The Great Silk Road

One of the major underlying bases for the connections between the cuisines of these countries that span thousands of miles is the trade and diplomatic relationships forged over thousands of years on the Silk Road. For several thousand years, these land and sea routes have linked China with lands as far away as Mediterranean Europe. Along with the goods that passed from one merchant to another, ideas, cultural and religious practices, and of course food and its methods of preparation flowed not only east to west, but west to east as well.

Geographically, the Silk Road is an interconnected series of ancient trade routes between Xi'an, China, with central Asia, the Indian subcontinent, Caspian and Caucasian states, as well as Europe and North Africa.

The northern and westward route extends through Xinjiang and into Kazakhstan, the middle westward through the Fergana Valley on the border of Kirgizstan and Uzbekistan before splitting into two routes.

Land and Maritime Routes of the Great Silk Road

The westward fork continued across central Asia and Iran before ending at ports in Mediterranean Turkey, while the southward fork skirted down through Pakistan and met with ships near Karachi that continued across the Arabian Sea towards the Levant and Africa. The route leading south out of Xi'an made a beeline down the eastern edge of the Tibetan plateau, through Burma, and into Bangladesh and Orissa to meet up with maritime routes in the ports of the Gangetic delta in the Bay of Bengal. Another easterly road travelled across north-central China before heading due south to ports in Hong Kong and Guangzhou, where it joined oceangoing ships that skirted down the edge of the South China Sea and into the Indonesian archipelago and Malaysia.

With all of this ancient contact going on, it is easy to see how cultures and cuisines separated by many thousands of miles influenced each other. Fortunes were made and commercial empires built on the flow of goods along these routes. In many places, trade was more important than politics: for example, in the early eighteenth century, the Bangladeshi ruler Nawab Alivardi Khan forced the British to pay an enormous fine for blockading Armenian and Mughal ships. The British never forgave the "cheekiness" of the fine, and that helped set the stage for their brutal reign over Bangladesh, which began only decades later.

Western and South Asian Trends

So what really are the western and southern Asian trends when it comes to ingredients and methods of preparation? Well, for starters, the two big dogs on the culinary influence block are the former Persian and Indian Empires, which dominate about half of the countries apiece. Most of western Asia owes large parts of its cookery to the Persians, which are represented today in part by the traditions of Iran and Azerbaijan. So, as one can see in Table I, which traces the origins of common ingredients used in southern and western Asian cooking, distinctive Persian elements such as pomegranates, sour cherries, sumac, and dried sour plums that are still used in Iranian and Azeri food are also important ingredients in Georgian, Armenian, and Afghan cooking. Sour grapes, on the other hand, which are a souring agent from southern Iran, are shared only with Afghanistan but are used only sparingly if at all in most Caucasus cooking. Also from the Persians comes the ubiquitous use of walnuts and lemons throughout the same region. Marigold petals are a unique Caucasian ingredient, adding color and a delicate but earthy flavor to recipes like saffron and turmeric. They are today found in the Caucasus and Azerbaijan but are not used in Iranian cooking. Quinces—which taste something like a cross between a tart apple and a sweet lemon—were first cultivated in Afghanistan and are eaten all across the region from Georgia into western Pakistan and north to Russia and central Asia.

Indian influence, of course, is felt in other subcontinent cuisines, such as that of Pakistan, Bangladesh, and Sri Lanka, but it also extends to Afghanistan and in part to Iran, as well. So the use of such native items as turmeric, oranges, curry leaves, and green cardamom is due largely to persisting Indian influence. Indian ingredients that have spread worldwide include sweet basil and black pepper. Surprisingly perhaps, quite a few of the "main ingredients" of Indian curries were first cultivated somewhere beyond the subcontinent, introduced in antiquity, and adopted by the Indians. Cilantro and coriander were cultivated first in Greece or elsewhere in the western Mediterranean, cumin comes from Iran, and tamarind is from Africa and brought north and east by traders from Arabia and the Levant states. Until fairly recently, Sri Lanka was the source of most of the world's cinnamon, and trade in the spice can be traced as far back as 1400 BCE, when the island nation traded their valuable commodity with the Egyptians.

Cross-continental trade in these flavorings is so old that it Is sometimes difficult for botanists to trace the region of origin of these plants and seeds. Written records, historical accounts, and modern methods of genetic analysis must be invoked to establish a clearer geographic picture of the spice trade in antiquity. Interesting perhaps is the number of important European and western Mediterranean seasonings in southern and western Asian food.

Table 1. Region of Origin of Ingredients Commonly Used in Southern and Western Asian Cooking

Region of Origin	Ingredient	Georgia	Armenia	Azerbaijan	Iran	Afghanistan	Pakistan	Bangladesh	India	Sri Lanka
New World	Potato	•	•	•	•	•	•	•	•	•
	Tomato	•	•	•	•	•	•	•	•	•
	Chili Peppers	•	•	•	•	•	•	•	•	•
	Allspice	•	•							
Pacific	Mace					•	•	•		
	Nutmeg	•		•	•	•	•		•	•
	Cloves		•	•	•	•	•	•	•	•
E & SE Asia	Lemongrass									•
	Coconuts					•	•	•	•	•
	Ginger			•	•	•	•	•	•	•
Indian Subcontinent	Cinnamon	•	•	•	•	•	•	•	•	•
	Curry Leaves						•		•	•
	Sweet Basil	•	•	•		•				
	Black Cardamom					•	•		•	
	Cardamom			•	•	•	•		•	•
	Turmeric	•	•		•	•	•	•	•	•
C Asia	Onion	•	•	•	•	•	•	•	•	•
	Garlic	•	•	•	•	•	•	•	•	•
	Tarragon	•	•		•					
	Dill	•	•	•	•	•				
W Asia or Persia	Marigold	•		•						
	Cumin	•	•	•	•	•	•	•	•	•
	Sour Plums	•		•	•	•	•			
	Sour Cherries	•		•	•					
	Sour Grapes			•	•	•				
	Fenugreek	•		•	•		•	•	•	•
	Sumac			•	•	•				
Europe or Western Mediterranean	Savory	•		•						
	Saffron	•	•		•		•		•	
	Oregano		•	•						
	Bay Leaf	•			•	•	•	•		
	Mustard						•	•	•	•
	Mint	•	•		•	•	•	•	•	
	Fennel	•			•	•	•	•	•	
	Cilantro	•	•	•	•	•	•	•	•	
	Coriander	•	•	•	•	•	•	•	•	•
Africa	Sesame	•	•	•		•	•		•	
	Tamarind				•	•	•	•	•	•

Coriander, cilantro, fennel, mint, and saffron—the use of these herbs and spices in Asia tells tales of habit and early trade rather than conquest or cultural commonality, and they were first cultivated in what is now Greece, Turkey, North Africa, or the Levant.

Using Table I to examine the origins of ingredients commonly used in southern and eastern Asian cuisines, we see that the country with the broadest complement of spices from around the Old World is Afghanistan, which incorporates flavors from Africa to the Pacific. This bespeaks Afghanistan's role as a crossroads between eastern and western Asia and also of the many peoples who have tried (and largely failed) to conquer it over the millennia. Both caravan traders and despots alike have left their marks on Afghanistan's cuisine. The next time you tuck in to a delicious Afghan kebab, breathe deeply and realize that you are about to consume thousands of years of history and cultural evolution in each bite.

Looking again at the ingredients mapped in Table I (which are reflective only of the recipes offered in this volume and do not represent an exhaustive list of flavors available in each country's cuisine), we can see important economic, cultural, and political connections between countries based on shared herbs and spices. Almost all of the cuisines in southern and western Asia use coriander or cilantro from the West, cumin from western Asia or Persia, onions from central Asia, turmeric and cinnamon from the Indian subcontinent, and cloves from the Pacific Rim. To a lesser extent, also common to most countries is the use of mint and saffron from the West, fenugreek leaves or seeds from Persia, cardamom from India, and ginger from China. So most of the variation between these cuisines is coming from the different proportions of the ingredients used and in the relatively fewer number of different spices not shared between them.

Combinations of spices are also fascinating to look at in terms of connections between cultures. One might argue that the masalas of western and southern Asia are simply the five-spice powders of the East, as can be seen by the side-by-side comparison of the two following recipes:

Afghan Char Masala
1 tablespoon black peppercorns
1 tablespoon cumin seed
1 tablespoon ground cinnamon
1 tablespoon black cardamom seeds
2 teaspoons whole cloves

Mongolian Five-Spice Powder
1 tablespoon Szechuan peppercorns
3 whole star anise corms
1 tablespoon broken cinnamon sticks
1 tablespoon fennel seed
1 tablespoon whole cloves

The proportions differ and some of the ingredients have been changed, but these two similar recipes undoubtedly were shared by the peoples that traveled and traded along the thousands of miles of the Silk Road that skirted the great mountains and deserts separating Afghanistan and Mongolia.

Examining how these connections play out in recipes—as will become more apparent as readers cook their way through the three volumes of *The Silk Road Gourmet*—we find connections between the Georgian cilantro-based **Garlic and Walnut Sauce** with the **Afghan Cilantro Sauce** and the sauce used in India's **Baked Fish with Lemon and Cilantro**. Rather than imagine that these similar sauces are independent inventions by cooks working thousands of miles apart, it is more likely that these sauces all come from the same common ancestor or that one of them was introduced and then adapted differently by each culture.

Likewise, Christian Armenia's **Zucchini-Egg Pie** is related to the egg pies still found in Muslim Azerbaijan and Iran in **Walnut Kuku** and in the **Kuku with Green Peas and Pistachios**. This style of cooking was probably introduced in Armenia during the Persian Sassanid dynasty, which ruled a territory from southern Russia and North Africa in the west to parts of India, Pakistan, and Kirghizstan in the east, from the third to the sixth centuries. The penchant for layering ingredients in casseroles such as **Fish and Vegetables with Black Pepper and Tarragon (*Kchuch*)** and **Vegetable Casserole with Garlic and Peppers (*Ailazan*)** may also have been introduced at this time, although the Armenians probably adopted it during one of the intermittent periods of Persian rule that took place between the fifteenth and seventeenth centuries. The Muslim Mughals also brought a similar love of layering east, as can be seen in rice preparations common throughout the Indian subcontinent, such as the **Chicken Biryani** offered in these pages.

My Favorite Recipes

I *like* all of the recipes in this volume of *The Silk Road Gourmet*, but I really *love* a few of them and want to bring those to your attention. Our Asian food journey begins in the western Asian nations of the Republic of Georgia, Armenia, and the Caucasus, and my favorite dishes from those regions are:

- **Grilled Chicken with Garlic and Walnut Sauce,** in which chicken marinated in lemon juice and a pungent spice mixture called *Khmeli-Suneli* that features the flavors of fenugreek and dill, is then blanketed with a spicy cilantro-garlic sauce

- The incredible **Fiery Lamb Chops in a Sweet and Sour Pomegranate Sauce,** with its blend of dangerously hot chili paste with a sweet and sour sauce

- **Meatballs in Lemon Sauce,** in which meatballs spiced with oregano and chili peppers are served in a thick and spicy lemon sauce similar to the Greek *avgolemono*

- **Beets with Sour Cherries** is a taste revelation that delicately blends sugary beets with apple cider vinegar and sour cherries with delicious results

- Your guests won't be able to get enough of the **Roasted Red Pepper Salad** with its combination of garlic and almonds in a light white vinegar dressing, and

- **Green Beans with Walnuts**, which blends the flavors of tomatoes with cinnamon and generous amounts of black pepper.

I have long enjoyed the many Persian-inspired dishes of the Caspian states, Azerbaijan, and Iran:

- **Lamb Chops with Sour Cherry Sauce**, which accents the natural, slightly sour flavor of the cherries with the addition of salt and cinnamon

- **Lamb in a Cardamom-Pomegranate Sauce** is a classic Iranian fesenjan that blends cardamom with cinnamon, pepper, and pomegranates and is further sweetened by the late addition of butternut squash to the mix

- For a change of pace, try the **Orange-Chicken Koresh,** in which orange and lime blend with almonds, pistachios, cinnamon, and cardamom in a delicious stew

- My husband simply insists that I include **Cinnamon Potatoes with Pine Nuts** on this list because he cannot get enough of this combination of cinnamon with apricots, currants, and potatoes

- Another Azeri treat can be found in the wonderful **Walnut Kuku,** which blends lemon and dill with walnuts and eggs for delicious results

- For a real change of pace on an everyday table, **Shiraz Tomato Salad** combines lime juice and grapeseed oil with almonds and mint for a real eye-opening dish.

From that wonderful crossroads of cuisines, Afghanistan, my favorite dishes are:

- **Meatballs with Garlic and Mint,** which is the first Afghan recipe I ever tasted and combines cilantro with lemon, garlic, and mint for a fantastic offering

- Although butternut squash may be prepared in many ways, the **Sweet and Spicy Squash** recipe is one of the most memorable I've encountered and blends ginger with sugar, garlic, and coriander.

From the part of the Indian subcontinent included in this volume, my favorite recipes are:

- The delicate Bangladeshi **Lamb Rezala** combines the sweet and sour flavors of sugar, vinegar, and a full complement of curry spices

- Also remarkable is the **Chicken with Pineapple Curry** that features a full complement of curry spices plus cloves, cinnamon, and pineapple

- **Cilantro Chicken**, with its lemony-cilantro sauce is a spicy Indian classic

- **Lamb or Pork with Vinegar and Spices (*Vindaloo*)** is another classic

- From Sri Lanka, **Curried Beef with Cinnamon and Lemongrass**, which is a remarkable blend of spicy, sour, and hot seasonings that is then moderated by sweeter flavors such as pandanus, cinnamon, cloves, and cardamom, and then blanketed in a delicious coconut sauce

- **Curried Scallops with Coconut and Lime** blends the sweetness of the red bell pepper, coconut milk, and sugar, with the crushed hot, dried peppers, lemongrass, and lime to bring out the very best in the scallops

- A delicate blend of northern beans and chickpeas can be found in the **Pakistani Mixed Bean Salad,** which brings together white vinegar, grapeseed oil, red bell pepper, and sugar for a sweet and cooling salad

- In **Tomatoes with Black Pepper and Cloves**, red peppers, cumin, and coriander provide the spicy curry base while the turmeric and black cardamom richen and deepen the flavor; a bit of *garam masala* sweetens the mix just before serving

- Potatoes to spice up any meal—Western or Eastern—can be found in the Indian **Ginger Potatoes** recipe in which ginger, fennel seeds, and turmeric are sautéed with potato chunks to yield this crunchy, spicy treat

- **Sri Lankan Spiced Rice** is a surprisingly delicate and flavorful rice blending black pepper, cardamom, turmeric, and cloves with lots of coconut milk. Great with a subcontinental curry or with a Western steak or chop.

Tastings

I come from a family of people who love to prepare and serve food, and I have fond memories of the days before major holidays or dinners spent in the kitchen getting everything ready for the feasts that would follow. An aspect of this traditional approach to major meals that is rapidly disappearing from a world in which people purchase food that has already been cooked is that these times spent in the kitchen together allow the women of a family to get together, share stories, and generally bond over the loving preparation of food.

To recapture some of this cuisine-oriented camaraderie, one great idea is to hold a themed tasting in which cooks bring a dish to share and taste that fits with the other dishes offered in a specific, preplanned way. For example, the theme could be an Azeri dinner in which a couple of people cook main dishes, a couple of people cook vegetables, and—you guessed it—a couple of people bring pilafs or salads. Around the table, you taste and talk about the food and the preparation and perhaps even the culture that inspired the cuisine while music from that country plays in the background. Diners learn about the food, about another culture, and about each other as they share ideas and stories over a richly appointed table. This approach brings me back to the long and lovely dinners in the garden that my mother used to host in which guests sang a song or recited a favorite poem or told stories over a wonderful dinner.

The three volumes of *The Silk Road Gourmet* lend themselves wonderfully to this type of activity. One can explore the cuisine of a country this way or even look for similarities or differences across countries by preparing, say, the five different stuffed pepper recipes offered in these three volumes for an informal get-together with some food-loving friends. The **Iranian Stuffed Pepper** combines the flavors of lime, mint, and cilantro in a nutty, rice stuffing; the peppers from Turkmenistan couple dill and mint with cumin and allspice; the stuffed peppers from Kirghizstan call for copious amounts of garlic and cheese with fenugreek and tarragon lightening up the mix; and the ones enjoyed in Tajikistan blend currants and nuts with cinnamon and star anise. The surprise stuffed pepper is, of course, the **Laotian Stuffed Pepper**, and the flavor combination of lemongrass and lime with onion, dill, and roasted peanuts will be an instant hit at any table.

Experiment, participate, communicate—but, above all, share the recipes offered in these pages with friends and family. As you cook and eat your way across Asia together, you may find yourselves growing closer over some really good food.

For more information about the Silk Road Gourmet, visit the blog at http://silkroadgourmet.com/blog

Metekhi Monastery, Tbilisi

Republic of Georgia

Main spices and flavors: sesame seeds, poppy seeds, sweet basil, bay leaves, caraway seeds, dill, fennel, tarragon, mint, fenugreek, savory, sour cherries, sour plums, marigold, saffron, savory, turmeric, coriander, cilantro, cumin, cinnamon, allspice, nutmeg

Souring agents: pomegranates, white wine vinegar, apple cider vinegar, lemons, oranges

The modern history of Georgia begins with two early Georgian kingdoms of late antiquity, known to ancient Greeks as Iberia in the east and Colchis in the west, around the shores of the Black Sea. It was to the wealthy kingdom of Colchis that Jason is said to have sailed the *Argo* in search of the Golden Fleece, which at that time lay at the reaches of the known Western world. Rome extended its reach east to include Georgia, Armenia, and several central Asian states by 66 CE, but before this time, eastern Georgia was strongly influenced by the Persians and western Georgia by the Greeks. Georgia remained a client state of Rome for several hundred years until the empire's ability to maintain its eastern territories disintegrated.

Sassanid Persians ruled Georgia and Armenia after Rome, and their rule was characterized by cosmopolitanism and tolerance. Georgian culture and Christian religious practice were allowed to flourish, as were the cultures in the rest of their empire, which ranged from North Africa to southern Russia and into parts of central Asia.

Persia and all of its holdings fell to Islamic conquest in the seventh century as Islam slowly spread. Arab rule during the hundred years of the Umayyad dynasty brought many elements of Arab culture to Georgia and Armenia, which were incorporated either by choice or by force. By the mid-eighth century, the mixed Persian-Arab Abbasids reasserted Persian control over the empire, and cultural tolerance was again extended to conquered territories. The Georgians quickly resumed most of their indigenous cultural practices, but many foreign practices and cultural elements—including some foods and dishes—that had been introduced were incorporated by choice. By the mid-tenth century, the Georgians had rebelled against the Persians and gained autonomous rule, creating the Georgian Kingdom, which one hundred years later was ruled by the Armenian Bagrationi dynasty.

By the mid-twelfth century, the Mongols swept through the region, destabilizing and subjugating it and causing Bagrationi central authority to wane and a period of local despotic rule to ensue. By the mid-fifteenth century, the Georgian Kingdom had completely dissolved, and the country was ruled by the Persians in the east and the Ottomans in the west. Seeking liberation from the Persians, the Georgians made allegiance with Russia and by the mid-eighteenth century were drawn into the Russian sphere of influence. Formal incorporation of Georgia into the Russian empire took place in 1801 but was not fully accepted by the Georgians until ten years later.

After the Russian Revolution, Georgia declared independence and had a brief period of self-rule that lasted until 1936 when it formally became part of the Soviet Union. Since 1990, when Georgia held the first multiparty democratic elections in the former Soviet territories, Georgia has been independent of Russia. Recent events in which Russia claimed to "protect" two of its provinces, however, throw its future independence into question.

Traces of all of these foreign influences on Georgian history can also be found in its material culture, including its culinary arts. For example, the Georgians share with the Persians many native Persian ingredients, including the common use of unsweetened pomegranate juice, sour cherries, and plums along with the use of fenugreek and cumin. Similar recipes can be found in the region as well, including vegetable and nut omelets called *kukus* by the Persians, the enjoyment of skewered meats both marinated and made with ground meats called kebabs, and similar types of layered rice pilafs.

Georgian cuisine is most closely related to Armenian cuisine—not only because of their shared border, but because Armenia (or its own rulers) ruled at least part of Georgia for almost one thousand years. From the seventh century onward, Georgians engaged in political, economic, and cultural contact with the Islamic world, and elements of Arab, Turkish, and Persian cuisines also can be found in the Georgian repertoire of flavors and foods. Although staunchly clinging to their Christian roots during periods of Islamic rule, the Islamic influence in Georgian food is undeniable.

Meat Dishes

Lamb, beef, and fowl of some kind are the most commonly eaten meats in Georgia. However, pork is eaten as chops, roast, or ground as part of a stuffing, and fish—usually whole or fillets—are also regular parts of the Georgian diet. Eggs of all sorts are also eaten—especially on a seasonal basis. When lamb is unavailable, the gamier, tougher mutton is used with extra steps taken to sweeten and tenderize the meat. Most meats are seasoned or marinated for hours (or even days) before cooking with pungent herbs and piquant spices—and more often than not, served with an accompanying sauce or as part of a flavorful stew.

Grilled Chicken with Garlic and Walnut Sauce

To begin on a high note, this is my favorite Georgian recipe. This meal once provided a welcome respite for me on a cold, wet evening in Moscow, and since that time it has been one of my all-time favorite meals. The flavor of chicken blending with the dill and fenugreek of the **Khmeli-Suneli** spice mixture is delicious and stands strongly on its own when either grilled or baked, and then there is the addition of the **Garlic and Walnut Sauce**—or *garo*—that produces a simply heavenly and original combination of flavors that I have experienced nowhere else.

I chicken cut into pieces or 2–3 pounds of meat on the bone, rinsed well and dried
1–2 teaspoons salt
I teaspoon freshly ground black pepper
I serving **Garlic and Walnut Sauce** (see Georgian Sauces and Spice Mixtures)

Marinade
½ cup light sesame oil or peanut oil
1 ½ cups lemon juice
2–3 tablespoons **Khmeli-Suneli** spice mixture (see Georgian Sauces and Spice Mixtures)
I teaspoon salt
I teaspoon ground black pepper

1. Salt and pepper the chicken with an even coat of spice. If using a whole bird, season the inside as well.

2. Combine marinade ingredients in a container large enough to hold all of the chicken pieces and whisk well. Add the chicken pieces and marinate in a cool or cold place at least overnight—turning the meat and spooning marinade over them occasionally. If the temperature is cold enough, feel free to marinate the meat for 24–48 hours to deepen the infusion of flavor. When the meat is done, remove it from the marinade, reserving the liquid.

3. The chicken will taste best if grilled outside over coals, but if using a broiler indoors, make sure the grill is very hot before placing the chicken on it. Grill for 10 minutes per side for most pieces and a bit more for the larger ones. Meat is done when the juices run clear on an average size piece of meat. Whole birds can be done on an indoor or outdoor rotisserie, if desired. When meat is done, remove from

the flame and arrange on a serving platter. Pour a bit of Garlic and Walnut Sauce (*Garo*) over them and serve.

Skewered Beef with Basil

This is a quintessentially Georgian skewered or "shish" kebab recipe that marinates the meat in unsweetened pomegranate juice spiced with onions, garlic, and a lot of fresh basil before grilling it over hot coals. The extra spices added to the meat just before cooking form a delicious crust around the tender, flavorful meat. Serve with rice or bread, chopped and lightly grilled tomatoes, and onions.

1 pound stew beef, cut into bite-size pieces
1 ½ cups of unsweetened pomegranate juice
2 tablespoons peanut oil
1 medium onion, peeled and diced
2 teaspoons garlic, peeled and diced
2 teaspoons salt
1 teaspoon ground black pepper
½ cup fresh sweet basil, chopped

1. In a large bowl or sealable plastic bag, combine the pomegranate juice, peanut oil, diced onions, garlic, and *half each* of the salt, black pepper, and fresh basil. Place meat inside bag and seal, ensuring the marinade evenly coats the meat. Place on a plate and marinate at least 3 hours, flipping the bag several times during the marinating process. The point is to infuse the flavors of the pomegranate and basil into the meat, not to appreciably soften the meat.

2. When meat is ready to cook, remove from the bag, discarding the marinade. String on skewers, leaving some space between pieces, and season with remaining salt, pepper, and basil (basil will have dried out somewhat—this is fine). Cook on a very hot grill or under a very hot broiler for about 5 minutes per side or until meat is browned outside and still pink inside. Serve with rice or a pilaf, and grilled onions and tomato wedges. Offer **Pomegranate Sauce** or other Georgian sauces for diners to use at will.

Grape Leaves Kebab

Grilled ground meats like this are eaten across the Caucasus, the Caspian, and Southwest and central Asia and do not belong exclusively to any one cuisine. I've adapted the original recipe so that it can be cooked in a Western broiler-oven instead of on the flat, swordlike skewers often used. If you'd like to try the traditional cooking method, skewers are available in most Persian markets. A helpful hint for skewering soft meat is to roll the meat right after blending, lightly flour, and then refrigerate for at least an hour before skewering. The cooking fire and grill must be very hot to cook the meat quickly and deeply. No matter how you cook them, the kebabs are great when served with plain rice or a pilaf with **Sour Plum Sauce** or a pickled vegetable nearby.

1 pound ground lamb or beef
1 medium-large red onion, peeled and chopped
2 teaspoons garlic, peeled and chopped
1 medium tomato, diced
1 teaspoon ground cumin
Zest of two lemons, finely diced
4 hot, dried, red chili peppers
20 grape leaves, well rinsed and stems removed
1 teaspoon ground coriander
1 ½ teaspoons salt
1 teaspoon ground black pepper

1. In a food processor, combine all ingredients—except the meat—and blend lightly so that the vegetables are chopped but still have their form. Then add the meat to the mixture and blend well. Transfer into a bowl and chill for several hours to firm the mixture up.

2. Preheat broiler on highest setting. Remove from refrigerator and roll the kebabs into sausages about 3 inches long and 1 ½ inches wide. Place on a baking sheet that has been oiled or sprayed.

3. Cook about 6 inches from the flame for 5 minutes per side. If meat still feels soft to the touch, cook another few minutes, but do not let the kebabs burn.

Beef and Mushrooms in a Tomato-Tarragon Sauce

This is one of my favorite dishes—especially on a chilly autumn afternoon. It's warm and flavorful with a rich tomato sauce of great depth—like one of Georgia's great fresh-water lakes. Once again, both sweet and sour flavors are evident. This time, tarragon provides the sweetness while sour plums offer up their tart essence. I like this dish in particular because the combination of spices from other cuisines—tarragon from the west, fenugreek from Persia, and coriander and cumin from South and Southwest Asia—come together to form a taste that is uniquely Georgian. Thousands of years of Georgian life went into this recipe, so sit back, relax, and taste the history with each bite.

2 tablespoons light sesame or peanut oil
1 pound stewing beef, cut into bite-size pieces
3 medium onions, peeled, and roughly chopped
1 cup beef broth (more as needed)
2 ½ tablespoons tomato paste
4 hot, dried, red chili peppers
1 tablespoon coriander seeds
1 teaspoon fenugreek seeds
1 ½ teaspoons dried tarragon
1 teaspoon ground cumin
1 teaspoon salt (or to taste)
2 teaspoons black peppercorns, cracked or coarsely ground
½ cup dried sour plums, pitted and chopped
1 ½ cups mushrooms, cleaned and thinly sliced
1 medium tomato, chopped
2 teaspoons garlic, peeled and coarsely chopped
½ cup walnut pieces, finely chopped or coarsely ground
1 small bunch fresh cilantro leaves, chopped (15–20 sprigs)
2 tablespoons butter

1. Heat oil in a sauté pan and when very hot, add beef and sauté quickly to sear the meat and seal the juices inside. When meat begins to brown on the edges, remove it from the oil with a slotted spoon and set aside. Lower heat to medium and add onions. Cook onions,

stirring occasionally for about 5 minutes or so, or until they start to become translucent and color.

2. Combine ¾ cup stock and tomato paste. Stir well until all of the paste is dissolved in the liquid. Grind coriander seeds, fenugreek seeds, and chili peppers into a fine powder. Add the tomato mixture to the onions together with the ground seeds, ground spices, salt, and peppercorns. Stir to mix well. Cook for 3–5 minutes to warm and blend spices.

3. Add meat and accumulated juices back to the pot and mix well. Reduce the heat to low and simmer covered until the beef starts to soften, about 30 minutes. Add more stock, a few tablespoons at a time, if the liquid in the sauté pan reduces too much.

4. In a separate pot, bring water to a boil and cook egg noodles until softened but still firm. Cover and remove from heat.

5. Add dried sour plums to the stew and mix well. Stir in the garlic, walnuts, mushrooms, cilantro and tomatoes; cover and continue to cook another 15 minutes or until the beef is tender. Drain egg noodles. Add butter and a pinch of salt and pepper, and place in serving dish.

Fiery Lamb Chops in Sweet and Sour Pomegranate Sauce

This dish combines the intense heat of lots of ground and slightly pickled red chili peppers in **Adzhika** with the rich sweet and sour flavor of **Pomegranate Sauce** to form a complex, layered taste for lamb or pork. When eaten, the heat is kept in check by the sauce, so it never overwhelms but rather teases and tantalizes diners for another bite. Free-range lamb would give this a truly authentic flavor causing diners perhaps to break out in song and ask you to refill their glasses with more Khvanchkara wine!

See recipe for **Adzhika** (see Georgian Sauces and Spice Mixtures)
See recipe for **Pomegranate Sauce** (see Georgian Sauces and Spice Mixtures)
4–6 lamb or pork chops (the thicker the better)
¼ cup beef broth

1. Wash and dry chops. Using a fork, pierce the chops on both sides in several places.

2. Spread the adzhika paste all over the meat. When the chops are lightly covered on both sides (the color of the meat should still be visible or it may become too spicy), place in a lightly oiled ovenproof pan or dish and refrigerate several hours or even overnight before cooking.

3. Preheat oven to 375°. Pour a small amount of beef broth to just cover the bottom of the dish and place in the oven. Cooking times will vary according to whether the chops have been boned or not. For chops with the bone in them, cook about 20 minutes on each side—gently turning them with a spatula to leave the *adzhika* crust intact. For chops without the bone, cooking times are approximately halved.

4. When chops are done, transfer them to a serving platter, ladle some hot pomegranate sauce over them, and garnish with chopped fresh cilantro leaves. Serve the remaining pomegranate sauce in a gravy boat so diners can add more if they desire.

Chicken and Tomato Casserole

This casserole has a flavorful red wine-, tomato-, and basil-based sauce that simply permeates the chicken, making it moist and delicious. I've adapted the original recipe from a stovetop-based one to an oven-based one to allow the flavors of the sauce to really work with the chicken instead of getting lost in the sauté. Wonderful when served with plain rice, simple pilaf, or boiled new potatoes.

2 tablespoons butter
1 chicken, cut into parts, or chicken parts on the bone, for 4 people
2 medium onions, peeled and diced
2 teaspoons garlic, peeled and diced
½ cup chicken stock
¼ cup red wine
¼ cup unsweetened pomegranate juice
2 tablespoons tomato paste
1 teaspoon salt
½ teaspoon ground black pepper
¼ cup fresh sweet basil, chopped

3 bay leaves
I small bunch fresh cilantro, chopped (15–20 sprigs)
2 medium tomatoes, chopped

1. Preheat oven to 350°. Lightly salt and pepper the chicken parts and set aside. Melt the butter in a deep sauté pan and sauté onions until they become translucent. Add garlic and cook until garlic swells and starts to color. Add chicken stock, red wine, and pomegranate juice and cook to heat.

2. When hot, add the tomato paste and stir well until dissolved. Add salt, pepper, basil, bay leaves, and cilantro and stir again. Add tomatoes and stir well. Cook covered for 5–8 minutes—stirring occasionally—or until the tomatoes start to give off their liquid. Remove from heat.

3. Spoon about ½ cup of the tomato sauce into a covered casserole. Add chicken parts and spoon the rest of the sauce over them, taking care to coat them evenly. Cover and cook in the preheated oven for 30 minutes, basting at least once as the chicken bakes. After 30 minutes, flip the chicken, baste, cover, and cook another 30 minutes, basting at least once during that time period. Chicken is done when it is loose on the bone to the touch.

A Stew of Lamb and Lemons

This lemony stew is sweetened by dill and celery, given an airy touch by the chopped cilantro, but kept earthbound by the lamb and of course by the last-minute addition of saffron. Serve it over rice or barley or in a deep bowl with a crust of bread to absorb the last of the sauce.

I pound of stew lamb cut into bite-size chunks
Salt and freshly ground black pepper, to taste
I tablespoon vegetable oil
3 tablespoons light sesame oil
I large red onion, chopped
2 large ribs of celery, including leaves, diced
3 teaspoons garlic, peeled and chopped
I heaping tablespoon finely chopped lemon zest
3 tablespoons fresh chopped dill (I tablespoon dried dill)
I small bunch coriander leaves, chopped (15–20 sprigs)

2 bay leaves
1 teaspoon salt (or more to taste)
2 teaspoons peppercorns, cracked or crushed
1–2 cups mixed chicken and beef broth
¼ cup fresh lemon juice
½ teaspoon saffron threads, dissolved in 2 tablespoons warm water

1. Heat oil in a saucepan and when very hot, add lamb and lightly brown it to seal in the juices. When lamb is seared, remove and set aside.

2. Reduce heat to medium, add the onion and the celery, and sauté until the vegetables start to soften.

3. Add the garlic, lemon zest, and two tablespoons of the chopped dill and stir well. Then add coriander, bay leaves, salt, and peppercorns and stir again to mix. Return lamb to the saucepan, stir again, and add enough mixed chicken and beef stock to cover (at least 1 cup). Bring stew to a boil and then lower heat to a gentle simmer. Cover and cook until lamb softens, about 45 minutes. Stir occasionally during cooking, and if more liquid is needed, add more stock.

4. After about ½ hour of cooking the stew, roll and juice lemons into a small bowl and add the remaining dill, salt, and pepper to taste. Add to the stew and stir well to mix.

5. Dissolve the saffron into the water and when lamb is soft and completely cooked, add the saffron and water mixture to it and stir well. Cook until contents return to full heat. Serve over cooked rice, barley, or other grain.

Vegetable Dishes and Salads

Eggplants, beets, and potatoes, you say? How can they form the backbone of unique and flavorful Georgian vegetable dishes? What could make them so special? My only response is to urge to you try these recipes, which are standouts on the rich Georgian table of vegetable dishes. What separate these vegetable dishes from the crowd are, of course, the unusual Georgian flavor combinations that create sweet and sour dishes unlike any others. Marigold petals and fenugreek leaves with a splash of pomegranate juice make the slightly bitter eggplant sing a rare, sweet tune in **Eggplant with Marigold Petals,** and with no added sugar, cider vinegar coaxes sugary syrup out of the vegetables in **Beets with Sour Cherries**. In **Walnut Potatoes**, on the other hand, the sweetness is offset by the chopped dill weed and the bitterness by the red wine vinegar.

Eggplant with Marigold Petals

This dish has such a rich and delicious flavor that it can stand alone as a main dish on vegetarian and omnivore tables alike. The spicy sweetness of the marigold petals mixed with the fenugreek and coriander brings out the best in the earthy eggplant, and it's like eating a slice of a lazy summer afternoon. Serve immediately after cooking for best and most balanced flavor.

I large eggplant, sliced crosswise into ½-inch slices
I medium red onion, peeled and chopped
3 tablespoons peanut oil
2 hot, dried, red chili peppers, diced
2 teaspoons garlic, peeled and chopped
I teaspoon ground coriander seed
I teaspoon dried marigold petals
I teaspoon dried fenugreek leaves
I teaspoon salt
½ teaspoon ground black pepper
2–3 tablespoons unsweetened pomegranate juice

1. Place eggplant on an oiled or sprayed baking sheet and cook in a preheated 400° oven for 20 minutes until done. When completely cooled, slice the roundels into quarters or eighths with a serrated knife.

2. Over low to medium heat, warm the peanut oil. When it is warm, add the chopped onions and diced chili peppers and sauté. When the onions start to soften, add the garlic and continue to cook.

3. Grind coriander, marigold, and fenugreek leaves to a fine powder and add to the sauté pan. Add salt and pepper and then add eggplant and stir well to coat with onions and spices. Add pomegranate juice and cook for a few minutes to fully warm the eggplant.

Beets with Sour Cherries

This combination of sweet and sour is, for me, a taste revelation! The full complement of the flavors—from apples and butter to dill, cherries, and beets—is amazing and truly unique! The one catch is that the dish has to be served immediately after cooking. If allowed to sit too long before serving, the beets overcome the other flavors and the dish tastes more vinegary than sweet.

3 medium-large beets, tops, bottoms, and greens removed, and rinsed well
I medium-large yellow onion, peeled and diced
2 tablespoons butter
2 tablespoons fresh dill, chopped (more if needed, depending on size of the beets)
¼ teaspoon salt (more if desired)
¼ teaspoon ground black pepper
I cup sour cherries, drained and rinsed
4 tablespoons apple cider vinegar

1. Wrap the beets in aluminum foil and place on a baking sheet. Put baking sheet in preheated 375° oven and bake for I hour, or until beets feel springy to the touch. Remove and let beets cool to room temperature.

2. When the beets are cool enough to handle, remove the skin with your fingers (if they are done, it should just slip off). Cut the beets into thick 1–2-inch-long julienne strips.

3. Heat butter in a large sauté pan and sauté onions. When the onions begin to soften, add the dill, salt, and pepper and mix well. Add cherries and any liquid that has accumulated after rinsing and mix again. Cook 3–5 minutes until the cherries start to break down and a sauce begins to form.

4. Add beets to the onion and sour cherry mixture and stir well. Add vinegar and stir again. Turn out of the sauté pan and serve immediately.

Stuffed Tomatoes with Walnuts and Dill

These tomatoes packed with walnuts and dill differ from most other stuffed vegetables in that they use cooked millet as the filling base. The Georgians traditionally ate lots of millet in porridges and pilafs until it was later replaced by corn and rice.

Stuffing
2 tablespoons butter
1 medium onion, peeled and diced
2 teaspoons garlic, peeled and diced
1 teaspoon salt
½ teaspoon ground black pepper
2 hot, dried, red chili peppers, diced
⅓ cup fresh dill, finely chopped
¼ cup vegetable broth or water
¾ cup shelled walnuts, finely chopped or coarsely ground
1 cup millet, cooked and cooled
4 large firm tomatoes, tops and insides removed

Stock
1 ½ cups vegetable stock or water
½ cup unsweetened pomegranate juice
2 tablespoons tomato paste
1 small bunch fresh cilantro leaves (15–20 sprigs) chopped
1 teaspoon ground coriander
½ teaspoon salt
¼ teaspoon ground black pepper

1. Melt butter in a large sauté pan and when warm, add onions and cook until they start to become translucent. Add garlic and cook until the garlic starts to swell and color. Add salt, pepper, dried chili peppers, and dill and stir well. Cook until dill begins to wilt. Add broth or water and ground walnuts and cook another minute or two. Add millet and mix well, lifting rather than stirring so you won't mash the millet.

2. When the ingredients are well mixed, remove from the heat and use to stuff the tomatoes. Stuff firmly but do not mash or rip the flesh of the tomatoes. Heat stock or water and pomegranate juice in a

large saucepan and when warm, stir in the tomato paste until fully dissolved. Add cilantro leaves, coriander, salt, and pepper and cook for 3–5 minutes to integrate the flavors. Add the stuffed tomatoes and cook uncovered for 20–30 minutes or until the tomato flesh is cooked but still holds its shape. Gently spoon broth over tomatoes at least once during the cooking process, but be careful not to add too much at once or the stuffing will overflow the tomato. Serve as a side or all by itself as a light meal.

Georgian Musician

Potatoes and Mushrooms in Clay Pots

Traditional Georgian cuisine uses clay pots to cook a wide variety of dishes. Baking in clay with broth allows for a combination of cooking and steaming to take place that results in dishes not unlike those cooked in tagines in North Africa. Most of the time meat is cooked together with vegetables, but on occasion, layered vegetables are cooked in this manner. Clay pots suitable for this sort of cooking are available at Asian groceries or from Internet retailers. Georgians use multiple small clay pots, but one larger one can be used as well. Regardless of the number of pots used, it is important to soak them in water for at least 15–20 minutes before using to let the clay absorb the water needed for steaming.

1 large onion, peeled and finely diced
3 tablespoons butter
2 tablespoons garlic, peeled and finely diced
2 teaspoons ground savory
¼ cup fresh tarragon leaves, finely chopped
2 hot, dried, red chili peppers, diced
¼ cup lemon juice
2 tablespoons tomato paste
1 ½ teaspoons salt
1 teaspoon ground black pepper
20 medium cherry tomatoes
1 pound king oyster or wild chicken mushrooms, cleaned and chopped*
20 medium new potatoes, parboiled or incompletely cooked in a microwave and halved
1 cup Kalamata or other dark olives (optional)
¼–½ cup water or vegetable broth (to top off layers)

1. Preheat oven to 350°. Soak clay pot(s) to be used in warm water for about 15–20 minutes. Remove the pots from the water and drain, inverted. In a large sauté pan, melt butter, add onion, and sauté until it starts to become translucent. Add garlic and cook until it starts to swell and color. Add savory, tarragon and diced chili peppers and mix well. Add lemon juice and tomato paste and stir well.

2. Cook 5 minutes to blend the flavors and then add salt, pepper, and cherry tomatoes and cook covered for 8–10 minutes, stirring occasionally, or until the tomatoes burst when pressed with a spoon. When tomatoes soften, add mushrooms and stir well. Cook covered another 8–10 minutes, stirring occasionally, until the mushrooms start to give off their liquid. Stir well and remove from heat.

3. Each pot should have at least three layers. On the bottom, place a thick layer of tomato and mushroom sauce. In the middle, place the potatoes (and olives, if using), and on the top, place more of the tomato and mushroom sauce. If using more than three layers, make sure that the top layer is the tomato and mushroom sauce. Repeat until all of the pots are constructed. Top each pot off with a tablespoon or two of

water or broth and cover. Bake in preheated oven for 1 ½ hours. Let stand to cool for at least 15 minutes before serving.

*Other types of mushrooms can be used if desired, but make sure to pick one that is full bodied and will stand up to cooking and baking, like the cardoncello or the wild chicken mushrooms. Alternatively, fish or another type of meat could be substituted for the mushrooms and cooking times adjusted accordingly.

Sweet and Sour Eggplant with Pomegranate Sauce

This dish combines the earthiness of eggplant with the sweet and sour magnificence of Georgian **Pomegranate Sauce** and is sure to change the mind of even the staunchest eggplant hater—as it did for my cousin Mary—about the tastiness of that vegetable. It goes especially well with **Grape Leaves Kebab** or a grilled meat, such as **Grilled Chicken with Garlic and Walnut Sauce** or **Fiery Lamb Chops in a Sweet and Sour Pomegranate Sauce.**

See recipe for **Pomegranate Sauce** (see Georgian Sauces and Spice Mixtures)
1 medium eggplant sliced crosswise into ½-inch slices

1. Place eggplant on an oiled or sprayed baking sheet and cook in a preheated 400° oven for 15–20 minutes until done. When completely cooled, slice the roundels into quarters or eighths with a serrated knife.

2. Heat 1 cup of Pomegranate Sauce in a sauté pan until hot, and add the eggplant slices. Stir to cover all of the slices with the sauce. Cook briefly, just enough to heat the eggplant, and serve. If needed, add more pomegranate sauce to the eggplants to moisten and add flavor, but do not saturate the slices. Serve additional sauce in a bowl or gravy boat for diners to add more as desired.

Beet Greens with Nutmeg Butter

This is a favorite dish from my childhood and I still love to make it, especially when the house is quiet and I have a chance to relax and reflect. It is one of my grandmother's recipes, acquired during her travels and shared with her daughters, who passed it on to their daughters. The nutmeg and the pepper in the butter nicely accent the slight bitterness in the greens. It works with almost any type of green, including spinach, but I like it best on beet greens.

½ pound beet greens or other greens, rinsed well
3 tablespoons unsalted butter
1 medium nutmeg corm, grated
¼ teaspoon salt
¼ teaspoon ground black pepper
¼ cup walnuts, finely chopped

1. Draw off any excess water from the greens by turning them in a salad spinner. Pack the greens tightly into a steamer and steam until greens begin to wilt. Remove from heat, and let drain.

2. When greens have drained, turn them into a sauté pan and distribute them to form as much of a single layer as possible. Dry fry them on very low heat for 2–3 minutes to help remove excess water. Add butter to the sauté pan and when melted, toss greens in the butter.

3. Add nutmeg, salt, black pepper, and chopped walnuts and stir to completely mix greens and spices. Continue to sauté until greens are completely cooked.

Potatoes with Walnuts and Dill

This robust dish is both sweet and sour at the same time! The sweetness comes from the dill and the sourness from the vinegar, which complement without interfering with each other. The depth is added by the diced or ground walnuts and the sautéed vegetables. This is a delicious stand-alone dish or one to complement a grilled meat dish, such as **Fiery Lamb Chops in a Sweet and Sour Pomegranate Sauce**.

1 tablespoon butter
1 medium onion, peeled and minced
1 teaspoon garlic, peeled and diced
1 teaspoon of salt
¾ teaspoon ground black pepper
4 medium potatoes, parboiled, cooled, and chopped

I cup of shelled walnuts, finely diced or ground
¼ cup water
¼ cup of finely chopped dill
4 tablespoons of unsweetened pomegranate juice

1. Melt butter in a sauté pan and when hot, add minced onion and sauté over medium heat until the onion starts to become translucent. Add garlic, salt, and pepper and stir well, then stir in the chopped dill and cook 2–3 minutes.

2. When onion is done, add walnuts and water and stir well. When the water heats and evaporates a bit, add the pomegranate juice and stir well. Add potatoes to the pan and mix, lifting rather than stirring to not break the potatoes. Then cook 5 more minutes or until potatoes are hot and serve immediately.

Green Beans with Eggs

This is Georgia's version of the Persian *kuku* or "anytime omelet" with vegetables along with herbs and nuts to flavor the eggs.

½ pound green beans, ends trimmed and cut into I-½-inch segments
I ½ cups water
2 tablespoons unsalted butter
2 small onions, peeled and finely diced
2 teaspoons garlic, peeled and diced
I teaspoon salt
½ teaspoon ground black pepper
2 teaspoons dried marigold
2 teaspoons dried tarragon, chopped
I tablespoon tomato paste
¼ cup walnuts, very finely chopped
Water or broth as needed
4 eggs, beaten

1. Place beans and water with a bit of salt in a medium sauté pan, cover, and heat. Water should not cover the beans but should come to about ¾ of their height. Boil and cook for 15–20 minutes, checking occasionally whether there is still water in the pan.

2. When water has almost boiled away, melt butter in the pan and sauté the onions until they begin to become translucent. Add garlic and cook until

garlic starts to color as well. Add salt, pepper, marigold, and tarragon and cook 3–5 minutes to blend the flavors. Add the chopped walnuts and the tomato paste and continue to cook another 2–3 minutes. If necessary, wet the ingredients with a tablespoon or two of water or broth.

3. Add eggs and stir once briefly to mix the beans. Lower heat and as the eggs cook, pull lightly at the edge of the pan and tilt to move liquid eggs from the center to the side of the pan. If desired, place the pan beneath a preheated broiler for a minute or two to firm up the top after removing the liquid eggs to the side.

Rice and Grain Dishes, Breads

Georgian cuisine has a full complement of rice and grain dishes and a wide spectrum of breads from the everyday **Lavash** and **Shoti** offered here, to more elaborate breads for holidays and special occasions, such as the **Bread Stuffed with Spinach and Cheese**. Nearly every Georgian meal I have been to has at least one pilaf offered along with the meat dishes or has meat incorporated into the pilaf and is the centerpiece of the meal itself.

Sweet Rice with Raisins

Here is the first sweet pilaf of our journey across Asia, and one that shows the Arab and Persian influences in the use of raisins and honey to sweeten the rice. It is particularly great with a sweet or a sweet and sour meat dish like the Georgian **Fiery Lamb Chops in a Sweet and Sour Pomegranate Sauce**.

4 tablespoons unsalted butter
I small onion, peeled and diced
½ teaspoon salt
¼ teaspoon ground black pepper
½ cup brown raisins
½ cup golden raisins
I cup uncooked basmati rice
2 ½ cups boiling water
¼ cup honey

1. In a medium saucepan, melt the butter and sauté the onion until it starts to color and become translucent. Add salt and pepper and stir well. Add both types of raisins and stir again.

2. Add rice in an even layer over the raisins and let steam for a few minutes. Boil water in a separate small saucepan as rice is steaming. When it is boiling, add it to the rice. Cover and cook over low heat for 20–30 minutes or until the rice is done.

3. When rice is done, place a plate on top of the saucepan and quickly turn the pan upside down, so raisins will lie atop the cooked rice. In a small saucepan, warm the honey and pour over the pilaf and serve.

Caraway Pilaf

Like the southern Russians, the Georgians adore the flavor of caraway seeds. Along with onions and garlic, caraway seeds provide a snappy spicy flavor for this simple but elegant pilaf.

2 tablespoons butter, melted
1 medium onion, peeled and finely chopped
1 tablespoon garlic, peeled and chopped
2 teaspoons caraway seeds
1 teaspoon salt
½ teaspoon ground black pepper
1 small bunch fresh cilantro (15–20 sprigs), finely chopped
1 cup rice, uncooked, rinsed
2 ½ cups water, boiled

1. In a large saucepan, melt butter and add chopped onions. Sauté until the onions start to become translucent. Add garlic and continue cooking until the garlic swells and colors. Add caraway seeds, salt, pepper, and cilantro and stir well. Cook over a low to medium heat until the caraway seeds swell.

2. Add the uncooked rice in an even layer over the onions and garlic and stir well. Cover and cook about 5 minutes to steam the rice a bit. As rice is steaming, heat water in a separate saucepan, and when it is boiling, add it to the rice. Cover and cook over low heat for 20–30 minutes or until the rice is done.

Lavash and Shoti

These two breads form the backbone of Georgian cuisine and are enjoyed with the wide variety of pickles, cheeses, and condiments that often grace Georgian tables, dipped in one of the cuisine's many flavorful sauces, or all by itself. The *lavash* is the round bread—like a crackly naan—and the *shoti* is the ∪-shaped bread that looks like Jason's ship, the Argo. The crusts dry and crack as the breads cool and age, providing a contrast between the harder outer surface of the bread and the soft middle. *Lavash* can be coated with any number of things but is most often enjoyed plain or with sesame or poppy seeds. The secrets to making these breads in a modern, Western oven is to preheat the oven to a very high heat at least 1 hour before baking and let it sit at high temperature until needed. Although it doesn't duplicate the conditions in a Georgian brick oven, it begins to come close.

1 package active, dry yeast
2 cups warm water
1 teaspoon sugar
3 ¼ cups unbleached flour
1 ¾ teaspoons salt
2 tablespoons peanut or corn oil
4 tablespoons toasted sesame seeds (optional)
3 tablespoons poppy seeds (optional)

1. Sprinkle yeast into warm water in large bowl and stir until dissolved. Add sugar and stir briefly again. Set aside and allow yeast to develop—about 10–15 minutes. While waiting for the yeast, combine the flour and salt in a large mixing bowl and mix to blend the salt with the flour. When yeast has begun to develop, mix it into the flour and salt and blend well. Turn out onto a bread board or a cutting board and knead for about 8–10 minutes. Oil a bowl that is at least twice the size of the dough mass and place the dough inside the bowl, flipping it to oil the top of the bread as well. Cover and place in a warm, quiet spot and let rise for 2 hours or until doubled in bulk.

2. Preheat oven to 450°. Turn the dough out onto the board and punch it down, dividing it into about 4–5 even pieces. Cover and let rise again for about an hour. When dough has risen for the second time, work

and flatten each piece of dough. Work the dough for each *lavash* into flattened circles by working it in a circular motion with your hands. Work the dough for each *shoti* into a flattened, elongated U-shape that is thicker in the middle than at the ends—sort of like an ancient boat. If desired, coat the *lavash* with sesame or poppy seeds or a mixture of both types of seeds.

3. Lower oven temperature to 400° and bake the breads on greased and floured baking sheets for 6–8 minutes for the *lavash* and 8–10 minutes for the *shoti*. Ovens vary, so keep a close watch on the bread and remove it when it reaches a nice golden brown color. I use one rack at a time, or if you wish you can use more than one, but allow for a slightly longer baking time for breads on lower racks.

(As an alternative baking method, you can turn an all-metal wok upside down in the center of the oven and "slap" the breads onto the side of the hot wok to cook. Make sure the wok is very clean and completely metal if you try this method.)

Bread Stuffed with Spinach and Cheese

The Georgians put lots of different things in bread, from meat to cheese, fruit, potatoes and other vegetables, along with onions, garlic, and spices with delicious results. These breads can be served at any time, but can also make a light meal in themselves when individually sized. In this example, spinach is combined with onions, garlic, just a hint of nutmeg, and Turkish whole-milk feta cheese, which is creamy and salty like the suluguni cheese that the Georgians use.

Pastry
4 cups all-purpose flour
1 teaspoon salt
½ pound butter
3 eggs
1 cup yogurt
½ teaspoon baking powder
1 egg yolk

1. Preheat oven to 450°. In a large mixing bowl, combine the flour and salt and cut the warm butter into the mixture. In a separate bowl, beat together the eggs, yogurt, and baking powder and combine with the flour to form the dough.

2. When all of the loose flour has come together, turn out dough onto a well-floured surface, lightly coat with flour, and then knead until smooth and elastic, about 5–8 minutes. Form into a ball and dust with flour. Let dough rest in a covered bowl in a warm place for an hour. Prepare filling while you wait.

Filling
4 tablespoons butter
10 spring onions, chopped (both white and green parts)
2 teaspoons garlic, peeled and diced
¼ cup finely chopped fresh cilantro
1 teaspoon salt
½ teaspoon ground black pepper
1 teaspoon freshly grated nutmeg
2 large bunches of fresh spinach, washed and drained
1 ½ cups Turkish feta cheese, diced
2 eggs, lightly beaten

1. In a large saucepan, melt butter and sauté the spring onions and cilantro until they wilt, and then add the garlic and cook until it starts to swell and color as well. Add salt, pepper, nutmeg, and then the spinach, all at once if possible. Mix well and cover. Cook for about 5–8 minutes, stirring occasionally, until the spinach is wilted. If spinach has given off a lot of liquid, drain and discard. When spinach is done, remove from heat and place in a strainer to drain. Press down on the spinach from time to time to facilitate the draining of the liquid.

2. In a mixing bowl, combine the feta cheese, drained spinach, and the beaten eggs and mix well. Add a little extra salt and pepper if desired. Form the spinach into the number of breads you want to make. The balls should be larger than a golf ball but smaller than a tennis ball.

3. Turn out dough onto floured bread board, lightly coat with flour, and then divide and flatten it until it is in pairs of disks about 8 inches

across. If you create an odd number of disks, simply take the last one and divide it into a pair of smaller disks.

4. Place filling in the center of one of the pairs of disks and spread it evenly over the surface of the bread, leaving ¾ inch around the edge that is just dough. Take the second dough disk and place it over the first to enclose the filling. Firmly seal the edges of the bread. Beat the egg yolk, brush the surface of the pastry, and place on a greased and floured baking sheet. Lower oven heat to 400° and bake for 20–30 minutes or until golden brown.

Desserts and Beverages

Georgia's cuisine is rich with desserts and sweets, such as the fruit and nut confection *churchkhela*—sweetened and flavored walnuts or hazelnuts strung together and dipped into fruit syrup and hardened over a series of days, which soldiers and men abroad would use to sustain them on long journeys. The few recipes offered here are those that a cook is most likely to use or to want to use on an everyday basis.

Ravane

Like *dolmas, ravane* is widely enjoyed from southwestern Europe and the Levant states through central Asia, although the recipe swirls and changes as it moves northward and eastward. The Georgians and the Armenians eat a more Persian *ravane* than a Greek one and use ground walnuts and almonds along with flour as the base of the cake.

Cake
1 cup unbleached white flour
1 cup ground walnuts
1 cup ground almonds, blanched and brown skins removed
2 teaspoons baking powder
6 eggs
½ cup sugar
½ cup butter, melted and cooled
Zest from 1 lemon, finely diced

Zest from 1 orange, finely diced
1 teaspoon ground cinnamon
¼ cup cream or half and half

Syrup
3 cups water
2 cups sugar
1 large cinnamon stick
½ lemon, sliced
½ orange, sliced

1. In a large mixing bowl, combine dry ingredients and mix well. In a separate bowl, whisk or beat eggs until frothy, then slowly add sugar a bit at a time until well mixed with the eggs. Add melted butter and diced lemon and orange zest, and mix again. Lastly, add the ground cinnamon and the cream or half and half. Combine wet and dry ingredients and mix well. The mixture is very dense and difficult to mix and you will probably have to stir by hand until well integrated.

2. Oil or spray a 9 x 12-inch baking pan and pour or spoon batter into the pan, spreading it evenly across the pan surface. Bake in a preheated 350° oven for 30–45 minutes or until a toothpick comes out clean from the center of the cake. When cake is done, remove from the oven to cool.

3. While cake is baking or at some time before baking, you can make the syrup. In a medium saucepan, heat water until boiling and then lower heat to a steady simmer and add sugar about a ¼ to ½ cup at a time. Stir constantly until sugar is dissolved and add cinnamon stick and citrus slices. Cook for 20–30 minutes to impart the flavors of the lemon and orange and cinnamon stick to the syrup, stirring often to make sure that the syrup is thickening nicely. Remove from heat and let cool about 15 minutes before removing cinnamon and fruit slices.

4. When syrup has cooled, prick the top of the cake with a fork or toothpick, but only go about halfway down—don't penetrate the cake completely. Little by little, pour the syrup in an even layer over the cake and wait for it to be absorbed. At first the cake will greedily take in the syrup and later it will absorb it more slowly. The point is

not to make the cake swim in the syrup but to provide enough syrup to moisten the cake and lend its fruity, cinnamon flavor. Cover tightly and let sit overnight before serving. Serve by cutting into diamonds or squares and placing onto individual serving plates. Garnish with chopped almonds or pistachios and a pinch of cardamom.

Apple-Walnut Cookies

If ravane is for holidays, then these easy-to-make cookies are for any time you please. In almost no time, these bake up into a delicious, healthful fruit and nut treat.

2 cups all-purpose flour
2 tablespoons baking powder
1 teaspoon salt
¼ cup sugar
1 teaspoon ground cinnamon
½ teaspoon allspice
¼ cup applesauce
¼ cup cream or half and half
1 cup cream cheese
1 cup lightly drained yogurt (*chaka*)
2 cups apples, peeled and diced
⅓ cup walnuts or hazelnuts (or a mix), chopped

1. Preheat oven to 300°. Mix the flour, baking powder, salt, sugar, cinnamon, and allspice together in a large mixing bowl. Add applesauce and cream or half and half, and begin to mix. Add softened cream cheese and lightly drained yogurt and mix again until dough begins to come together.

Georgian Clay Wine Bottle

2. Add apples and walnuts and work them in with your hands to make sure that they are evenly distributed. Use a folding motion and mix until all ingredients are thoroughly blended together. Make small 1-½-inch balls out of the dough and place on a greased or oiled baking sheet. Pat the balls to flatten them just a bit and bake in the preheated oven for 30–35 minutes or until done. When done, place on a rack to cool and enjoy.

Orange-Hazelnut Brittle

This is a variation on a traditional Georgian confection that is enjoyed particularly during the holidays, when well-wishers tell each other to "Grow old in sweetness," and pass some of this candy around. It is simple to make and can of course be enjoyed at any time of the year.

For variations, try different varieties of nuts or honey, such as clover or orange blossom.

1 pound hazelnuts, skins removed and roughly chopped
1 cup honey
2 teaspoons sugar
Zest of 1 orange, very finely minced

1. Dry roast the hazelnuts either in a sauté pan or spread out on a cookie sheet and under the broiler until they are very lightly toasted. Be careful not to burn them.

2. In a large saucepan, heat honey to a boil and stir in sugar and orange zest. Stir constantly and cook over medium heat for 2–3 minutes. Then add the hazelnuts and cook for another 10–15 minutes, stirring constantly. Line a cookie sheet or cutting board with wax paper and spread the nuts and honey onto the paper, forming a large square as you do. Let cool until not sticky to the touch—at least 1 hour.

3. When the brittle has cooled but has not become cold, cut into squares or diamonds and place on a plate to continue drying. If storing, keep in a covered box and store in a cool place or in the refrigerator.

Flavored Waters

With meals, Georgians traditionally drink wine and lots of it. No wonder, because they have so many flavorful varieties. Sometimes vodka is also shared, especially during toasts. As far as nonalcoholic beverages are concerned, however, the most quintessentially Georgian type are the flavored waters. These delicious treats are enjoyed across the country at home or in old-fashioned soda shops—Just like the ones that have all but vanished from the American landscape and been replaced by franchise coffee houses. The flavored waters come in many different flavors, from peach to pomegranate and coriander, but tarragon and citron are perhaps the most popular. You can make them with bottled water or, for a more traditional taste, homemade or store-bought seltzer. I like the natural flavor of the tarragon and the citron and so have made sugar optional.

2 quarts cold spring water or seltzer*

6 springs fresh tarragon, crushed
Salt or sugar as desired (optional)

Peel of one medium ripe citron or lemon, sliced
Sugar as desired (optional)

Let flavorings steep in the water for an hour or two, remove (strain if needed), and serve ice-cold or over ice.

*If using homemade seltzer, carbonate after flavoring has had a chance to steep in the water for a while.

Appetizers and Condiments

It is impossible not to *linger* at a Georgian table—both the food and the camaraderie is so fantastic! The meal has a rhythm all its own, waxing and waning as dishes come and go and glasses are filled—and emptied. Many meals are started with a "cold" fish course, which is really more a "cool room temperature" fish, such as **Freshwater Fish in Cilantro Sauce**. Also enjoyed are **Stuffed Grape Leaves** and **Pork and Onion Dumplings**, a variety of cheeses, olives, and homemade pickles such as the **Pomegranate Pickled Garlic** and **Red-Pepper Pickle** offered here. Above all, the starters for a meal provide a sampling of sweet, sour, spicy, and hot flavors for diners' palates that will be features of main-course dishes.

Freshwater Fish in Cilantro Sauce

This is a great starter for a large multicourse meal or can even be a light meal unto itself. The Georgians eat a great deal of freshwater fish, and an ideal fish to use with this recipe is river trout, river carp, or even catfish. The Georgians eat this dish chilled, but I prefer it at room temperature. A popular variation is to add about a half-cup of chopped fennel while sautéing the onions and garlic, which gives the dish a wonderful licorice-like flavor.

1 ½–2 pounds of trout, carp, or catfish filet, cut into serving-size pieces
1 ½ teaspoons black peppercorns, crushed
2 teaspoons salt
2 cups water
1 large onion, peeled and diced
2 teaspoons garlic, peeled and diced
2 bay leaves
1 small carrot, finely diced or shredded
1 cup of fresh cilantro leaves, very finely chopped
½ cup white vinegar
½ cup unsweetened pomegranate juice

1. Rinse filets well, pat dry, and season on both sides with *half* the salt and pepper. Heat water in a large saucepan and add onions, garlic, bay leaves, carrot, and remaining salt and pepper. Cook for 10 minutes on a strong, steady simmer to infuse the flavors into the broth.

2. Add fish by sliding the fish into the hot broth from a spatula. Poach fish for 5–8 minutes so it is still firm but nicely cooked. When done, remove from the broth and set fish aside.

3. Mix finely chopped cilantro with vinegar, pomegranate juice, and ¼ cup of the broth the fish cooked in. Pour cilantro sauce and fish into a coverable container and seal as the fish cools.

A Plate of Hinkali

Sautéed Feta Cheese

This is a classic Georgian appetizer with the flour and herbs forming a crispy crust and the Turkish feta a warm and creamy center. The Georgians use a salty, aged feta called suluguni that is similar to the whole-milk Turkish feta available in Persian grocery stores.

½ pound Turkish feta cheese, cut into ¼ to ½ inch slices
½ cup all-purpose flour
½ teaspoon salt
¼ teaspoon ground black pepper
I teaspoon dried tarragon (or other dried herb)
½ stick butter

In a mixing bowl, combine flour, salt, pepper, and herbs and mix well. Pour flour onto a flat plate. Rinse the slices of cheese in water and dredge lightly in flour on both sides. Melt butter in a medium sauté pan, and when melted, lower heat to medium-low. Place floured cheese into the butter for several minutes a side, and when crust starts to color, remove from pan and place on a plate to drain.

Pork and Onion Dumplings (Hinkali)

Meat- or cheese-stuffed dumplings are a Georgian specialty enjoyed all across the country. Recipes vary from region to region and even between households, from meat dumplings with caraway seeds to cheese with lots of ground black pepper to mixed fillings spiced with dill or other greens. This recipe blends pepper and the greens-based meat filling with delicious results. Serve as an appetizer in a multicourse meal, as part of a "tapas" Georgian dinner with lots of little bites, or even as a light supper.

½ pound ground pork
2 medium-large onions, peeled and finely diced
2 teaspoons salt
I teaspoon ground black pepper
I teaspoon fenugreek leaves
I teaspoon tarragon leaves
2 hot, dried, red chili peppers, finely diced

2 cups whole wheat flour, sifted
1 cup warm water

1. In a large bowl combine ground meat, onions, 1 ½ teaspoons of the salt, and pepper and mix well with your hands. Add the fenugreek, tarragon, and diced chili peppers and mix again. Set aside.

2. Place flour in a bowl and indent the top. Add the remaining ½ teaspoon of the salt and pour about half of the water into the bowl and mix. Add remaining water as needed to fully moisten the flour and to get it to form a ball. You shouldn't need quite the whole cup. Knead the dough for about 5 minutes and roll it out and cut it into circles or grab small golf-ball-sized pieces of dough and work them by hand into thin circles of dough. You should not be able to see through the dough if you hold it up, but it needs to be close. Dough too thin will probably not stand up to filling and cooking.

3. Place about a tablespoon or two of filling in the center of the dough circles and gather the edges together in the center, pinching and twisting until they form a flower bulb shape. Make sure that the dumpling is fully sealed before moving on to the next one.

4. When all the dumplings are done, boil enough water to completely cover the dumpling in a large saucepan. When water is boiling, turn heat down until water enters a steady slow boil. Then drop dumplings in one by one and boil for about 10–12 minutes. Set on a rack or paper towels to drain and serve as soon as they're dry with lots of ground black pepper.

Stuffed Grape Leaves (Dolma)

Dolmas or *dolmades* are eaten from Greece through central Asia and, although not uniquely Georgian, are enjoyed regularly as part of large meals or as a light snack to accompany a glass or two of Georgia's strong red wine. Can be made with any meat, but lamb and beef are by far the most commonly used.

½ pound ground lamb or beef
½ cup rice, cooked and cooled
1 medium onion, peeled and very finely diced

⅓ cup freshly chopped dill
Zest of 1 lemon, finely diced
1 teaspoon salt
½ teaspoon pepper
2 dozen grape leaves, unrolled, rinsed, and patted dry
2 tablespoons butter
1 ½ cups beef stock (plus enough to top off the grape leaves as they cook)

1. In a mixing bowl, combine meat, rice ,onion, dill, lemon zest, salt, and pepper and mix well until spices and other ingredients are evenly integrated into the meat. Trim the hard stems from the grape leaves and lay out flat on a cutting board.

2. Depending on the size of the leaf, place a tablespoon or two of filling in the center of the leaf and first fold in the left and right edges of the leaf to enclose the meat. Then, fold up the bottom edges, and roll the leaf, from the bottom up, tucking the edges in as you roll to fully jacket the meat.

3. When all *dolmas* are rolled, place each one seam side down in a sauté pan large enough to hold them in a single layer. In a small saucepan, combine the beef stock and the butter and when hot, pour it over the dolmas. Simmer covered over very low heat for about 45 minutes to 1 hour, topping off the broth as needed. The *dolmas* shouldn't be swimming in the broth, but they do need to be moist or they won't cook evenly. When they're done, there should be very little liquid left in the pan. Remove to dry and serve on a platter with sour cream or yogurt spiced with garlic and salt.

Pomegranate Pickled Garlic

This is a wonderful and very strong accompaniment to a Georgian meal. Eat as one of several appetizers with bread or use as a condiment for meat dishes. The garlic cloves are made sweet and sour by the addition of pomegranate juice and vinegar and spiced up with peppercorns and chili peppers with delicious results.

2 large heads of garlic (about 60 cloves), peeled
3 tablespoons salt

2 teaspoons sugar
I cup of unsweetened pomegranate juice
¼ cup of white wine vinegar
I tablespoon black peppercorns, cracked or lightly crushed
3 hot, dried, red chili peppers
I tablespoon fresh dill, chopped

1. Place the peeled garlic in a sterile glass jar and add the salt and sugar. Cover and shake to mix. Let stand on the counter for 1–2 hours, shaking every now and then to get the garlic to start to break down and give off its liquid.

2. Heat the pomegranate juice and the vinegar in a small saucepan to bring to a boil. Add the peppercorns, the sliced or torn chili peppers, and the dill to the garlic and then top off with the pomegranate juice and vinegar mixture. Cover and shake well. Store refrigerated for at least 2 weeks before eating.

Northern Beans with Sour Plum Sauce

This condiment is both flavorful and cooling and nicely offsets most Georgian meat dishes. Although sliced red onions are usually served as a garnish for the dish, this recipe finely dices them and adds them directly to the salad. Also, the authentic Georgian condiment is usually made with kidney beans, but I prefer it with great northern beans or chickpeas to appreciate the flavor of the sauce. Best served at room temperature or slightly cooler to allow the full flavors to shine through.

3 tablespoons **Sour Plum Sauce**
I cup northern white beans (drained, rinsed, and drained again)
½ cup red onion, finely diced
I small bunch of coriander leaves, finely diced (15–20 sprigs)
½ teaspoon lemon juice
Salt and pepper to taste

1. Combine the beans with the sour plum sauce and stir to coat. Add the onions, coriander, lime or lemon juice, salt, and pepper and stir again.

2. Let cool in the refrigerator for several hours. Take out and let stand about 45 minutes–1 hour before serving to bring toward a cool room temperature.

Jonjoli

Jonjoli are the pickled flowers of the Georgian bladderwort bush (*Staphylea colchica*) that are enjoyed as appetizers. In truth, although they appear to be, jonjoli aren't really pickled flowers, they are pickled seed pods that have formed at the base of the flower that taste citrusy—sort of like capers. They are difficult to find in stores in the West but are available at some Armenian specialty stores, farmer's markets, and in the wild—if you are a forager. If using a wild source, watch the flowers bloom and the seed pods begin to ripen and pick the stems just before the flower has fallen away. The flowers clump together several on a stem.

2 cups jonjoli flowers and seed pods
1 cup water
¼ cup salt
1 cup sugar
1 cup cider vinegar

1. Rinse flowers by dipping into still water and agitating just enough to clean them. In a separate jar or crock, mix water and salt and stir until the salt is dissolved. Grab the bunch of jonjoli by the stem and place them into the crock, flower side down. Cover and let stand 2 days, then remove from the brine.

2. Heat vinegar and sugar until sugar has completely dissolved and mixture begins to boil, and pour into a sterile jar. Place jonjoli flower stalks into the vinegar, flower side down, and seal.

Red Pepper Pickle

Here's another sweet and sour pickled vegetable that tastes so familiar that it's almost European.

4 large red bell peppers, quartered, seeded, and defleshed
¾ cup white wine vinegar
½ cup unsweetened pomegranate juice
½ cup grapeseed oil or other fruit oil
1 small head of garlic (about 20 cloves), peeled and finely diced
1 medium bunch of cilantro, chopped very finely

1 teaspoon salt

1 teaspoon sugar

2 teaspoons black peppercorns, cracked or lightly crushed

1. Quarter the peppers and seed them. Place on a baking sheet skin side up and put under the broiler until the skins have blackened. Cool, then peel off the skins and discard them. Slice the peppers into strips.

2. In a mixing bowl, combine the vinegar, pomegranate juice and oil and whisk well. Add the garlic and cilantro and continue to stir. Add the salt, sugar, and peppercorns and mix again. Add the pepper strips and mix again. Place into plastic or glass containers and refrigerate for at least 3 days before using. Serve with bread.

Sauces and Spice Mixtures

Shakespeare might have said, "The *sauce* is the thing," if he had dined on Georgian cuisine—so rich in its array of sweet and spicy sauces. Often presented simultaneously at the table, a variety of sauces allows diners to choose which flavor they want to use on each dish, offering a certain amount of customization of food to take place at the table according to the diner's whimsy. For those wishing a spicy, lemony twist to their meat or vegetable there is Georgia's famous **Garlic and Walnut Sauce (Garo)**, while those wishing a bit of sweet and sour can opt for the **Pomegranate-Basil Sauce** instead. Although more of a condiment than a sauce, the dangerously hot **Adzhika** is amazing on both meat and vegetables, especially when paired with a sweet and sour sauce such as **Sour Plum Sauce** or **Satsivi**. I find that most Georgian sauces age spectacularly, and I recommend preparing them at least a day or two in advance of the meal.

Garlic and Walnut Sauce (Garo)

Georgians use this sauce in one form or another on almost everything! They use it on a wide variety of hot or cold meats; they use it on fried or baked vegetables. I've even tasted it on egg dishes or as a spread on a hearty slice of crusty bread. The principal flavors come from the ground fenugreek and the lemon and how they give depth and brightness to the mass of fresh cilantro leaves and walnuts ground up with them. The *Garo* will taste better if it is prepared a day or two in advance and reheated for the meal.

2 small to medium bunches of fresh cilantro leaves
1 heaping tablespoon chopped garlic
1 ½ cups walnuts, chopped
1 ½ cups chicken stock
4 tablespoons lemon juice
1 generous teaspoon ground coriander
2 generous teaspoons fenugreek seeds
1 level teaspoon ground turmeric
1–2 dried red chilies crushed (optional)
Add salt and black pepper to taste

1. Place washed fresh cilantro leaves, chicken stock, lemon juice, garlic, and walnuts in a blender or food processor and grind until you have a thick sauce, carefully adding more chicken broth if needed for smoothness. When desired consistency is achieved, add fenugreek seeds, coriander, turmeric, and chilies (if desired) and continue blending until seeds are roughly ground.

2. Empty contents of container into a medium saucepan and heat over medium heat until it just starts to boil, stirring often. Then lower temperature to simmer and cook sauce for about 10–15 minutes to allow flavors to blend. When done, cover and remove from heat.

3. Just before roasted or grilled meats and vegetables are served, reheat the sauce, add enough to the dish to flavor without saturating the meal, and pour into a gravy boat to allow guests to add as little or as much additional sauce as they wish.

Pomegranate Sauce

This wonderful sweet and sour sauce is a Georgian-Armenian take on a common Caucasian and Caspian flavor. Throughout northern Iran and through Azerbaijan, pomegranates are used as "souring agents" for dishes and sauces, not unlike how tamarind is used in South, Southwest, and Southeast Asia.

The take that the northern Caucasus and Caspian countries offer is a slightly sweetened pomegranate. In this sauce, the sweetness is provided primarily by sweet basil, but a bit of sugar can also be used. My advice, however, is to hold off on the sugar until you've tasted the sauce without it.

1 bottle pomegranate juice (unsweetened) (4 cups)
½ cup red onions, finely diced
1 heaping teaspoon coarsely chopped garlic
⅛ cup finely chopped fresh basil or 1 heaping teaspoon dried basil
1 small bunch fresh cilantro leaves, finely chopped (15–20 sprigs)
1–2 hot, dried, red chili peppers, crushed
1 teaspoon sugar (optional)
Salt and pepper to taste (if desired)

1. Empty the pomegranate juice into a medium saucepan and cook over medium heat. After the juice has come to a boil, reduce heat, bring to a steady simmer, and cook uncovered until reduced by half until about 2–2½ cups of juice remain.

2. When sauce is at least halfway reduced, add onions, garlic, basil, and coriander. As the coriander begins to thicken the sauce, add crushed pepper (if desired) and cook for another 15 minutes or so. Remove from heat and add salt and pepper, if desired.

3. Just before roasted or grilled meats and vegetables are served, reheat the sauce, add enough to the dish to flavor without saturating the meal, and pour into a gravy boat to allow guests to add as little or as much additional sauce as they wish.

Sour Plum Sauce (Tkemali)

This is another one of the Georgian sauces with a multitude of uses. It is commonly used to complement heartily spiced grilled meats and brings sweetness and light to earthy beef or pork kebabs. Other uses include lifting the flavor of red beans and other legumes. It is also often a part of an ordinary table, so diners can use it on whatever they please. The plums themselves are both sweet and sour, the fennel and mint offer further sweetness and depth, and the lemon juice and garlic bring up the tartness.

8 ounces of dried sour plums (available at Persian food stores or via the Internet)

1 small bunch of fresh cilantro (15–20 sprigs)
1 tablespoon mint, chopped
1 teaspoon chopped garlic, peeled and diced
1 ½ teaspoons coriander seeds
1 teaspoon fennel seeds
2 hot, dried, red chili peppers, very finely diced
¼ cup water or beef broth
2 teaspoons fresh lemon juice
¼ teaspoon salt (optional)

1. Place prunes in a saucepan and just cover with water. Bring to a boil and then reduce heat to a high simmer for 5–10 minutes. Remove prunes and discard liquid.

2. When prunes have cooled enough to touch, remove the pits. I find that removing the pits is easier to do if one waits several hours or even a day after boiling. Waiting also seems to yield more prune meat.

3. In a blender or food processor, combine coriander seeds and leaves, garlic, fennel seeds, chili pepper(s), and lemon juice and grind until the base of a sauce has formed. Add the prune meat and half the water and broth and mix on pulse until all ingredients combine to form a sauce. Add additional water as necessary.

4. Pour mixture into a saucepan and heat to a slow boil. Cook for 2–3 minutes and remove from heat. Cool and store in a container until use. Makes about ½ cup.

Satsivi

This is a sweet and flavorful sauce that Georgians use on a wide variety of meats. It is usually served at room temperature after the freshly cooked meat has been covered with generous amounts of sauce and allowed to cool slowly. Works particularly well with poultry, beef, or lamb.

1 cup walnut kernels
¼ cup white wine vinegar
½ cup chicken stock
1 medium onion, peeled and minced very finely
3 cloves garlic, peeled and diced

½ teaspoon ground cinnamon
1 teaspoon dried marigold
1 teaspoon ground coriander
1 teaspoon dried fenugreek leaves
2 bay leaves
2 hot, dried, red chili peppers, diced
½ teaspoon ground black pepper
½ teaspoon salt

1. Grind walnuts, white wine vinegar, and chicken stock in a blender. Then add minced onions, garlic, cinnamon, marigold, and coriander and grind again. Add fenugreek, bay leaves, red chili peppers, ground pepper, and salt and mix again.

2. Pour contents of the blender into a small saucepan and heat over low heat. Cook 10–15 minutes to blend flavors and then another 15 minutes to thicken slightly. When done, remove from heat until needed. If necessary, warm again before serving.

Khmeli-Suneli

This is Georgia's ubiquitous five-spice powder that has many uses in the kitchen and on the table. It is a delightful blend of earthy fenugreek leaves and airy dill, with savory and marigold bringing up the bass. Its most common use is for a flavorful rub or a marinade ingredient for meats prior to cooking, but it can also appear on the table to be used at the discretion of diners. There are many different recipes for it, and even within a single household spice proportions will change according to what is being cooked or simply to reflect individual preference. For example, if used as a fish rub, you might wish to increase the proportion of dill; when used as a rub for lamb or beef, savory and fenugreek could become the strongest flavors. Variations or additions to the recipe below include dried basil, bay leaves, or parsley.

1 tablespoon coriander seeds
2 teaspoons dried dill
2 teaspoons dried savory
2 teaspoons dried fenugreek
2 teaspoons dried marigold

Grind coriander seeds in a food grinder. Add dried spices; grind again briefly to blend.

Adzhika

This is a hot and spicy ground paste of chili peppers, sweet peppers, and spices that is widely used in the Georgian kitchen and on the table. It is usually prepared in large batches and used over the course of several weeks. Cooks use it to add spice to dishes; diners use it like a condiment to add a little heat to dishes that lack a bit of zing. Sometimes it is even used as a main spice in meat recipes, like the chop recipe offered earlier in the chapter. The ingredients lend many layers of flavor, which become deeper and richer as the days pass—so prepare it several days in advance of using it.

1 cup hot, dried, red chili peppers
1 celery stalk
1 red sweet bell pepper, cored and defleshed
1 heaping tablespoon chopped garlic
1 cup fresh dill, roughly chopped
½ cup fresh cilantro leaves, roughly chopped
¼ cup red wine vinegar
1 teaspoon dried tarragon
1 teaspoon dried fenugreek
½ teaspoon salt

1. In a blender or food processor, combine the sweet red pepper, celery, chili peppers, chopped garlic, and vinegar, and grind until you have a light pink paste.

2. Add the dill, tarragon, fenugreek and the coriander and grind again until well blended. Add salt (if desired).

3. Spoon into a container, seal, and refrigerate until needed for use. Makes about 1 cup.

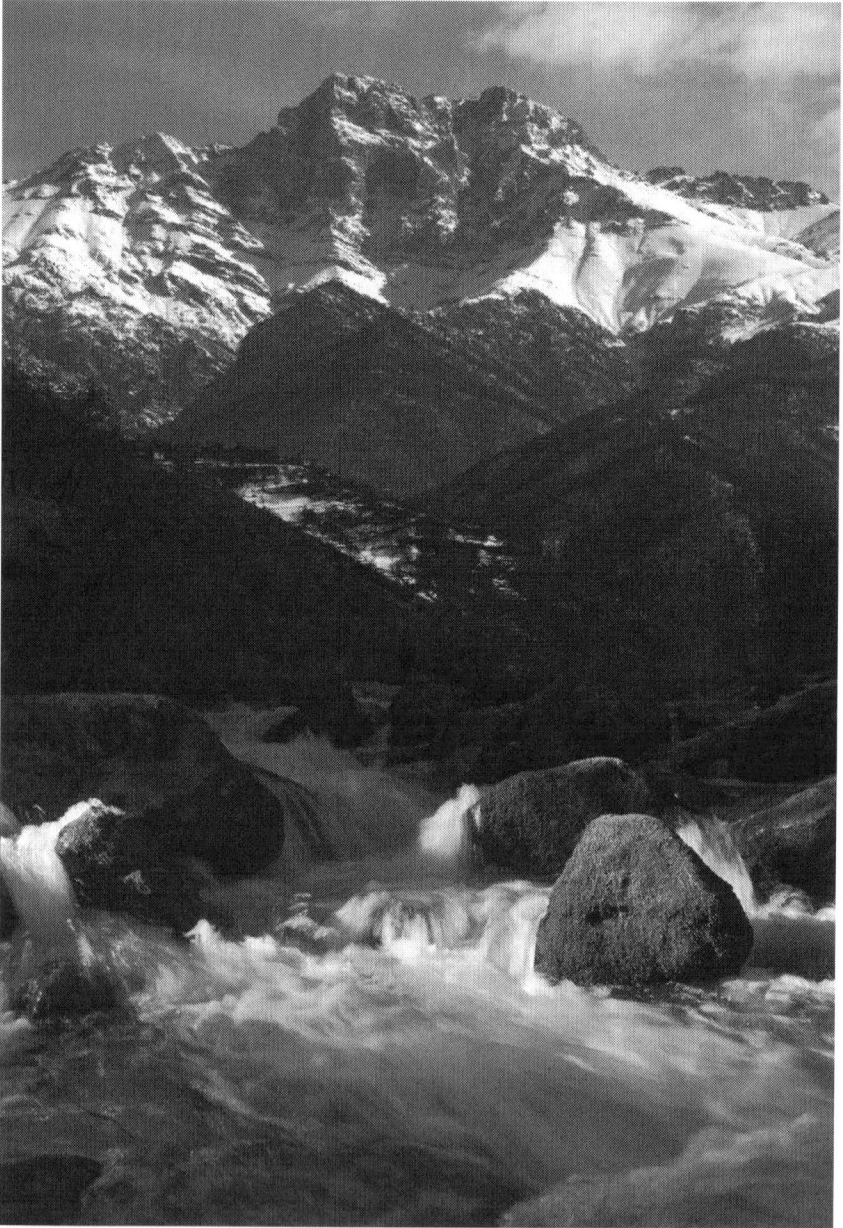

The Mountains of Armenia

Armenia

Main spices and flavors: sesame, sweet basil, mint, oregano, bay leaves, fenugreek, saffron, dill, tarragon, turmeric, coriander, cilantro, cinnamon, cloves, allspice

Souring agents: pomegranates, lemons, white vinegar

Over the years, Armenia's lush mountains and valleys have been ruled by the Greeks, the Romans, Persia, Turkey, and Russia. In turn, it has—either for itself or for a foreign power—ruled portions of Georgia, Azerbaijan, Iran, Turkey, and Syria. All of these cultural contacts have left marks on what is today considered Armenian cuisine.

In 301 CE, Armenia was the first nation to adopt Christianity as its national religion. Armenians felt so strongly about their religion that they entered into an unwinnable war with the Sassanid Shah in the fifth century, who met them with an army of over 200,000 fighters—some riding war elephants. Despite their military defeat, the Armenians won the right of religious freedom from their Sassanid masters—with tolerance having won a great victory.

Every hundred years or so until the middle of the ninth century, Armenia changed hands, and it wasn't until the Bagrationi dynasty took power that the borders of the country became more settled, occupying the lands currently known as Armenia and southern Georgia. In the late eleventh century, Seljuk Turks defeated the remains of the Byzantine Empire, and Armenia fell to Ottoman rule once again. Given its strategic significance as a pathway between the Black Sea and the Caspian, Armenia was tossed around between the Turks and the Persians periodically between 1500 and the mid-seventeenth century.

It wasn't until the early nineteenth century that Armenian borders became really settled as the Republic of Armenia in the Union of Soviet Socialist Republics. Russian cultural domination led to the suppression of many things Armenian, and it wasn't until 1991 that Armenia resumed its course, abandoned in the eleventh century as a free republic.

Given all of these relationships, Armenian cuisine has elements of all of these cultures in it. Shared with the Greeks is their wonderful lemon sauce, evident in **Meatballs with Lemon Sauce**. With Syria and other Arab states, they share the **Pine Nut and Sesame Pilaf**; with Persia and modern Iran they share the use of pomegranates, fenugreek, and walnuts, as seen in **Skewered Pork with Pomegranates** and in many of the stewed meats and vegetables. With the Turkmen of central Asia they share the use of bulgur wheat in place of rice for making pilafs. With Armenia's strategic position near the northern Silk Road, it shares many, many foods and methods of preparation with other cultures, despite the sometimes negative political influence that contact brought to the Armenians.

Meat Dishes

Lamb is by far the most commonly eaten meat in Armenia with beef following a far second and chicken or other fowl taking up the slack. Traditionally, pork was not eaten, given their strict Christian roots, but most modern Armenians eat it without compunction, and it falls somewhere in between beef and chicken in its popularity.

Like Georgian meats, Armenians often accompany their meat with flavorful sauces such as those seen in **Meatballs in Lemon Sauce** and

Skewered Pork with Pomegranates. Another trend that Armenia shares with other western and southwestern Asian nations is the use of spices traditionally considered "sweet" in the West, such as cinnamon, nutmeg, and cloves to season meats—evident in the recipes for **Lamb Chops with Mint and Sweet Basil** and **Lamb or Beef Kebabs** offered in these pages. As far as I am aware, the dough covering used when cooking **Fish and Vegetables with Black Pepper and Tarragon (Kchuch)** is a uniquely Armenian preparation method, although the layering of ingredients is a generalized trend seen throughout western and central Asia and probably was adopted during one of the several periods of Persian rule.

Meatballs in Lemon Sauce

This is a great introduction to the wonders of the Armenian table! The zesty, spicy meatballs in a rich lemon-flavored sauce are truly delicious. Match with plain fluffed basmati rice or with one of the pilafs offered here, such as **Red Pepper and Mushroom Pilaf** or the **Traditional Armenian Pilaf**, and you will have the basis for a great meal.

1 pound ground lamb or beef
1 medium onion, coarsely chopped
Zest from 2 medium lemons
2 hot, dried, red chili peppers
1 egg
2 tablespoons tomato sauce
1 small bunch fresh cilantro (15–20 sprigs)
1 teaspoon dried oregano
2 teaspoons salt
1 teaspoon ground black pepper
1 ½ cups vegetable broth
1 cup water
2 tablespoons unsalted butter
2 egg yolks
1 tablespoon lemon juice

1. In a food processor, combine onion, chili peppers, lemon zest, egg egg, tomato sauce, cilantro, oregano, salt, and pepper. Mix well. Add meat and blend again until well mixed. Refrigerate 1 hour before

rolling. Shape into 2-inch meatballs. Refrigerate for 1 hour before cooking.

2. In a large sauté pan, bring the broth to a boil over medium-high heat. Melt butter in the broth. Add meatballs and reduce the heat to medium-low. Cook covered, until meatballs are tender, about 30 minutes. Spoon broth over meatballs several times during cooking and turn meatballs over after about 15 minutes. If may be necessary to lower the heat to low to keep them cooking only gently.

3. In a small bowl, beat the egg yolks. Stir in lemon juice. Add ½ cup hot broth and mix well. When meatballs are done, remove from the broth, reduce the sauce if necessary, and add the egg-lemon mixture—stirring or whisking steadily as you dribble the mixture in. When the sauce is done, heat until it starts to thicken and add meatballs back into the sauce. Cook to warm meatballs and serve.

Skewered Pork with Pomegranates

Just making the marinade for this dish produces a beautiful aroma in the kitchen! The fragrance of warm pomegranates mixed with oregano smells like a long-overdue homecoming. And the taste of the marinated pork cooked on skewers, with just a little broiled crust around the edges, is heavenly! Served over a simple rice or pilaf, this is a truly wonderful supper.

1 pound boneless lean pork, cut into 1 ½ - to 2-inch cubes
3 cups pomegranate juice
1 tablespoon olive oil
3 teaspoons oregano
2 teaspoons salt
1 teaspoon ground black pepper
2 tablespoons plain yogurt
1 large onion, cut into chunks
12 cherry tomatoes
½ teaspoon onion powder
½ teaspoon garlic powder

1. In a small saucepan, heat unsweetened pomegranate juice until it boils. Lower heat until the juice simmers. Cook uncovered for about 1 hour

until it has reduced to about ¾ cup. Stir occasionally to make sure that the juice does not burn.

2. In a large bowl, combine *half each* of the oregano, salt, and black pepper with the yogurt and olive oil and ½ cup of the pomegranate syrup. Add the pork, stir thoroughly, and pour into a sealable, gallon-size plastic bag. Marinate at room temperature for 3 to 4 hours, or overnight in the refrigerator, turning the pork about in the marinade every hour or so to keep it well moistened.

3. Remove the pork from its marinade and without rinsing, string the cubes on skewers. Season meat with remaining salt, pepper, and oregano. String tomatoes and onions on separate skewers and season with garlic and onion powder. Broil 4–6 inches from the source of the heat for 10–15 minutes, turning the skewers frequently so that the pork browns well on all sides. The vegetables may be done sooner and should be removed from the oven when done.

4. Briefly reheat leftover pomegranate syrup. Remove from heat and serve skewered meat and vegetables and spoon the extra pomegranate syrup over the meat or serve separately.

Lamb or Beef Kebabs with Cinnamon and Cloves

These delicious kebabs have a partial litany of what Westerners consider "sweet" spices in them. Yet they are simply flavorful and delicious. Serve with a pilaf and a side vegetable or pickle for the foundations of a wonderful meal.

1 pound ground lamb or beef
1 medium onion, peeled and chopped
5 spring onions, sliced
8 cloves garlic, peeled
1 ½ teaspoons ground cinnamon
2 tablespoons white peppercorns, ground
2 teaspoons fresh thyme
5 bay leaves
¾ teaspoon ground cloves
1 small bunch fresh cilantro leaves (15–20 sprigs)
2 teaspoons salt

1. Grind pepper and cloves until they form a fine powder. Then in a food processor combine all ingredients except the meat and blend lightly so that the vegetables are chopped but still have their form. Add meat to the mixture and blend well. Roll the meat into 4-inch sausages, place the sausages on a plate, and chill for several hours to firm the mixture up.

2. Preheat broiler on highest setting. Remove sausages from refrigerator and place them on an oiled or sprayed baking sheet and place pan under broiler about 4–6 inches from the flame.

3. Cook about 5–8 minutes on each side. If meat still feels soft to the touch, cook another few minutes, but do not let the kebabs burn. Serve with rice pilaf, and a salad or pickled vegetables.

Lamb Chops with Mint and Sweet Basil

Another nice way to prepare lamb that is flavorful and easy to prepare. The long time in the marinade allows the flavors of the mint and basil to really infuse the meat that just pops when the meat is grilled. It works well with a bulgur or rice pilaf and a salad or a vegetable.

4 lamb chops (the thicker the better)
1 cup dry red wine
1 yellow onion, peeled and diced
1 small bunch fresh cilantro, chopped (15–20 sprigs)
1 teaspoon salt
½ teaspoon ground black pepper
1 teaspoon dried mint
1 teaspoon dried sweet basil

1. Pour the wine into a large covered casserole and then add the onion, cilantro, salt, pepper, mint, and basil and stir or whisk well. Add lamb chops and tuck underneath the onions and cilantro. Spoon wine over the chops, cover, and set aside.

2. Marinate 3–4 hours at room temperature or overnight in the refrigerator. When ready to cook, remove the chops and discard the marinade. Grill over coals or place beneath a broiler for 5–8 minutes per side. Serve hot.

Fish and Vegetables with Black Pepper and Tarragon (Kchuch)

This is a delicious and slightly spicy way to prepare fish that has come in handy many times during Lent in our family. The overwhelming flavor of the black peppercorns gives spice to this dish, not unlike some of the wonderful Portuguese fish dishes. Then lifting it to new heights, the tarragon and wine temper the pepper just enough to make this a new taste sensation. In the traditional dish, it is cooked covered with a dough lid, which functions as a semipermeable membrane. It is a meal unto itself but can be served with a little extra rice or a simple pilaf and a salad for a well-rounded meal.

1 pound meaty, white fish, filleted
2 large onions, peeled, sliced, and separated into crescents
4 tablespoons butter
3 medium tomatoes, diced
1 tablespoon black peppercorns, crushed
1 ½ red bell peppers, cored, defleshed, and thinly sliced
1 cup precooked rice
½ cup dry white wine
½ teaspoon ground red pepper
3 tablespoons tarragon
2 teaspoons salt

1. Preheat oven to 375°. Salt and pepper the fish fillets, then cut them into large chunks; set aside. Melt 2 tablespoons butter in a large, covered, ovenproof casserole, and tilt to spread butter up the sides of the dish. Remove from heat.

2. In layers, place the following from the bottom up: rice, half the sliced onions, half the diced tomatoes, and peppercorns. Add half the salt, tarragon, and red pepper. Then, place peppers on top of the tomatoes and the fish slices above them. Place remaining onions and tomatoes in two layers above the fish. Season with remaining spices and a pinch or two more peppercorns, and cover with wine. Cover tightly and bake in a preheated oven for 15 minutes. Then uncover and bake another 40–45 minutes or until fish is done. Baste with liquid from the cooking casserole occasionally.

Vegetable Dishes and Salads

Armenians simply love their vegetables and eat them as main dishes or significant side dishes whenever possible. Even their pilafs have generous portions of vegetables in them—all a consequence of them living on some of the most fertile farmland that Asia has to offer. The most western Asian or even European influence is seen in the simple **Mushrooms with Cilantro and Dill** recipe offered in these pages. More common Armenian uses of vegetables are those baked in casseroles, such as in the **Armenian Vegetable Casserole (*Ailazan*)** or those made into tomato-based stews, such as **Stewed Okra with Apricots** or **Green Beans with Walnuts**. With the Persians, the Armenians share the type of egg and vegetable preparation known as a kuku—seen in the **Zucchini Pie** recipe—but more so than the Azeri or the Iranians, the Armenians tend to use a lot of cheese with their eggs.

Vegetable Casserole with Garlic and Peppers (Ailazan)

Ailazan is a traditional Armenian vegetable casserole—but with an unusual array of spices, including red pepper, that give it an extra kick. It works well as a side dish to roasted chicken or lamb or as the centerpiece to a lovely vegetarian meal.

1 medium eggplant
2 medium potatoes, sliced crosswise
2 medium onions, peeled and sliced lengthwise and separated into crescents
3 medium tomatoes, chopped
2 red bell peppers, sliced thinly
2 tablespoons fresh sweet basil, chopped
2 tablespoons fresh thyme, chopped
1 medium bunch cilantro leaves, chopped (25–30 sprigs)
3 tablespoons garlic, peeled and diced (1 medium head)
1 teaspoon ground black pepper
½ teaspoon ground red pepper
2 teaspoons salt
2 tablespoons unsalted butter

1. Preheat oven to 375°. Slice eggplant crosswise and place cut side down on a sprayed or oiled baking sheet. Bake in preheated oven for 20–30 minutes until dry to the touch. Let cool and cut into smaller bite-sized pieces as other vegetables and spices are prepared.

2. In an oiled, covered casserole dish, layer vegetables starting from eggplant and potatoes on the bottom, followed by onions and tomatoes, and lastly by red bell peppers. In between each layer, add a bit of salt and pepper, some of the chopped herbs, and garlic.

3. Dot with butter and cover tightly. Bake covered in preheated oven about 15 minutes, then cook uncovered another 30–40 minutes or until done.

Okra with Apricots

This is an interesting recipe in which the apricots provide a blast of sweetness when you bite down on them in an otherwise tart dish. The sauce blends lemon and tomato with fenugreek and a bit of cinnamon for very tasty results. The secret to making it is getting the freshest, smallest okra you can find in the market and cooking them that day.

1 pound okra, sliced crosswise
3 tablespoons unsalted butter
2 medium onions, sliced and separated into crescents
1 ½ cups vegetable broth
¼ cup tomato paste
1 teaspoon salt
½ teaspoon ground black pepper
¼ cup lemon juice (about 1-2 lemons)
12 dried apricots, soaked and diced
½ teaspoon dried fenugreek leaves
¼ teaspoon ground cinnamon
½ teaspoon sugar

1. Heat butter in a sauté pan over medium heat and sauté onions until they start to soften and color. Add vegetable broth, tomato paste, salt, and pepper. Continue to cook until broth heats up, then add lemon juice and okra.

2. Bring to a near boil, then cook covered for 10 minutes, stirring occasionally. Then uncover and add apricots, fenugreek, cinnamon, and sugar and continue to cook another 5–10 minutes or until okra is done. Serve with rice or bulgur.

Armenian Roasted Red Pepper Salad

This is a really lovely salad! The softness and smokiness of the roasted peppers works with the roasted almonds, garlic, and white vinegar to transcend the usual pepper salad flavor. This is a great accompaniment to roasted meats, kebabs, and stews.

3 red bell peppers, cored, defleshed, and cut in half or quarters
2 teaspoons garlic, peeled and chopped
2 tablespoons white wine vinegar
¼ cup grapeseed or other fruit oil
½ teaspoon salt
¼ teaspoon ground black pepper
¼ cup slivered almonds, roasted

1. Preheat broiler to high. Dry fry the almonds over low heat, stirring constantly, until the almonds take on a light golden color. When done, remove from heat and set aside.

2. Flatten the pepper halves or quarters onto an oiled baking sheet, skin side up. Place under a preheated broiler until skin chars brown and black. When charred, remove from the heat and set aside until cool enough to handle.

3. Peel the charred skin off of the peppers and discard. Then slice the peppers into thin strips and place in a mixing bowl. Add the diced garlic to the peppers and fold them together.

4. Whisk oil, vinegar, salt, and pepper together and pour over the peppers and mix well. Sprinkle the slivered almonds over all and mix again. Let sit for at least 30 minutes. Serve slightly cooled.

Armenian Woman in the Field

Stuffed Apples

Although Westerners may look askance at a baked, stuffed apple being included in a section on vegetables, it is an important cultural difference between East and West. This apple is sweet and uses cinnamon, nutmeg, and raisins, but it is most often served with kebabs, a meat chop, or roast as a vegetable. Further south and east, the Afghans enjoy quinces, stuffed

73

and baked in this manner, and the Azeris and Iranians will often serve sweet or sweet and sour fruit-based jams to accent a spicy meat dish. So relax and enjoy a familiar dish in a new way as you continue your journey through Asian food.

3–4 large tart or all-purpose apples, cut and cored
1 cup uncooked rice
2 ½ cups water
1 teaspoon salt
½ cup raisins
½ teaspoon cinnamon
½ teaspoon freshly grated nutmeg
⅓ cup granulated sugar
¼ cup melted butter

1. Add salt and rice to the boiling water and cook covered until rice has absorbed most of the water—about 20 minutes. Add raisins to the cooking rice, cover, and cook until rice is done. Remove from heat and set aside to cool.

2. Prepare apples so that the tops are removed and they are hollowed out to leave ¾ of an inch of apple around the empty center. Sprinkle 2–3 tablespoons of sugar inside the cored apples, then combine remaining sugar and melted butter with the cinnamon and nutmeg and pour all over the rice and raisins and mix well.

3. Fill the apples with the mixture and add a pinch of cinnamon to the top of each. Replace the apple tops and arrange in a baking dish. Add a small amount of water around the apples and bake in a preheated 350° oven until the apples are done—about 30–40 minutes. Baste occasionally as the apples cook.

Mushrooms with Cilantro and Dill

This is a delicious and quick-to-make vegetable side dish that adds a flavorful, tangy accent to your table. Whether paired with Asian meat dishes or other vegetable dishes, this is an unusual way to prepare mushrooms that will even go well with a thick steak or other European-based fare.

1 pound white mushrooms, cleaned and thickly sliced
3 tablespoons unsalted butter
6 spring onions, diced crosswise
1 teaspoon garlic, peeled and diced
2 tablespoons vegetable broth
1 medium tomato, chopped
1 teaspoon salt
¼ teaspoon ground black pepper
1 tablespoon lemon juice, warm
¼ teaspoon saffron
1 small bunch fresh cilantro leaves, chopped (15–20 sprigs)
1 tablespoon fresh dill, chopped

1. Heat butter in a sauté pan and sauté the onions until they start to soften and color. Add the garlic and continue to cook until the garlic swells. Add the vegetable broth to just moisten the mixture, then add the tomato, salt, and pepper and cook until the tomato softens. Heat lemon juice in a small saucepan or in a microwave until warm, and dissolve the saffron into it.

2. Add the cilantro and the dill to the tomato mixture and cook until they wilt, stirring constantly. Add the lemon juice and the dissolved saffron and stir again. When the lemon juice is hot, add the sliced mushrooms and stir in until well mixed. Cover and cook the mushrooms for about 10 minutes over medium heat until they give off their liquid, stirring occasionally. Then uncover and cook another 5–8 minutes or until they are done. Do not overcook. Serve hot with rice or bulgur if desired.

Zucchini Egg Pie

This is an example of the egg-vegetable or egg-meat combinations eaten throughout the Caucasus and Caspian, called "kuku," after the Persian word for egg. Sometimes kukus contain meat and cheese and sometimes they just contain nuts and spices, so a wide variety of flavors are offered in these baked omelets. Enjoy them at any meal, not just breakfast!

2–3 medium zucchini, very thinly sliced crosswise
1 medium onion, very finely diced
¾ cup sharp cheese, grated (feta, cheddar, or gruyere)
5 eggs, beaten

I teaspoon salt
½ teaspoon ground black pepper
½ teaspoon dried basil

Preheat oven to 350°. After slicing zucchini, arrange in a round buttered casserole in a circular fashion, with each slice slightly overlapping the one before it. Then add onion and cheese, sprinkling them liberally over the zucchini. Beat eggs and add salt, pepper, and basil to them. Beat again. Pour over zucchini and cheese. Bake casserole in a preheated oven 30–45 minutes or until done.

Green Beans with Walnuts

This dish blends the flavors of string beans with tomato sauce, cinnamon, and walnuts—with delicious results. Its spiciness comes from freshly ground black pepper accenting the cinnamon instead of from some form of red pepper, and the turmeric only adds to the warm blanket of flavor surrounding the beans. Serve hot with a roast meat or kebab dish or enjoy it all by itself for a quick lunch.

I pound green beans, stemmed
2 tablespoons unsalted butter
2 medium onions, peeled and diced
I medium tomato, chopped
I teaspoon salt
½ teaspoon ground black pepper
½ teaspoon turmeric
I teaspoon cinnamon
½ cup chopped walnuts
I cup water
I cup tomato sauce

1. Heat butter in a sauté pan and sauté onions until they start to soften and take on some color. Add tomatoes and sauté until the tomatoes start to break up. Then add salt, pepper, turmeric, walnuts and cinnamon and stir again.

2. Mix the water and the tomato sauce together and add to the onions and tomatoes. Cook to warm, then add the green beans and cook covered for 10–15 minutes, stirring occasionally, until the green beans

start to soften. Then cook uncovered until the beans are tender but still firm. Serve over rice.

Rice and Grain Dishes, Breads

Rich pilafs, crusty, crunchy breads, and soft, sweet rolls—the range of Armenian rice and grain dishes and breads is an entire spectrum of cuisine color! The pilafs offered here have a strong Saudi influence, such as the **Roasted Pine Nut and Sesame Pilaf** and the bulgur wheat dishes, which were probably brought to Armenia during the Umayyad dynasty. Armenians enjoy a simple *lavash* as often as the Georgians do, but their unique **Braided Sourdough Bread** is offered here as an Armenian centerpiece bread and the **Sweet Orange Rolls** can be a delicate snack or even a light dessert for those wishing to avoid sugar-filled options.

Roasted Pine Nut and Sesame Pilaf

A delicious plain pilaf with a touch of nutty flavor that really complements the roasted or skewered meat dishes and kebabs offered in this book. It probably came to Armenia from Arabia during one of the periods of Islamic conquest of the region and is still eaten in Arabia and in several Muslim countries around Asia.

3 tablespoons butter
1 medium onion, peeled and diced
1 cup rice
1 cup chicken or beef broth
1 cup water
½ cup pine nuts, lightly roasted
¼ cup sesame seeds, lightly roasted
1 teaspoon salt
½ teaspoon pepper
1 teaspoon fenugreek leaves

1. Melt butter in a large sauté pan and sauté the onion until it softens and starts to color, then add the fenugreek and the roasted seeds and nuts and mix well. Cook over medium until the onions have wilted completely.

2. Add salt and pepper to the onions along with the stock and water and bring the mixture to a boil. When the water is hot, add the rice and return to a boil. Then lower heat and cook covered 15–20 minutes or until the rice is done.

Bulgur Pilaf with Currants and Almonds

This is a delicious change of pace from an ordinary rice pilaf. Bulgur wheat is eaten in place of rice in many western and central Asian countries and is especially good when mixed with the fruits and spices offered below. For a real treat, chop some walnuts or pistachios and add them into the mix as well.

1 cup coarse bulgur wheat, rinsed and drained
½ cup sliced almonds
2 tablespoons butter
1 medium yellow onion, peeled and diced
1 cup currants
12 dried apricots, diced (and soaked if necessary to soften)
1 teaspoon salt
¼ teaspoon ground black pepper
2 teaspoons sugar
¼ teaspoon dried sweet basil
½ teaspoon lemon juice
2 cups water

1. Dry fry the almonds over medium flame until they become golden, stirring constantly. When they are done, remove from heat and set aside. Melt butter in a sauté pan and sauté onions until they start to soften and color.

2. Add the currants, apricots, salt, and pepper and mix well. Cook for 3–5 minutes and add the sugar, basil, lemon juice, and almonds and cook for another minute or two. Add the water and bring the mixture to a boil. When nearly boiling, add the bulgur and stir into the fruit and vegetables.

3. Return to a boil then cover and lower heat and cook on low for 15–20 minutes until the bulgur is nearly done. Cook another 10 minutes or so, making sure not to burn the bulgur and then turn off heat and leave covered until ready to serve.

Tabooleh

Here is Armenia's version of the often-consumed Middle Eastern dish. It follows the Saudi recipe fairly closely but has more of most ingredients and subsequently a much stronger flavor than the gentler taboolehs of the Gulf States and Middle East. Serve as an opener to a large meal with bread, olives, and other appetizers.

2 cups medium or coarse bulgur wheat, rinsed and drained
4 cups green onions (both white and green portions, chopped)
2 large bunches fresh cilantro leaves, chopped (35–40 sprigs)
I cup fresh mint leaves, chopped
I tablespoon chopped fresh sweet basil
3 medium tomatoes, diced
2 teaspoons salt
I teaspoon ground black pepper
¼ teaspoon cayenne pepper (optional)
¼ teaspoon paprika
Juice of 3 lemons
¼ cup extra virgin olive oil

Lettuce or grape leaves—rinsed and dried to scoop up and eat the tabooleh

1. Soak coarse bulgur wheat in enough warm water to cover for 5 minutes. Drain and begin to prepare other ingredients.

2. Mix together in a food processor the spring onions, cilantro, mint, and basil and pulse to grind. Then add the tomatoes and pulse again until tomatoes are diced but still have some form. Add salt, pepper, cayenne pepper, and paprika and mix together.

3. In a cup or small bowl whisk together the lemon juice and the olive oil until it becomes cloudy and starts to emulsify. Pour over the mixed greens and tomatoes and stir well.

4. Combine dressed greens with bulgur wheat and toss together with forks to ensure even mixing without smashing the bulgur. Allow to sit to absorb the juices of the fruits and vegetables. If more moisture is needed for the bulgur, add hot water or broth to the mixture and

let sit an additional 10–15 minutes. To serve in the traditional manner, arrange tabooleh on a serving plate and serve with lettuce and grape leaves to pick up bits of the salad with. In a more modern fashion, use a serving spoon instead.

Red Pepper and Mushroom Pilaf

This pilaf gets its color and soft but zingy flavor from turmeric that is then lifted to new heights by dried basil and fenugreek leaves. Lastly, the mushrooms and red peppers add depth and breadth to the flavor. Match it with a flavorful kebab or enjoy it all by itself!

2 tablespoons butter
1 medium onion, finely diced
1 teaspoon garlic, peeled and diced
½ teaspoon dried basil
½ teaspoon dried fenugreek leaves
½ teaspoon ground turmeric
1 red bell pepper, thinly sliced
1 cup mushrooms, thickly sliced
1 medium tomato, diced
1 cup basmati rice, uncooked
1 cup vegetable stock
1 cup water
1 teaspoon salt
½ teaspoon pepper

1. Melt the butter in a large, heavy sauté pan over moderate heat. Add the onion and sauté until it starts to wilt. Add the garlic, basil, fenugreek, and turmeric and stir to blend and warm spices. Add pepper and mushrooms and stir again. Cook 3–5 minutes until the pepper starts to soften, and then stir in the diced tomato and cook another 3–5 minutes to soften.

2. Now add the rice and stir well to blend. Cook 2 minutes to steam the grains, then pour in the broth, add the salt and pepper, and stir well. Bring to a boil, stirring. Then, reduce the heat to low, cover and simmer for approximately 20–30 minutes or until all the liquid has been absorbed and the rice is well cooked. Spoon onto a serving platter or into a bowl and serve.

Braided Sourdough Bread

Here's as delicious a sourdough bread as you could ever ask for and presented as a beautiful braid—no wonder it's one of Armenia's most popular traditional breads! The yogurt in the dough lends the sourness along with the yeast, and the poppy or sesame seeds deliciously dress the bread for your table.

½ cup warm water
2 packages dry, active yeast
1 teaspoon salt
⅛ cup sugar
4 cups flour
½ cup butter, melted and cooled
1 teaspoon baking powder
1 teaspoon baking soda
1 cup plain yogurt, drained
1 egg, lightly beaten
½ cup sesame or poppy seeds

1. Place yogurt in a coffee filter and allow it to drain some of its liquid. After about ½ hour, enough water will be drained, and the yogurt is ready to use.

2. Dissolve the sugar and the salt in the warm water and then add the yeast and stir well. Set aside and allow the yeast to activate. Mix the butter, baking soda, and baking powder together until blended and then add the lightly drained yogurt. Add yeast to mixture and blend well.

3. Stir in the flour and knead for about 5–6 minutes. Cover the dough and let rest for 15–20 minutes. Then divide the dough into thirds and roll each ball into an 8–10 inch cylinder of dough.

4. Line the cylinders up on a bread board or counter top and braid them together by alternatively crossing each end over the middle piece. Place on a lightly greased cookie sheet. Cover and let rise for 20–30 minutes. Lightly brush with the beaten egg and sprinkle with sesame or poppy seeds. Bake in a preheated 350° oven for 20–25 minutes.

Armenian Sweet Orange Rolls

Sweet and buttery with a touch of orange—it's a wonder these rolls aren't seen more widely on anxious tables. A delicious way to indulge your guests at any point in the meal, from appetizer to dessert, these rolls are versatile enough to work as any part of the meal.

1 package dry, active yeast
½ cup warm water
2 tablespoons sugar
1 cup plus 1 teaspoon butter, melted and cooled
½ cup whole milk, warm
2 eggs, beaten
1 teaspoon salt
Zest of 1 orange, finely chopped
4 cups flour
1 teaspoon baking powder
1 egg, beaten (for glaze)

1. Dissolve yeast in warm water and mix well. Add sugar and mix again. Set aside and allow yeast to activate for 15–20 minutes. Combine melted butter with milk, eggs, salt and orange flavoring and mix well. Add dissolved yeast and mix again.

2. Add flour and baking powder to make a soft dough. Knead for 5 minutes and let stand for at least 30–40 minutes or until double in size. Punch down and knead for a minute or two.

3. Form rolls into desired shapes and let rise on trays about 30 minutes. Brush lightly with the beaten egg and sprinkle with sesame or poppy seeds and bake in preheated 375° oven until golden brown for 10–12 minutes.

Desserts and Beverages

The desserts in this section range from the simple (**Sesame Butter Cookies**) to the more complex (**Date and Nut Crescents**). All are delicious and reveal Christian Armenia's ties to other Caucasus nations or to the Muslim Levant.

Date and Nut Crescents

Here is a delicious Middle Eastern–inspired dessert! Dates and nuts tucked gently into a light but sour pastry crust and baked until lightly golden.

Pastry
2 cups sifted flour
½ cup butter, room temperature
1 cup cream cheese, room temperature

Filling
1 ½ cups dates, chopped
¼ cup warm water
½ cup nuts, chopped

1. Preheat oven to 375°. In a medium-sized mixing bowl, combine flour, butter, and cream cheese together. Work dough until all of the ingredients are integrated. Divide dough into 3 or 4 balls. Roll each one out into a square or rectangle. You should not be able to see through the dough when you hold it up, but it should be close. Divide each rectangle in half or thirds.

2. Mix dates, warm water, and chopped nuts together until you have a smooth paste. Take about ⅓ cup of filling and spread it lengthwise down the center of the pastry, mounding it as you go. Leave about 1 inch at either end to seal the pastry. Fold dough over filling and seal, crimping the edges together. Leave straight, or shape into a crescent and bake on a sprayed or oiled baking sheet for 20–25 minutes.

Hazelnut Bastegh

This is Armenia's much-easier-to-prepare version of Georgia's confection *Churchkela*. Instead of dipping strings of nuts into a mixture of flour and juice, the Armenians prepare the mixture spread out on a lined baking sheet. Of course, the results are not the wonderfully strange salami-shaped confections that the Georgians love, but neatly cut diamonds or strips of candy instead. Still, the taste is sweet and nutty and simply wonderful.

1 quart applesauce
¼ cup sugar
2 cups hazelnuts, chopped
½ quart grape juice
1 cup flour

Place applesauce into 4-quart saucepan. Blend small amount of flour (½ cup) in 1 cup of grape juice in jar and shake. Put through strainer into applesauce. Repeat process until all flour and grape juice are used up. Blend.

1. Bring to a boil, stirring constantly, until mixture thickens. Add sugar and stir while boiling for 1 minute. Remove from heat and let cool. Line several baking sheets with wax paper, and when the mixture is cool enough to spread, spread it over the paper, covering it evenly.

2. When cool but not cold and crackly, peel from the wax paper and cut into desired squares or diamonds.

Mixed Fruit and Barley Pudding

This is a delicious traditional "pudding" made with barley and fruit that satisfies the Armenian soul! It is sweet and nutty and a delicious treat at the holidays or any time at all.

1 cup prunes
1 cup golden raisins
1 cup dried apricots
4 cups water
1 cup barley
1 cup sugar

Soak barley overnight. The following day, drain barley, chop fruits, and add all to the 4 cups of boiling water. Bring to a boil and then simmer for 1 ½ hours. Serve warm or cold with chopped walnuts or almonds and a bit more sugar on top.

Sesame Butter Cookies

A simple, mildly sweet butter cookie with a nutty twist that should satisfy most sweet-toothed diners, whether Armenian or not. This is another great example of the links between Saudi cooking and that of western and southern Asia.

½ cup butter
½ cup sugar
1 egg
⅓ cup evaporated milk
¼ teaspoon vanilla
1 teaspoon baking powder
2 ½ cups flour
Sesame seeds (as needed)

Melt butter and add sugar and beat until smooth. Add eggs and beat 3 minutes. Add evaporated milk, vanilla, and baking powder and beat 5 minutes more until fluffy. Then slowly add the sifted flour and knead. Roll dough with the palm of your hands into ropes 1 inch in diameter. Cut into 3-inch pieces. Dip individual pieces in sesame seeds and place on greased cookie sheet. Bake for 20 minutes in a preheated 350° oven. To make a crisp cookie, turn oven off and let cookies sit in oven for 3 to 4 minutes longer.

Rose Petal Preserves

This recipe reveals Armenia's connection to the Greeks, who also still make and eat preserves from masses of rose petals. From Greece, the use of rose petals has moved as far east as India and Bangladesh in the easy use of rose water, especially in desserts.

1 pound rose petals
1 liter water
1 pound sugar
2 teaspoons citric acid (also called lemon salt)

Cut the lower (white) part of petals with scissors; make sure there are no dry petals. Place the petals in strainer and rinse them thoroughly with cold water. Place petals in cooking pan, add water, bring to boil, and cook for 5 minutes. Add sugar and cook until thickened. Add citric acid to keep the petals' vibrant color. Place in sterilized jar and seal until needed.

Mint Tea

Here is a simple and commonly enjoyed beverage in Armenia that is also good for your digestive health and can guard against the effects of bacterial and viral infections. Sweetened or with only the mint's natural sweetness, this tea is a great addition to any meal.

6 cups water
4 teabags of your choice
2 tablespoons dried mint

Boil water and pour over teabags and mint and let steep for 3–5 minutes depending on how strong you like your tea. Remove teabags, strain, and serve.

Appetizers and Condiments

These recipes represent a variety of different types of appetizers used to start a meal or even to make small meals unto themselves. The savory pies offered—**Spinach and Cheese Turnovers** and the **Spicy Lamb or Beef Turnovers**—are dipped in yogurt or sour cream sauce and can be enjoyed along with a hearty soup or as only the first stop on a multicourse meal. The **Armenian Northern Bean Salad** is a familiar beginning on most tables, as is the **Yogurt and Cucumber Dip** for use with a good crusty bread. Lastly, the **Armenian Mixed Pickles** are standard parts of most Armenian meals.

Spinach and Cheese Turnovers

This is the Armenian version of a spinach-and-cheese-stuffed turnover or dumpling eaten widely throughout the region. It is given the uniquely Armenian twist of a blast of ground coriander to spice up the filling.

Pastry

Filo dough, warmed enough to separate and handle the sheets without tearing them

Melted butter as needed (at least 1 stick)

Filling

1 ½ pounds spinach, sautéed and chopped

1 pound feta cheese, chopped or shredded

2 medium bunches fresh cilantro leaves, chopped (25–30 sprigs)

1 teaspoon ground coriander

2 eggs, beaten

1 teaspoon salt

1 teaspoon ground black pepper

2 teaspoons lemon juice

1. Combine filling ingredients together and mix well to blend.

2. Brush melted butter on bottom and sides of pan. Place a sheet of filo in the pan, lightly butter it, and place another sheet on top. Repeat to yield 4 individually buttered layers of filo on the bottom of the pan.

3. Spoon about ⅓ of the filling and spread across filo surface but not all the way to the edges of the pan. Cover with two sheets of filo, with butter between them and on top. Spread more filling and cover with another two layers of filo. Put last layer of filling in place and then cover with 4 individually buttered pieces of filo.

4. Brush butter on top of the last layer and bake in a 450° oven for 20 minutes. Lower the heat to 300° and bake another 20 minutes. When it is golden, remove from the oven and let cool. Cut into diagonals or squares and serve.

Spiced Lamb or Beef Turnovers

This flavorful turnover is a meal unto itself, with the cumin-based spice mixture made spicier with the addition of large amounts of black pepper and allspice. Keep a sour cream or yogurt dip or sauce nearby to dip these in and enjoy!

Pastry

Filo dough, warmed enough to separate and handle the sheets without tearing them

Melted butter as needed (at least 1 stick)

Filling
1 pound ground beef or lamb
2 tablespoons butter
2 medium onions, peeled and diced
2 tablespoons **Armenian Spiced Meat Rub** (see Armenian Sauces and Spice Mixtures)
1 teaspoon salt
1 teaspoon ground black pepper

1. Combine filling ingredients together and mix well to blend.

2. Brush melted butter on bottom and sides of pan. Place a sheet of filo in the pan, lightly butter it and place another sheet on top. Repeat to yield 4 individually buttered layers of filo on the bottom of the pan.

3. Spoon about ⅓ of the filling and spread across filo surface but not all the way to the edges of the pan. Cover with two sheets of filo, with butter between them and on top. Spread more filling and cover with another two layers of filo. Put last layer of filling in place and then cover with 4 individually buttered pieces of filo.

4. Brush butter on top of the last layer and bake in a 450° oven for 20 minutes. Lower the heat to 300° and bake another 20 minutes. When it is golden, remove from the oven and let cool. Cut into diagonals or squares and serve.

Armenian Northern Bean Salad

This is a light, mild but flavorful salad to tease the palate and prepare it for the main course. It brings a bit of Islamic cookery into western Asia and will be encountered in a different permutation south and east in Pakistan.

2 cups cooked and cooled northern beans
1 medium bunch fresh cilantro leaves, very finely chopped (20-25 sprigs)
1 medium tomato, diced
3 teaspoons garlic, peeled and chopped
¼ cup olive or grapeseed oil
1 teaspoon tomato paste
½ teaspoon salt
½ teaspoon ground black pepper

In a medium bowl, combine the beans with the cilantro, garlic, and diced tomato and toss well. In a separate small bowl, whisk together the oil, tomato paste, salt, and pepper and pour over the beans. Toss until ingredients are well mixed with the dressing.

Yogurt with Cucumbers

A cooling dip or sauce enjoyed throughout western and southwestern Asia in one form or another. Great with bread, turnovers, dumplings, or even as a sauce for kebabs and other roasted meats and vegetables.

2 cups cucumbers, peeled, seeded, and diced
2 cups yogurt
1 teaspoon salt
½ teaspoon black pepper
2 teaspoons garlic, peeled and diced
1 teaspoon dried, crushed mint leaves

A Dish of Matsoon Yogurt

Combine yogurt with salt, black pepper, garlic, and mint and mix well until evenly blended. Let sit for 10–15 minutes to allow flavors to blend. Add cucumbers and mix again. Serve as soon as possible after adding the cucumbers so mixture will not get watery. Serve with bread or turnovers.

Mixed Pickled Vegetables

These wonderful mixed pickles decorate many an Armenian table and are enjoyed in many an Armenian home! Now available for you to enjoy, they are just a bit sweet and sour and 100 percent delicious.

Brine
1 gallon water
½ cup **Armenian Pickling Spices** (see Armenian Sauces and Spice Mixtures)
½ gallon cider vinegar
1 cup salt

Pickles
2 cups cauliflower florets
2 cups celery, cut in 1 ½ inch lengths
2 cups carrots, cut crosswise or quartered
½ head garlic broken into cloves and peeled
Brown sugar as needed

1. Add pickling spices to water and bring to a boil. Let boil for 3–5 minutes and then turn off heat. Let sit for about 30 minutes or so while you prepare the vegetables. When ready to prepare the brine, strain pickling spices from the water and pour water into a clean pot or vessel. Add cider vinegar and salt and mix well.

2. Combine cauliflower, celery, and carrots with the garlic cloves and mix well. Fill jars or bottles with this vegetable mix as much as you can, leaving space above vegetables for brine. Pack tightly, but do not smash vegetables.

3. Into each quart bottle pour brine to about 1 inch from top. If necessary, pack additional vegetables; if they settle too much, add a few more

vegetables. Place a teaspoon of brown sugar on the top of each jar or bottle and seal. The pickles will be ready in about 2–3 weeks.

Sauces and Spice Mixtures

Although not as broad as Georgia's array of sauces and spices, Armenia's offerings are every bit as varied and delicious. Spanning the spectrum of flavor from the **Sweet Orange-Saffron Sauce** to the sweet and sour **Armenian Pomegranate Sauce**, the spice combinations also bring diners hot and spicy offerings in the **Spiced Meat Rub** to the more sour and sweet combination in **Armenian Pickling Spices**.

Sweet Orange-Saffron Sauce

In addition to eating flavorful pilafs, the Armenians use a variety of sauces to flavor rice and bulgur wheat as well. This sauce can be used to brighten any pilaf or can even be used on chicken, fowl, or lamb for a sweet treat.

¼ cup butter
¼ cup sugar
½ teaspoon saffron
I cup water or broth
I teaspoon salt
Zest from 2 oranges, finely minced
¼ cup pistachio nuts, skinned and slivered
¼ cup slivered almonds
I tablespoon lemon juice

To melted butter, add sugar, saffron, salt, and water. Bring to a boil and then reduce to a steady simmer and add nuts, orange zest, and lemon juice and cook gently until it thickens. If it becomes too thick, add a bit more water or broth to thin. Serve soon after preparing.

Armenian Pomegranate Sauce

This pomegranate sauce is very different from the one used in Georgia with its fresh basil creating so much of the flavor. This is a sweeter, more Asian sauce that has variations in Azerbaijan's fesenjan cookery and Uzbekistan's sweet and sour cherry sauce.

2 cups fresh pomegranate juice
3 tablespoons lemon juice
1 teaspoon ground cinnamon
2 tablespoons sugar

In a small saucepan, heat the pomegranate juice over low heat, stirring often, until it begins to reduce by about ⅓. Then add the lemon juice, ground cinnamon, and sugar and continue to cook, stirring often, over low heat until the mixture reduces by half of the original amount and begins to thicken into a sauce.

Armenian Spiced Meat Rub

A wonderful meat rub—used here in the **Spicy Lamb or Beef Turnover**s—but one that can be used to flavor meat chops and steaks as well as kebabs and even vegetables. As handy as any five-spice powder, this rub is an essential part of a complete Armenian kitchen.

2 tablespoons sweet paprika
½ teaspoon red pepper
1 teaspoon salt
2 teaspoons cracked black pepper
2 teaspoons ground cumin
½ teaspoon ground allspice
3 teaspoons garlic, peeled and diced

Mix dry spices together and then add garlic and mix again. Use as a meat rub or to flavor ground meats as filling for pastries or dumplings. Works particularly well for lamb and beef.

Armenian Pickling Spices

This is how Armenian cooks get that wonderfully distinctive flavor into their pickled vegetables. Plenty of black pepper accents cinnamon and cloves along with healthy amounts of allspice.

2 tablespoons whole allspice
2 tablespoons black peppercorns
2 tablespoons coriander seeds
1 tablespoon whole cloves
4 bay leaves
1 cinnamon stick
3–4 hot, dried, red chili peppers

Combine in a pestle and only lightly crack before using. Do not grind, or balance of flavors will change.

Mosque with Two Minarets in Baku, Azerbaijan

Azerbaijan

Main spices and flavors: coriander, cilantro, mint, saffron, savory, sumac, fenugreek, sour grapes, sour cherries, sour plums, cumin, marigold, dill, garlic, onion, cardamom, sweet basil, cinnamon, cloves, nutmeg, mace, chili peppers, tomato, potato

Souring agents: lemons, pomegranates, limes, red wine vinegar, white vinegar

Situated on the western coast of the Caspian Sea, Azerbaijan is another one of the Asian continent's strategic crossroads between east, west, north, and south. As such, it has been occupied by many foreign rulers and peoples who have left their mark on its modern culture. As with its Georgian and Armenian neighbors, influences as diverse as those of Rome, Alexander, the Uzbek Tamerlane, and Genghis Khan, can be found—both in and outside of the kitchen. Like Georgia, Azerbaijan has a wide variety of climatic zones as well. In fact, nine of eleven climatic zones are represented, and in Azerbaijan one can simultaneously see all four seasons just by traveling from one end of the country to the other. High mountains, fertile foothills growing tea and citrus, dry steppes, luxurious forests, and Caspian shores—Azerbaijan has it all! So, in addition to a long history of foreign occupation, a widely varied climate has led to one of western Asia's most diverse cuisines.

In addition to being a strategic crossroads, Azerbaijan is also the land of magic fire. Its abundant supply of natural gas produces bogs of self-igniting gas that have been noted by travelers since ancient times. Seeking the source of the fires, travelers of old often sought monsters or mythical beasts such as dragons as the cause. Imagine cooking your kebabs by dragon fire—what a remarkable meal that would be!

Although there are no dragon-fire kebab recipes offered here, there is an incredibly tasty one to be found in the **Kebabs of Lamb or Beef with Mint**—which is one of my all-time favorites! Likewise the **Lamb or Pork Chops with Sour Cherry Sauce** are a delicious take on the Persian sour-cherry theme and are the sour cousin to Uzbekistan's **Meatballs with Sweet and Sour Cherries**. Along those same lines, I have to offer the incredible **Baked Fish with Sour Cherries** and **Lamb with Quinces and Capers**. Last but not least is the remarkable **Hens with Dill and Pomegranates** that is a take on the Iranian fesenjan style of preparing meat. This is one of my favorite cuisines where, for me, the Asian theme of sweet and sour comes together perfectly. So please, enjoy!

Meat Dishes

Watch out for that signpost up ahead; in Azerbaijan, one begins to enter "The Lamb Zone"—a vast swath of territory that stretches from the Caspian across central Asia and the northern part of South Asia and into Mongolia where lamb, mutton, or even kid are by far the most commonly eaten set of meats. It is eaten almost daily in kebabs, in stews, ground in meatballs, or, in the case of young animals, even on the bone at celebrations or as an everyday meal for those who can afford it. Mutton from adult or older animals is eaten more frequently than the lamb or kid from younger animals, and its pungent, gamier flavor will bring a different aspect to many of these recipes, but I have substituted lamb for most mutton recipes because of the Western familiarity with its gentler flavor and tender texture. If you are a brave and curious soul, however, work backwards and try the recipes with mutton—just be sure to take steps to tenderize the mutton and extend most cooking times.

Not to paint too wooly a picture of Azeri meat dishes, fowl and fish are also eaten. Generally the fowl eaten is game hen, quail, or smaller, free-range chickens, not the meaty, breasty brutes we have in the West. Generally hens are seasoned, split, and roasted on large, swordlike skewers, but they can also be roasted in a brick or conventional oven. Fish is prepared a myriad of different ways. It could be baked whole, skewered in large chunks, filleted, or even fried as cakes with other vegetables. In this chapter, I have tried to offer a range of representational recipes that illustrate the roots of Azeri cuisine and that will be unique and welcome additions to the modern Western table.

Lamb Chops with Sour Cherry Sauce

It wasn't an apple that Eve offered to Adam, it was a bowl of sour cherries—I'm sure of it! Either that or God must have created sour cherries for himself and accidentally let their secret slip out some other way. However this wonderful fruit came to be, it is simply delicious when paired with meat or fish! This recipe is a wonderfully simple way to prepare lamb or pork chops, which—in larger quantities—can also be used to make a wonderful roast as well. This recipe accents the natural, slightly sour flavor of the cherries with the addition of salt and cinnamon, while recipes from central Asia tend to offset the sourness of the cherries with sugar, as in the Uzbek **Meatballs with Sweet and Sour Cherries**. Widely used throughout western and central Asia, sour cherries are a taste sensation you'll not want to miss!

Chops
4 lamb or pork chops, the thicker the better
½ teaspoon salt
½ teaspoon freshly ground black pepper (or more to taste)
½–1 corm nutmeg, grated
¼ cup beef broth (more or less as needed)
I serving **Sour Cherry Sauce** (see Azeri Sauces and Spice Mixtures)

1. Preheat oven to 375°. Season the meat on both sides with salt, pepper, and nutmeg and place in a baking pan. Pour a small amount of beef broth to just cover the bottom of the dish and place in the oven. Cooking times will vary according to whether the chops have been

boned or not. For chops with the bone in them, cook about twenty minutes on each side. For chops without the bone, cooking times are approximately halved.

2. Make the sauce while the lamb is cooking. Just before serving, pour a bit of warm or hot sauce on the chops, offering the rest of the sauce as a side.

Lamb with Quinces and Capers

Quinces and capers form the flavor backbone of this dish, with each bite alternating between the lemony sweetness of the quinces and the sourness of the capers. Helping these fruits along are dill, offering its sweetness, and sour grape powder, which makes the capers pucker! All in all, the earthy lamb is blanketed along with these flavors with a light touch of saffron. Serve with plain basmati rice, barley, or with noodles for an authentic Caucasian treat!

¾ pound stew lamb, cut into bite-size chunks
1 medium onion, peeled, sliced, and separated into crescents
4 tablespoons butter
2 tablespoons sour grape powder
¼ teaspoon saffron
1 cup beef broth, hot
1 cup chicken broth
3 hot, dried, red chili peppers, diced
1 cup spinach, rinsed and dried
2 quinces, peeled and chopped
½ cup fresh chopped sorrel or 1 tablespoon dried, ground sorrel
1 tablespoon dill
1 tablespoon cilantro leaves, chopped
1 teaspoon salt
1 teaspoon pepper, coarsely ground
2 teaspoons sugar
1 tablespoon lemon juice
4 tablespoons capers, drained

1. Heat butter in a saucepan and sear lamb over high heat for 3 minutes to seal in the meat's juices. When done, lower heat and remove from

the pot with a slotted spoon and set the meat aside. Dissolve the saffron in the hot beef broth and set aside.

2. Lower heat to medium and add the onions to the butter and sauté until they start to soften. Add the dissolved saffron and the sour grapes and stir. Then add the sorrel, dill, and cilantro and stir again. Add the salt and pepper and the seared lamb along with any juices that have collected and stir again. Add chicken broth and mix well. Cook to rewarm lamb and then cook covered over low heat 20–30 minutes or until lamb begins to fall apart.

3. When lamb is almost done, add the quinces and spinach, and cook until wilted. Then add the capers, sugar and lemon juice and mix well. Re-cover and cook another 5–10 minutes until the meat is really tender and the flavors have blended together.

Baked Fish with Sour Cherries

"Delicious! Incredible!" and just, "Wow!" are some of the things that my guests have said when sampling this dish. If you love fish, this is one of the recipes you've been waiting for! If you are new to Caspian cooking, I can guarantee that you have never had fish prepared this way before. I've adapted the recipe to work as a casserole instead of as a stuffed, baked, whole fish to make it easier to prepare and allow the stuffing's sweet and sour flavors to mix with the fish instead of being overcome by it. Also, traditionally, the fish used is likely to be sturgeon, but I recommend using sea bass (or rockfish) or snapper because they are easier to find and more familiar to the Western palate.

3 sea bass (or rockfish) or other meaty fish filets, rinsed and dried
Salt, pepper, and red pepper flakes to lightly season the filets
1 medium eggplant, cut crosswise into ½-inch slices
1 tablespoon vegetable oil
3 tablespoons light sesame or peanut oil
2 medium yellow onions, sliced into thin crescents
1 tablespoon chopped garlic
1 tablespoon lime juice
¾ teaspoon ground cinnamon
½ teaspoon ground black pepper
¼ teaspoon ground cumin

1 pinch of ground cloves
¼ cup beef broth
¼ cup water
1 ½ cups walnut pieces, diced
2 cups sour cherries, rinsed and pitted (with liquid that accumulates after rinsing)
2 teaspoons sugar
1 teaspoon salt (or to taste)

1. Slice the eggplant crosswise into ½-inch roundels, lightly salt, and bake on an oiled or sprayed baking sheet in a 375° oven for 20–30 minutes. When done, cool completely and then slice the pieces into pie-shaped, bite-size pieces; set aside. Sprinkle salt, pepper, and cayenne over the filets and set aside.

2. Heat oil in a sauté pan; add onions and sauté until they start to soften. Add garlic and lime juice and stir to coat. Add eggplant pieces and walnuts and stir again. Add some beef broth to prevent the eggplant from burning as it starts to cook.

3. Cook covered until the eggplant softens and then add the sour cherries and cook to warm ingredients. Add the ground spices and stir to distribute. If it seems too dry, add a little water to the mix until a thick, stewlike consistency is achieved. Add sugar and remove from heat.

4. Butter a covered casserole dish and place a layer of stuffing ½ to 1 inch thick at the bottom of the dish. Place salted and peppered fish filets on top of stuffing; dot with butter. Cover fish with an additional layer of stuffing of equal thickness. Unused stuffing can be served separately as a garnish for the fish.

5. Cook covered in a preheated oven for 30 minutes and then uncover and cook for an additional 10–15 minutes depending on the size of the filets. Serve a complete layer of stuffing, fish, stuffing.

Kebabs of Lamb or Beef and Mint

This kebab is so spicy and flavorful, I simply love it! The mint and the basil work with the vinegar to really make the meat zesty, and the chili peppers add their special spice as well. I've adapted the original recipe so that it can be cooked in a Western broiler-oven instead of on the flat, swordlike skewers often used. If you'd like to try the traditional cooking method, skewers are available in most Persian markets. A helpful hint for skewering soft meat is to roll the meat right after blending, lightly flour, and then refrigerate for at least an hour before skewering. The coals or grill must be very hot to cook the skewered kebabs quickly without them falling into the grill. No matter how you cook them, the kebabs are great when served over rice with a pickled vegetable or salad.

I pound ground lamb or beef
I medium onion, peeled and coarsely chopped
2 teaspoons salt
I teaspoon ground black pepper
3 hot, dried, red chili peppers
2 tablespoons crumbled dry mint
I tablespoon dried basil
3 tablespoons red wine vinegar
½ teaspoon cumin

1. In a food processor, combine all ingredients except the meat and blend lightly so that the vegetables are chopped but still have their form. Then add the meat to the mixture and blend well. Roll the meat into 4-inch sausages, and place the sausages on a plate and chill for several hours to firm the mixture up.

2. Preheat broiler on highest setting. Remove sausages from refrigerator and place them on an oiled or sprayed baking sheet and place pan under broiler about 4–6 inches from the flame.

3. Cook about 5 minutes on each side. If meat still feels soft to the touch, cook another few minutes, but do not let the kebabs burn. Serve with rice, powdered sumac, and pickled vegetables.

Hens with Dill and Pomegranates

This is perhaps my favorite roast fowl recipe—ever! Over the lightly browned dill-flavored hens, a robust, crimson, sweet and sour pomegranate sauce is poured. Serve the extra sauce and let diners add more, and the silence at the dinner table will be one of satisfied awe. This wonderful dish is an example of how the Azeris often roast meats—with plentiful layered vegetables and delicious fruity overtones.

2 medium Cornish game hens, rinsed and dried
1 teaspoon salt
½ teaspoon pepper
¼ cup fresh dill, chopped
1 small bunch fresh cilantro leaves, chopped (15–20 sprigs)
1 medium onion, peeled, sliced, and separated into crescents
10 cloves garlic, separated and peeled
1 cup carrots, julienned
2 medium potatoes, well washed and chopped
2 cups pomegranate juice
3 tablespoons butter
1 teaspoon sugar
3 tablespoons sour cream

1. Combine *half each* of the salt, pepper, and dill and rub both inside and out of the hens with the mixture; set aside. Preheat oven to 375°.

2. Heat pomegranate juice in a saucepan over medium heat. When it comes to a boil, reduce heat to low and cook to reduce the juice by about half. This will thicken the juice and concentrate the flavor. When the juice is reduced, set aside.

3. Oil or spray a deep baking pan and place a layer of potatoes at the bottom. Follow this with a layer of garlic and a layer of sliced onions. Over all, lightly sprinkle the julienned carrots. Combine remaining salt, pepper, and dill with the chopped cilantro and distribute over the vegetables in the pan.

4. Place hens, breast side up, directly on top of the vegetables and place into the oven. Cook 20 minutes, then cut the butter up into pats and place on the skin of the bird. Cook for another 20 minutes and baste well with the pan juices.

5. Cook another 20 minutes, baste again, and then flip hens and cook another 15–20 minutes. Just *before* flipping the hens, check the vegetables to see if they are done. If done, transfer the hens to a plate, spoon out the vegetables into a serving bowl, and then put the hens back in the baking pan and resume cooking. (If you like crisper vegetables, check them sooner than 1 hour.)

6. Warm the pomegranate sauce, add the sour cream and sugar, and whisk until the sour cream is well integrated. Baste hens with pan juices, flip back over and pour about half of the pomegranate sauce around the hens, and then spoon the rest gently over the birds so as to not disturb the herbs on them. Place them back in the oven and continue to cook for another 15 minutes or until done. Baste once or twice with the thickened pomegranate sauce before transferring the hens to a serving platter. Pour remaining sauce (if any) into a serving bowl and place on the table. Serve over plain rice or with a simple pilaf such as **Chickpea and Dill Pilaf**.

Vegetable Dishes and Salads

Forget about the limp overcooked vegetables that far too many of us grew up with—Azeri vegetable dishes are an absolute delight! They are not meant to be shy companions to the meat dish all-stars. They are in fact wonderfully flavorful unto themselves and are meant to shine on vegetarian and omnivore tables alike.

My favorite of the recipes offered here is the **Cinnamon Potatoes with Pine Nuts**—simply because of the surprise combination of flavors and how it whispers of the wonders of Persian cuisine to come in the next chapter. Another rich surprise is to be found in the stuffed vegetable recipe, **Eggplant Stuffed with Pomegranate Seeds** where the pomegranates, ground coriander, and fenugreek leaves lift and lighten the earthy eggplant. One of the themes common in Azeri vegetable recipes is the use of dill and lemon or pomegranate juice to provide a sweet and sour flavor blast, as in **Walnut Kuku** and **Spinach with Dill**. Lastly, I offer the **String Beans in a Spicy Tomato Sauce**, which is reminiscent of India's **Spicy String Beans**.

Cinnamon Potatoes with Pine Nuts

This delicious dish combines flavors rarely experienced together in the West. The cinnamon, coriander, and cardamom bespeak an Eastern influence, the pomegranate juice is Caspian and western Asian, and the fruits added to the mix are a Persian phenomenon. Think of it as thousands of years of cultural evolution in each bite! This dish is a regular visitor to our table, and I often pair it with a simple grilled lamb or beef to really let it take center stage. It also works well paired with Azeri **Lamb or Pork Chops with Sour Cherry Sauce** or **Lamb Chops Afghan Style**.

3 medium russet potatoes, parboiled or incompletely cooked in a microwave oven and cooled
1 medium yellow onion, peeled and chopped
2 tablespoons unsalted butter
2 tablespoons light sesame or peanut oil
¼ cup lightly roasted pine nuts
2 hot, dried, red chili peppers
Seeds from 8 cardamom pods (about ¼ teaspoon)
1 teaspoon ground coriander
2 teaspoons ground cinnamon
2 teaspoons granulated sugar
¼ cup beef broth (more if desired)
½ cup dried apricots, soaked and thinly sliced
½ teaspoon salt
½ teaspoon ground black pepper
1 tablespoon pomegranate syrup

Antique Azeri Tableware

1. Heat the butter and the oil in a sauté pan and sauté the onions until they start to soften and become translucent. Add pine nuts and continue to cook.

2. Grind chilies and cardamom seeds. Then add ground coriander, cinnamon, and sugar and grind briefly again until blended. Add spices to the sauté pan and stir well. Add some beef broth to moisten if the sauté pan contents become too dry. Lower heat to medium-low and cook to warm the spices.

3. Add diced apricots and salt and pepper; stir again. Add pomegranate syrup and mix again. Slice potatoes into bite-size chunks and add to the sauté pan. Mix by lifting rather than stirring so as not to mash the potatoes. Cook for 3–5 minutes and scrape the brown bits off the bottom of the pan.

Peas and Sour Plums

This is an Azeri take on the Georgian **Northern Beans with Sour Plums** that builds its sweet and sour flavors with herbs and fruit and then explodes them with dashes of vinegar and sugar just before serving. The earthy peas are accented by the light, sweet dill and the passing dash of sourness offered by the sour plums. It's quick to prepare, light, and works with just a bit of rice to make a nice vegetarian lunch. The secret is the firmness of the peas, so get them fresh if you can.

1 pound fresh or 1 large can firm green peas, drained and rinsed*
2 tablespoons butter
6 shallots, peeled, sliced, and separated
½ cup sour plums, pitted and chopped
1 cup water, hot
¼ teaspoon saffron dissolved in water (above)
1 tablespoon fresh dill, chopped
½ teaspoon salt
¼ teaspoon ground black pepper
½ teaspoon cumin
2 teaspoons white vinegar
1 teaspoon sugar

1. If necessary, pit the sour plums by boiling them in hot water for 10 minutes and then, when they are cool, working the pits out of the meat with your fingers. This is best done well in advance of cooking.

2. Heat water and dissolve saffron in it; set aside. Melt butter in a sauté pan and add sliced shallots and sauté until they start to soften. Then add chopped sour plums and cook 2–3 minutes to warm the plums. Add water (with the saffron in it) and when it is hot add dill, salt, pepper, and cumin. Add white vinegar and sugar and cook until the broth starts to thicken and become a sauce.

3. Then add peas and cook to warm them. Cook another 5–8 minutes if fresh, half that time if canned, and serve.

*If using canned peas, try to get green pigeon peas. They hold up to cooking fairly well.

Eggplants Stuffed with Pomegranate Seeds

This is the punk-rock dish of the Caucasian states, with the pomegranate seeds studding the stuffed eggplant like magenta-colored spiked hair. Similar eggplant preparations are found throughout the region, but this is one of my favorite takes on a stuffed vegetable, so I had to share it! The marigold and the fenugreek broaden and deepen the flavor of the eggplant, while the pomegranate and mint lift it and transform it into something new.

1 medium eggplant
3 tablespoons butter
1 small-medium onion, chopped
1 rib of celery, chopped
2 teaspoons garlic, peeled and chopped
1–2 hot, dried, red chili peppers
½ cup walnuts, chopped
1 teaspoon dried mint leaves
2 teaspoons dried fenugreek leaves
1 teaspoon ground coriander
6 tablespoons pomegranate juice
½ teaspoon marigold petals
½ teaspoon salt (or more to taste)

½ teaspoon ground black pepper

½ cup pomegranate seeds (fresh is best)

1. Slice eggplant lengthwise and hollow out the fleshy insides, leaving a ¼-inch shell all around. Set fleshy meat aside; salt and pepper the shell and place into a baking dish, hollowed side up.

2. Heat butter in an sauté pan and add chopped onion. Sauté for 2–3 minutes and add the hollowed-out portion of the eggplant. Stir well, then lower heat, and cook covered until the eggplant begins to soften and darken. Add celery, garlic, and chilies and cook until eggplant is very soft.

3. Transfer mixture from sauté pan into a food processor and pulse until onions and celery are well integrated into the eggplant but still retain some form. Return to sauté pan and continue cooking over low heat.

4. Add walnuts, mint, fenugreek, coriander, and marigold and stir well. Add about half of the pomegranate juice and stir again. Cook for about 5 more minutes. Add salt, pepper, remaining pomegranate juice, and pomegranate seeds and cook another couple of minutes.

5. Remove from heat and spoon stuffing into eggplant shells. Heap the stuffing high. Add a small amount of water mixed with pomegranate juice to the baking dish and bake in a 350° oven for 20–30 minutes or until eggplant loses form when pinched or poked with a fork.

Spinach with Dill

This is a wonderfully simple vegetable dish from the Caspian. In Azerbaijan, this is made with fresh spinach or sorrel or a combination of the two greens. If you love, say, beet greens like I do, add some into the mix—this is just a general way that greens of all types are prepared. Greens made like this are also used as stuffing for grape or cabbage leaves, dumplings, or (along with rice or ground meat) to stuff vegetables like tomatoes or onions that are then stewed slowly on the stovetop.

1 pound spinach, rinsed, drained, and spun dry in a salad spinner

2 tablespoons butter

1 tablespoon chopped, packed, fresh dill

1 medium onion, peeled and diced
3 cloves garlic, peeled and diced
1 teaspoon salt
½ teaspoon pepper
1 small bunch fresh sorrel or 2 tablespoons dried ground sorrel
3 tablespoons pomegranate juice
½ teaspoon sour grapes
2 tablespoons plain yogurt
3 tablespoons pistachios, finely chopped

1. Melt butter in a sauté pan and add the diced onion. Sauté over medium heat until the onion softens, then add the garlic, salt, pepper, and dried sorrel. Cook 2–3 more minutes and add the pomegranate juice, sour grapes, and yogurt and stir. Cook until a sauce forms.

2. Add spinach and cook covered for 2–3 minutes, stirring a couple of times. Then cook uncovered another 2–3 minutes until the spinach has wilted. If sauce is thin, pour some off and cook spinach until done. Garnish with chopped pistachios and serve.

String Beans in Azeri Tomato Sauce

I really like string beans and think that they are underappreciated in much of the West. If you either agree with me or are a certified bean-hater, please try them this way. It will open up doors of flavor for you and prepare you for some of the other great ways that Asians prepare green beans. This is a delicious and tangy way to prepare string beans that go well with so many other dishes—I hope you agree!

1 pound fresh string beans, trimmed
4 tablespoons butter
2 onions, sliced thinly into crescents
1 batch **Azeri Tomato Sauce** (see Azeri Rice and Grain Dishes, Breads)

1. Melt the butter in a sauté pan set over medium heat. Add the onions and lower the heat, stirring occasionally for 3–5 minutes. Add the green beans, stir, and cover to cook for 20 minutes, stirring occasionally, or until the beans start to soften.

2. Stir in the tomato sauce and half of the basil and all of the pepper.

Stir in yogurt and sour cream, cover, and cook beans until done. Stir in remaining basil; salt to taste and serve.

Rice and Grain Dishes, Breads

A stunning array of pilafs are presented in this chapter that range from those sweetened by fruits, as in the **Sweet Pilaf of Apricots and Almonds** to the spicy and sour **Pilaf with Currants, Cinnamon, and Pepper** to the **Dill and Chickpea Pilaf** with the lightness of dill and lemon to lift it to new heights. There is even a new take on the Arab-influenced pilaf first encountered in Armenia with the **Pilaf of Sesame and Almonds**. Each dish goes wonderfully with grilled or roasted meats or kebabs and will even form the center of a table laden with vegetarian specialties. Azeri oven bread is also offered as an alternative to the rice dishes to brighten your table.

A Sweet Pilaf of Apricots and Almonds

This pilaf is delicious and sweet and well matched with sweet or sour kebabs or roast meats or even by itself. The apricots, currants, and prunes along with the almonds, onions, and broth make this a wonderful, balanced rice dish.

1 cup uncooked basmati rice
2 cups water
3 tablespoons butter
1 medium onion, peeled, sliced, and separated into crescents
2 tablespoons currants
4 medium prunes, pitted and cut lengthwise into narrow strips
½ cup dried apricots, cut into narrow strips
¼ cup chicken or vegetable broth
¼ cup sliced, blanched almonds
1 teaspoon salt
½ teaspoon ground black pepper
1 tablespoon sugar
½ cup orange juice

1. Soak rice in enough water to cover it in a bowl. Heat butter in a large

sauté pan and add the sliced onions. Sauté until they begin to soften, and then add the currants, prunes, apricots, and chicken or vegetable broth and cook gently until the fruit starts to get tender. Add the salt, pepper, and sugar and stir. Add orange juice and almonds, and cover to cook 5 minutes over medium-low heat.

2. In a small saucepan, bring the water to a boil. Drain rice and add it in a single layer over the onion-fruit mix and cover and let it steam for a few minutes. Then, place pot of boiling water on the side of the cooking pot and pour the boiling water by increments into the pot. Pour at several different places to ensure even distribution of the water. Cover and cook on low flame for 45 minutes or more or until done. Check mixture every 15 minutes or so, but do not stir.

3. When done, spoon rice and onion mixture into two separate bowls and have diners layer the onion and fruit mixture over the rice. Alternatively, you can use the method I prefer and place a large, round serving dish over the mouth of the pot and quickly invert the pot contents onto the plate. This second method allows the flavor and juices of the onions to flow down into the rice and spread more evenly around.

Pilaf with Raisins, Cinnamon, and Pepper

In this delicious pilaf, cinnamon is paired with ground black pepper to bring out its spicy side and then the dish is accented with the sweet flavor of brown and golden raisins and chopped chestnuts or hazelnuts to finish. A delightful "dirty rice" to serve with a wide variety of meat and vegetable dishes.

1 cup long grain rice, uncooked
2 ½ cups water
3 tablespoons butter
1 medium onion, peeled and sliced
1 teaspoon salt
½ teaspoon ground black pepper
¼ teaspoon cinnamon
¼ cup water or broth
½ teaspoon saffron dissolved in 1 tablespoon of milk

¼ cup chestnuts or hazelnuts, peeled and chopped
¼ cup brown raisins or mixed brown and golden raisins

1. Rinse and drain rice and then add to water in a medium saucepan and bring to a boil. After it comes to a boil, reduce to a steady simmer and cook for 20–30 minutes until the rice is tender. When rice is done, remove from heat and keep covered until needed.

2. In a medium sauté pan, melt butter and sauté onions until they start to become translucent and color. Add salt, pepper, cinnamon, and water or broth and stir well. Dissolve saffron in a tablespoon of milk, let sit for a minute or two, then add to the pan. Lastly, add the nuts and raisins and cook for another 5–8 minutes or until the raisins start to soften and plump up.

3. Spoon rice out into a bowl or onto a platter and pour the raisin and onion mixture over it. Garnish with a bit more cinnamon and pepper and serve.

Chickpea and Dill Pilaf

This is a delicious and simple pilaf that highlights the trio of dill, lemon juice, and black pepper with wonderful results. Simple to prepare, it is a home-style dish that is eaten widely from Azerbaijan through central Asia, with the chickpeas taking the place of meat. To adapt this for the vegetarian table, trade out the chicken stock for vegetable broth and enjoy.

1 cup rice
2 cups water, boiling (to cook pilaf)
2 tablespoons butter
1 medium onion, peeled, sliced, and separated into crescents
2 cloves garlic, peeled and diced
1 medium tomato, diced
¼ cup chicken stock
1 8-oz. can chickpeas, drained, rinsed, and drained again
2 tablespoons lemon juice
2 tablespoons fresh dill, chopped
1 teaspoon salt
½ teaspoon ground black pepper

1. Soak rice with enough water to cover; set aside. Heat butter in a large saucepan. When hot, add chopped or diced onions and sauté over medium heat. When onions start to become translucent, add garlic, tomato, and chicken stock; heat and stir. Cook for 5 minutes.

2. Add salt, pepper, dill, and lemon juice and stir again. Now add the chickpeas and a little more broth, if needed, just to moisten the mixture. Cook another 5–10 minutes. Taste and adjust flavor if desired by adding more spices. Drain rice completely.

3. Add uncooked rice in a thin layer on top of cooking meat mixture, lower heat, and cover to let rice steam for a few minutes. Place pot of boiling water right on the side of the cooking pot and pour the boiling water by increments into the pot. Pour at several different places to ensure even distribution of the water. Cover and cook on low flame for 45 minutes to 1 hour until done. Check mixture every 15 minutes or so, but do not stir.

Pilaf of Sesame and Almonds

Another Levantine pilaf that is simple, elegant, and really good. In this dish, ginger and black pepper spice up the rice littered with almonds and roasted sesame seeds. A delicate dish that goes with everything.

½ cup blanched almonds
2 tablespoons butter
1 cup long-grain rice
2 cups chicken stock, fresh or canned
1 tablespoon white sesame seeds, dry roasted
1 teaspoon ground ginger
¼ teaspoon salt
Freshly ground black pepper

1. Preheat the oven to 350°. Spread the almonds on a cookie sheet in a single layer and toast in the oven for about 5 minutes. Watch for any sign of burning and regulate the heat accordingly. Set aside.

2. Melt butter in a large saucepan set over moderate heat. Add the rice and stir with a wooden spoon until the rice turns somewhat white and opaque. Stir in the sesame seeds, then pour in the chicken stock, ginger, salt, and a few grindings of black pepper.

3. Stirring constantly, bring to a boil, then cover the casserole tightly and bake in the center of the oven for 20–25 minutes, or until the liquid has all been absorbed and the rice is tender. Sprinkle the reserved almonds over the rice and serve at once.

Azeri Oven Bread

This is a simple, everyday bread in Azerbaijan that is easy to make and will be a great addition to your Azeri or globalized table.

1 package dry yeast
1 ½ cups warm water
1 teaspoon salt
3 cups bread flour, plus extra as needed
1 egg yolk, for garnish
1 tablespoon poppy or sesame seeds (black or white)

1. In a small bowl, mix yeast with water until the yeast is dissolved; set aside until the yeast activates. Preheat oven to 375°.

2. Sift flour into a large bowl. Add salt and mix well. Gradually add the yeast-water mixture and stir in using your hand until a rough ball forms. Turn the dough onto a lightly floured surface and knead the dough, folding it over and turning for about 5–8 minutes, or until smooth and elastic. Shape the dough into a ball and put it back into the large bowl. Cover the bowl with a kitchen towel and let the dough rest for about 1–1 ½ hours, or until the dough has doubled in bulk.

3. Transfer dough to a lightly floured surface and punch it down. Knead for about another 2–3 minutes and shape the dough into a ball. Then using a rolling pin, start rolling the dough until it measures about 12 x 8 inches and is about ½ inch thick.

4. Transfer the bread onto a greased and floured baking sheet and, using a knife, make shallow crosshatching slashes on the bread. Let it rest for about 20 minutes before baking. Just before popping the bread in the oven, brush it with the beaten egg yolk and sprinkle with the sesame or poppy seeds.

5. On the middle rack of a well-preheated oven, bake for about 30–35 minutes or until it is golden in color.

Desserts and Beverages

A real sampling of Azeri desserts awaits, from the delicious nut-filled and honey-infused **Pakhlava** to **Sweet Apricot Crescent Rolls** to represent pastries; a simple and sweet pudding called **Sweet Cinnamon Pudding** for an everyday dessert; and a delicious sweet and tart **Tangy Lemon Sherbet** for a cooling drink anytime.

Pakhlava

This is Azerbaijan's version of Greco-Turkish baklava. Instead of making it with paper-thin filo dough, however, the Azeris prepare it with a thicker, yeasty dough that flakes when cooked. Other differences between this dessert and others from the west are the use of pistachios or almonds instead of walnuts, and vanilla flavoring instead of citrus-infused syrup. A great end to a multicourse meal or an unusual addition to a dessert table, this dish is a western Asian standard.

Dough
1 cup wheat flour
½ cup milk, room temperature or lukewarm
1 egg, lightly beaten
2 teaspoons sugar
1 ½ teaspoons yeast

Filling
¼ cup honey
¾ cup pistachios, almonds, or other nuts, peeled and very finely chopped
¼ cup sugar
¼ teaspoon vanilla
Water as needed (optional)

4 tablespoons butter, melted
¼ teaspoon saffron

1 egg yolk
Pinch or two of sugar (if desired)

¼ cup honey, warmed for garnish (optional)
Whole peeled nuts for garnish (optional)

1. Whisk the milk, sugar, and egg together and add the yeast, stirring gently. Set aside and allow the yeast to activate for about 10–15 minutes. Add flour and mix well. Knead dough for 5–8 minutes and set aside for about 45 minutes to 1 hour in a warm, quiet area.

2. Prepare the filling for the pakhlava by mixing the honey with the nuts, vanilla, and sugar in a medium saucepan and warming over low heat, mixing until the nuts form a spreadable mass. If necessary, add a teaspoon or two of water to thin the filling.

3. Punch down dough and separate it out into 8 balls. Flour and roll each ball out into a thin sheet slightly larger than the pan to be used. Melt butter and spread a thin layer on the pan with a baker's brush or small paintbrush. Place the first sheet of dough at the bottom of the pan and spread a thin (less than ¼ inch) layer of filling over the surface of the dough. Place the second layer of dough over the filling, brush with melted butter, and add another layer of filling. Repeat until all the filling has been used.

4. Place final layer of dough over the top, trim and tuck edges to make them neat, and cut into diamonds or squares. Brush some melted butter on the top sheet and let it absorb for a minute or two. Mix egg yolk and saffron together with a pinch or two more sugar and brush over the surface of the pastry. Bake in a preheated 375° oven for 35–40 minutes or until done. If desired, warm a little honey and pour over the top and sprinkle lightly with nuts.

Sweet Apricot Crescent Rolls

Crescent rolls are earth-bound crescent moons—the Ottoman Osman's symbolic gift to Muslim iconography—and are said to represent the spread of the Islamic faith around the world. You may wish to share these delicious little sweet rolls with everyone you know, and that at least is a start. Easy to make, these crescent rolls are good at any time of day.

1 cup milk, room temperature or lukewarm
2 teaspoons yeast
1 teaspoon salt
¼ cup sugar
1 cup all-purpose flour
2 eggs, lightly beaten
½ cup butter, softened or melted and cooled
¾ cup apricot jam
¾ cup walnuts, finely chopped
½ teaspoon vanilla
Confectioners' sugar for garnish (optional)

1. Dilute yeast in milk; add salt and about 1 tablespoon of sugar and let sit in a quiet dark place until activated, about 10–15 minutes. Mix flour, eggs, and butter and mix well. Add yeast mixture and knead for 5–8 minutes. When done, place dough in warm place for 1 ½ hours.

2. Mix remaining sugar with chopped nuts, apricot jam, and vanilla. Flour and roll dough into ¼-inch-thick sheets and cut into large right triangles. Put the stuffing in the center of the triangle and roll up from the edge opposite the right angle first, turning as you roll. Bake in hot oven for 10–13 minutes. Cool and sprinkle with confectioners' sugar if desired.

Sweet Cinnamon Pudding

Here is another version of the milk pudding enjoyed from the Caucasus to Cathay. Sometimes it's flavored with rosewater or orange water, but here in Azerbaijan, cinnamon and sugar take the lead. Firmi is a very simple, relatively healthy (as desserts go) alternative to end a meal.

6 tablespoons rice flour
2 cups milk
2 tablespoons sugar
2 tablespoons butter
¼ teaspoon cinnamon
¼ teaspoon salt

In a medium saucepan, bring milk to a boil then return to a steady simmer. Dissolve rice flour into the milk, stirring constantly. Add sugar, butter, cinnamon, and salt and continue stirring as the pudding begins to firm up.

When it is starting to firm up, pour into bowls or cups and let firm up and cool. Just before serving, sprinkle with an additional pinch of cinnamon.

Tangy Lemon Sherbet

This is a recipe for real sherbet—not the ground and frozen flavored ice treat you may remember from childhood, but a delicious lemony drink that is poured over large amounts of crushed ice and enjoyed mostly as a liquid until you get to the bottom where the ice slush lies. An Azeri and Iranian standard and enjoyed widely in other parts of the Muslim world as well.

2 quarts water
Juice and zest from 3 lemons
1 teaspoon coriander seeds
3 tablespoons sugar
1 small pinch saffron
Crushed ice as needed

Finely chop the lemon zest and add to the 2 quarts of boiling water. Remove from heat, add coriander seeds, and stir. Allow to steep for several hours to infuse flavors and cool. Strain and add sugar, lemon juice, and saffron and mix well. If still warm, place in refrigerator to cool. When ready to serve, fill each glass about ⅓ to ½ of the way full with crushed ice and pour sherbet liquid over the top.

Appetizers and Condiments

Cabbage rolls, turnovers stuffed with herbs and onions, a delicious walnut-flavored omelet, a salad, and some pickles are to be found in the following pages to introduce you to the breadth of flavors to be found in Azeri appetizers. Keep in mind that all of the dishes presented work wonderfully as an introduction to a large meal and can also become the centerpiece of a small meal with some bread and sauces to accompany them.

Cabbage Rolls Stuffed with Chestnuts and Dill

This is a different sort of *dolma*—made with cabbage leaves instead of grape leaves—but just as tasty and wonderful, with a lamb, rice, and quince stuffing flavored with dill and cilantro. The garlic and the chili peppers lend a bit of spice and heat to this wonderful dish that is at home as an appetizer but can also serve as a light meal.

2 cups ground lamb or beef
⅓ cup cooked rice
I medium onion, finely chopped
I tablespoon garlic, peeled and chopped
I medium tomato, diced
I quince, peeled and chopped
3 tablespoons chestnuts, chopped (substitute walnuts or other nuts if chestnuts are unavailable)
¼ cup chopped cilantro
¼ cup fresh dill
I teaspoon salt
½ teaspoon ground black pepper
1–2 hot, dried, red chili peppers
10–12 large cabbage leaves to wrap

Broth
1 ½ cups beef broth
2 tablespoons unsalted butter
3 teaspoons vinegar
I teaspoon sugar

1. In a food processor, combine onion, garlic, tomato, quince, chestnuts, cilantro, dill, salt, pepper, and hot chili peppers. Pulse grind until well mixed, but ensure the vegetables still have their shape. Do not overgrind. Add meat and rice and mix again until well integrated.

2. If using bottled leaves, rinse and dry each leaf. If using fresh leaves, separate leaves and boil in lightly salted water until tender but still firm. Drain and dry freshly cooked leaves. If desired, cut the extremely large leaves into more manageable sections. I like to use leaves that are about 4–6 inches long for appetizer-size rolls and leaves that are 6–8 inches long for larger dinner-size dolmas. Depending on the width of the leaf, place 2–3 tablespoons of filling about 2 inches from

one edge and then roll the leave lengthwise, tucking in the top and bottom as you roll to make compact squarish rolls.

3. Melt butter in a large saucepan or sauté pan and add vinegar, sugar, and about half of the broth. Place rolled leaves in the pan and cover with the remaining broth. Cook covered over low heat until done, about 40 minutes. Serve with rice or boiled potatoes.

Turnovers with Herbs and Onions

Like the flaky turnovers with spinach and cheese, these Azeri pastries are stuffed with copious quantities of herbs and onions—not too dissimilar from an Iranian Gormeh Sabzi stew. Simply flavored with salt and pepper, enjoying the natural flavor of the herbs is the point of these delicate pastries.

Pastry
I cup wheat flour
½ cup water
I egg
I teaspoon salt

Filling
3 tablespoons butter
I medium onion, peeled and finely diced
I large bunch dill (20–25 sprigs)
I small bunch fresh cilantro leaves (15–20 sprigs)
I teaspoon dried fenugreek leaves
1–2 tablespoons beef or vegetable broth (as needed)
2 tablespoons dried sour plums,, finely diced
I teaspoon salt
½ teaspoon pepper
I small bunch spinach

Yogurt for dipping as needed

1. Make pastry by combining flour, water, egg, and salt in a medium bowl; mix ingredients well. Knead dough for about 5 minutes and then set aside for about 30 minutes as you prepare the filling.

2. In a medium sauté pan, melt butter and sauté the onions until they

start to become transparent. Then add the chopped dill and cilantro, and sauté until the spices wilt. Add fenugreek, broth if mix is too dry, chopped sour plums, salt, and pepper and mix well. Add spinach and mix well. Cover and cook until spinach is tender, stirring often, about 5 minutes.

3. Divide dough into several similarly sized balls. Flour and roll out balls to form circles about 8 inches in diameter. Place a few tablespoons of filling along a line in the center of the circle and fold the circle in half, pressing the edges together as you go. Seal the edges with a fork and curve the pastries slightly into crescent shapes as you place them on a greased or sprayed baking sheet. Make all of the pastries in this manner.

4. Bake in a preheated oven at 375° for 15–20 minutes or until the pastries start to color. When done, remove from oven to cool for a few minutes and, if desired, pour a bit of melted butter over the pastries just before serving for an authentic touch. Serve with slightly drained yogurt for dipping.

Walnut Kuku

This is another wonderful example of the baked vegetable-omelets eaten throughout the region. Here, the lemon juice and dill work with the walnuts to form a delicious and filling meal. Tasty and easy to prepare, kukus will convince you that eggs aren't just for breakfast anymore.

3 eggs, beaten
2 tablespoons butter
3 spring onions, finely chopped
½ cup shredded spinach, washed and spun dry
3 teaspoons ground coriander
1 teaspoon dried dill
2 teaspoons lemon juice
½ cup walnuts, finely chopped
½ teaspoon salt
¼ teaspoon pepper

1. Preheat oven to 375°. On the stovetop, melt butter in a covered, ovenproof casserole over medium-low heat and add spring onions and spinach when the butter is warm. Stir well and cook covered

for 3 minutes to get spinach to wilt. Keep cooking until the spinach is limp.

2. Combine coriander, dill, lemon juice, walnuts, salt, and pepper with the beaten eggs and beat again until all ingredients are well integrated. Pour egg-spice mixture into the casserole with the spring onions and the spinach and stir well until onions and spinach are blended. Cover and bake for 15–20 minutes.

3. When done, loosen the edges of the omelet by running a knife around the edge of the casserole. Serve in casserole, or place a serving plate over the mouth of the casserole dish and quickly invert. Then cover the bottom of the omelet with another serving plate and invert again, so the puffy, baked side faces upward.

Azeri Salad

This is a recipe for the national salad of Azerbaijan and loved by almost all Azeris! It is also representative of the many sour cream dressed salads eaten throughout western Asian and into southern Russia. The sour cream and dill blend seamlessly together to form a wonderful dressing for the fruits and vegetables. It is enjoyed at every festive occasion and eaten often at home as well. Very simple to prepare and can be made as a quick appetizer to a main meal in a flash.

2 medium-large tomatoes
1 small cucumber, peeled, seeded, and chopped
3 spring onions, chopped (white and green parts)
1 small to medium onion, peeled and diced
4–6 medium red radishes, sliced into paper-thin rounds
2 tablespoons sour cream
1 tablespoon fresh dill, finely diced and packed
1 teaspoon salt
½ teaspoon ground black pepper

Whisk together the sour cream, dill, salt, and pepper until smooth. Toss vegetables together and pour dressing over all and toss lightly again. Chill lightly and serve arranged on a plate or in a serving bowl.

Samovars in Baku

Azeri Pickled Garlic

Here's a pickled garlic that is enjoyed as an appetizer or snack with a bit of flat bread or a sour roll. It is much more sour than the related Iranian dish that uses pomegranate juice to pickle the garlic, but just as tasty.

50–60 cloves of garlic, peeled and rinsed
1–2 cups red wine vinegar
2 teaspoons salt
2 teaspoons sugar
1 tablespoon whole black peppercorns
6 cloves
3 bay leaves

Pack garlic cloves into a clean, sealable jar. When about halfway filled, add salt, peppercorns, cloves, and bay leaves. Add the rest of the garlic cloves and pack them in the jar tightly. When done, pour vinegar over all and seal. Let sit in a cool or cold place for at least 1 month before enjoying.

Sauces and Spice Mixtures

To round out the chapter, here are some simple sauces. The first one, **Sour Cherry Sauce**, is used by the Azeris on meats, but it also works well on vegetables. The second one, the **Sour Tomato Sauce** is generally used on green beans and other vegetables, but I've found it makes a lovely sauce for chicken and other fowl as well as lamb. The last sauce is a dipping sauce that you can offer with bread or grilled meats and vegetables for a tasty, cooling treat.

Sour Cherry Sauce

Here is a delicious sauce that you will want to use again and again on roasted meats, chops, and kebabs. Works wonderfully with roasted vegetables as well. The sweet and sour flavor of the cherries is offset by the cinnamon, pepper, and lemon juice and mellowed just a bit by the butter. A really amazing and simple sauce to accent a wide variety of dishes.

2 tablespoons butter
½ teaspoon salt
1 tablespoon lemon juice
½ teaspoon ground pepper
½ teaspoon ground cinnamon
1 small pinch ground cloves (no more than ⅛ teaspoon)
1 cup sour cherries, chopped

To make the sauce, melt butter in a saucepan and dissolve salt in it. Stir in pepper, cinnamon, cloves, and lemon juice and add chopped cherries. Stir until cherries start to break down, about 5–7 minutes.

Azeri Tomato Sauce

Here is a wonderful tomato sauce, made slightly sour by the yogurt, sour cream, and vinegar but sweetened by the addition of sweet basil. Commonly used to flavor vegetables such as green beans and peas, but can also be used on meats as well. Works particularly well with chicken and fowl as well as lamb.

8 ounces tomato sauce
2 tablespoons finely chopped fresh basil
1 teaspoon salt
½ teaspoon ground black pepper
¼ cup plain yogurt
¼ cup sour cream
2 teaspoons white vinegar

In a small to medium saucepan, stir in the tomato sauce, half of the basil, and all of the pepper. Cook 3–5 minutes or until warmed. Stir in yogurt and sour cream, cover, and cook another 5 minutes, stirring often. Stir in remaining basil and salt, cook another 3–5 minutes, and pour over your favorite vegetables.

Cucumber and Yogurt Sauce

Cool and refreshing with a zing from the herbs and sumac, this condiment will cool down your mouth when eating spicy kebabs! An example of the yogurt-cucumber preparations eaten throughout the Caucasian and Caspian territories, this dish may even remind you of a more highly spiced Indian *riata*, its distant cousin.

1 ½ cups whole-milk plain yogurt
2 teaspoons garlic, peeled and chopped
2 medium cucumbers, peeled, seeded, and grated
2 tablespoons fresh mint, chopped
1 tablespoon fresh cilantro, chopped
¼ teaspoon sumac

Combine in a bowl the yogurt, garlic, cucumbers, mint, and cilantro. Cover and refrigerate for several hours or overnight to allow the flavors to blend. Before serving, stir in some sumac and garnish with mint leaves.

A Mountain Road in Western Iran

Iran

Main spices and flavors: tamarind, sesame, coriander, cilantro, mint, saffron, sumac, fenugreek, sour grapes, sour cherries, sour plums, cumin, dill, tarragon, garlic, onion, turmeric, cardamom, cinnamon, ginger, cloves, nutmeg, chili peppers, tomato, potato

Souring agents: lemons, pomegranates, oranges, white vinegar, Persian limes, sour grapes

Civilization in Iran goes back over eight thousand years, with evidence from archaeological sites in the southwestern part of the country showing significant agricultural communities that had links to better-known settlements in the Fertile Crescent. Empire building began in earnest with Cyrus the Great's Achaemenid Dynasty in the fifth century BCE and at its greatest extent ran from Greece and Thrace in the west, to the Indus River in the east, and included Libya and Egypt as well. During this time, the first declaration of human rights guaranteeing legal and political rights was codified and gold and silver coinage was introduced.

Alexander conquered the Achaemenids in 333 BCE and during the hundred years of Greek rule, Greek language, philosophy, and art came to Iran with colonists from the west, Buddhism flowed westward from India and flourished in Afghanistan and Iran, and Zoroastrianism flowed outward from Iran to surrounding countries. Native Persian rule was resumed in the second century BCE with the rise of the Parthian Dynasty, which ruled the country for almost five hundred years when the Sassanian Dynasty assumed control. The Sassanids ruled from North Africa and southern Russia in the west to parts of India, Pakistan, and Kirghizstan in the east, and their rule was characterized by the same cosmopolitan tolerance for other cultures and religions that distinguished Cyrus's rule almost one thousand years earlier.

The Sassanid rule of Persia was influential far beyond the borders of the empire, with cultural elements reaching as far as Byzantine Europe and China. Even when the empire fell to Islamic conquest in the sixth century, the empire slowly became Muslim, but it retained its Persian cultural identity. Much of what we now identify as Islamic culture was in large part influenced by the converted Sassanid Persians.

Arab rule during the hundred years of the Umayyad Dynasty brought many elements of Arab culture—including the Arabic language—to Iran, which were incorporated either by choice or by force. Enforcement of foreign culture and customs caused unrest in the polity of the empire and continued until the Abbasid takeover in 750 CE. The mixed Persian-Arab Abbasids reasserted Persian control over the empire by allowing the rise of semi-independent Persian states. This loose confederation lasted for several hundred years but gradually fell sway in the eleventh century to a confederation of Turkic tribes called the Seljuks, who ruled from Anatolia to central Asia for two hundred years.

The Mongol conquest of Persia, which began with the genocide of millions of people from deliberate extermination and famine, also brought many Far Eastern cultural practices to Iran. Around the turn of the fourteenth century, the Mongols began rebuilding the empire and encouraged renewed work in art, architecture, and public works. The Uzbek Tamerlane conquered the Persian Empire piece by piece beginning in 1381 and held it until the mid-fifteenth century when it fell once again to the Turkmen. The Safavid Persians ruled from the sixteenth century until the mid-eighteenth century, made Sh'ia Islam the official religion of the state, and are responsible, in large part, for the formation of the modern state of Iran.

All of these foreign contacts—whether they were with conquerors or the conquered—have left marks on what we now know as Iranian cuisine and likewise brought elements of Persian cookery to many faraway places. As ingredients go, the native complement of Persian items such as pomegranates, walnuts, sour grapes, sour cherries, dried sour plums, sumac, lemons, and cumin were supplemented by contacts and trade with other nations. Early contacts with the Greeks probably brought cilantro and coriander to Iran, and trade in antiquity with India brought black pepper, oranges, and cardamom. Indo-Pacific spices and souring agents such as cinnamon, cloves, nutmeg, and limes were likely later additions brought to Iran along the Great Silk Road, while favorite herbs such as dill and tarragon entered Iranian cuisine via contact with the central Asian states of Turkmenistan and Uzbekistan.

As rich as its native tradition of ingredients is, it is hard to imagine Iranian cuisine without all of the foreign herbs and spices that have been incorporated into the dishes over time. For example, the recipe for **Advieh** would be left with only Persian lime powder, and **Sour Meat and Vegetables** and **Rice with Herbs** would be very different dishes without dill, cilantro, black pepper, and saffron. The tradition of rice-stuffed vegetables as seen in **Stuffed Tomatoes** and **Iranian Stuffed Peppers** is at least shared with the Turkmen, if not inherited from them, and the use of rhubarb as in **Lamb and Rhubarb Stew** is also acquired from central Asia as well.

Meat Dishes

Meat dishes in Iranian cuisine are almost always slow cooked with vegetables either as stews called koreshes or baked in casseroles. A uniquely Persian way of preparing meat that spread far and wide across western, central, and parts of South Asia as well as into the Levant is to pair meats with fruits as well as vegetables in most dishes. So, oranges are a significant addition to **Orange-Chicken Koresh** and pomegranates are the basis of the flavoring in **Lamb Fesenjan** while rhubarb lends its sour flavor to **Lamb with Rhubarb**. Even at a distance, the Persian way of mixing meats and fruits persists to the present day, and in later volumes of *The Silk Road Gourmet*, we encounter a strongly Persian-influenced dish from Kirghizstan and other nations as well

Orange-Chicken Koresh

Orange and chicken with hints of lime, almonds, and pistachios are some of the incredible combination flavors you'll experience in this dish. It is really delicious, rich, and complex—the orange blends beautifully with the sweet nutmeg and cardamom, while the vinegar and lime powder balance this with a hint of sourness. All in all, an excellent introduction to Iranian cuisine.

3 medium-large chicken breasts, cut into bite-size pieces
3 tablespoons light sesame or peanut oil
2 large onions, peeled, sliced, and separated into crescents
2 tablespoons orange zest, finely chopped
1 ½ cups orange juice (4–5 oranges)
½ teaspoon ground cinnamon
½ teaspoon ground cardamom
½ teaspoon ground nutmeg
½ teaspoon cumin
½ teaspoon coriander
1 teaspoon salt
½ teaspoon ground black pepper
½ teaspoon Persian lime powder
2 medium carrots, julienned or matchsticked
3 teaspoons slivered almonds
2 teaspoons chopped pistachio nuts
3 medium oranges, peeled, cleaned, and separated into segments
2 tablespoons white vinegar
¼ cup lime juice (2–3 limes)
¼ cup sugar
¼ teaspoon saffron threads, dissolved into 2 tablespoons of hot water

1. Heat oil in a deep saucepan and sauté chicken over high heat until it becomes firm and starts to color—the point being to sear the meat

but not completely cook it. When done, remove from the pan with a slotted spoon and set aside. Lower heat to medium and add the sliced onions and cook until they soften and start to color.

2. When the onions are done, add the orange zest and stir well. Add the chicken back into the pan along with any juices that have collected. Then add the orange juice and bring to a near boil. Then add the cinnamon, cardamom, nutmeg, cumin, coriander, salt, black pepper, and Persian lime powder and lower heat and cook covered for 20–30 minutes, stirring occasionally, or until chicken starts to become tender.

3. Combine the vinegar, lime juice, sugar, and saffron water in a medium saucepan and heat for 10 minutes or so until hot. Then remove from heat and add orange segments and stir well. Set aside until needed.

4. Next, add the julienned carrots, slivered almonds, and chopped pistachios to the chicken mixture and cook for another 15 minutes or so. When done, remove from heat and pour in lime juice mixture used to soak orange segments and stir. Then add orange segments to the stew and stir again.

Lamb in a Pomegranate-Cardamom Sauce (Fesenjan)

This is a new twist on a classic Persian recipe that is simply phenomenal! The lamb is stovetop roasted in pomegranates, lemons, onions, and spices, including cinnamon and cardamom. There's also the spice of a few hot peppers and the added sweetness of some sugar and butternut squash that is cooked along with the meat. The flavors are richer and more complex than those in the related Azeri **Hens with Pomegranate Sauce**, and some cooks will find the stovetop cooking easier than oven roasting. If you like this recipe, it is easy to adapt to other meats by adjusting the cooking times.

2–2 ½ pounds lamb roast
3 tablespoons light sesame or peanut oil
2 tablespoons butter
I large onion, minced

4 hot, dried, red chili peppers, diced
½ teaspoon turmeric
I cup walnuts, coarsely chopped
⅓ cup water
I ½ cups pomegranate juice
4 tablespoons pomegranate syrup (also called concentrate)
2 teaspoons salt
I tablespoon sugar
½ teaspoon ground cinnamon
I ½ teaspoons ground cardamom
2 tablespoons lemon juice
½ medium butternut squash, peeled and chopped

1. Heat oil in a large, heavy saucepan and sear the roast over very high heat until it is browned on all sides. When roast is browned, lower heat and remove it from the pan and place it on a plate. Then, melt butter, sauté the onions until they begin to soften, and add the diced peppers and the turmeric. Stir well to blend and add the walnuts and stir again.

2. Add water, pomegranate juice and syrup, salt, sugar, cardamom, cinnamon, and lemon juice and stir well. When sauce has warmed, place roast back into the saucepan and cook covered for 30 minutes. Stir and spoon the sauce over the meat occasionally. Add peeled and chopped squash around the roast and cook covered until roast is done, about another 30 minutes, stirring occasionally.

3. When the roast is done, let sit covered for 5 minutes, stirring occasionally. Then put roast on a serving plate and either place the squash around it or serve in a separate bowl. Serve with white rice or a simple pilaf.

Beef with Dried Lemons and Herbs (Gormeh Sabzi)

Unlike a lot of meat dishes offered in this chapter, this dish is mildly sour and tasty without any hint of sweetness. The large amount of herbs and green vegetables give it a unique and "green" taste, and the beans mellow the sour lemons just enough to make them delicious. With a little bit more turmeric and chili powder stirred in just before serving, this dish provides a wonderful exploration into Iranian cuisine.

1 pound stew beef, cubed
3 tablespoons cooking oil
1 medium onion, finely diced
3–4 stems fresh leek greens, chopped (greens only)
8 spring onions, chopped crosswise
¼ cup water or beef broth
1 bunch fresh cilantro leaves, finely chopped (15–20 sprigs)
1 bunch fresh dill, finely chopped (25–30 sprigs)
1 tablespoon dried fenugreek leaves
1 ½ teaspoons salt
1 teaspoon ground black pepper
1 large bunch fresh spinach or 1 bag, rinsed and spun dry
1 cup water
1 cup beef broth
4 dried lemons, 1 hole poked in each one
1 8-oz. can northern beans, drained, rinsed, and drained again
1 ½ teaspoons turmeric
1 ½ teaspoons cayenne pepper
1 tablespoon lemon juice (optional)

1. Heat oil in a medium saucepan and when hot, sear the cubed beef, stirring constantly, over high heat until it becomes firm and starts to get a golden color around the edges. When the beef is done, remove from the pan with a slotted spoon and set aside.

2. Lower heat and sauté onion until it softens and starts to color. Add leeks and spring onions and sauté until the leeks are tender. And cilantro, dill, and fenugreek and stir well, then add water or beef broth to moisten the mix and cook for 2–3 minutes or until herbs wilt. Add the salt and pepper and stir well and then add the spinach and cook covered, stirring occasionally for 2–3 minutes until the spinach starts to wilt.

3. Add beef broth and water and heat. When the liquid is hot, add the beef back into the stew and stir well. Then add the dried lemons and mix again. Cover and cook over medium-low or low heat for 30 minutes, stirring occasionally. Cook uncovered another 30 minutes over low heat; if necessary, add a bit more broth or water. When beef

is just about done, add the turmeric and chili powder and stir well. Then add the beans and cook another 3–5 minutes or until beans have warmed. If you like the sour taste, add a bit more lemon juice (optional) and cook to warm it. Serve over rice or with a rice-stuffed vegetable.

Baked Fish with Pomegranates and Oranges

Sweet, sour, slightly spicy, and simply delicious—this is another one of the meat dishes that will always please and garner copious compliments for the cook. It's a Caspian recipe that, in an unusual twist, combines both pomegranate and sour grape powder as souring agents. It's great served with either a plain or spiced rice, such as **Rice with Sour Cherries** or **Rice with Herbs**.

4 thick steaks of a fleshy white fish, such as sea bass (or rockfish) or trout
3–4 tablespoons pomegranate syrup (also called concentrate)*
3 tablespoons light sesame or peanut oil
12 spring onions, chopped crosswise
1 cup pomegranate juice
1 teaspoon sour grape powder
1 cup orange juice (about 3–4 oranges)
1 cup tomato sauce
1 teaspoon salt
¼ teaspoon black pepper
1 teaspoon red pepper flakes
2 teaspoons sugar
2 teaspoons **advieh**
1 medium bunch fresh cilantro leaves, chopped (25–30 sprigs)

1. Preheat oven to 375°. Brush or pour 2 tablespoons of pomegranate syrup over the fish steaks. Then season with a little bit of extra salt and ground black pepper and set aside. Heat oil in a sauté pan and sauté the spring onions until they are wilted. Add the pomegranate juice, remaining pomegranate syrup, and sour grape powder and mix well.

2. Add orange juice, tomato sauce, salt, black pepper, red pepper, sugar, advieh, and cilantro and mix well. Cook for 5–8 minutes or until the liquid starts to evaporate and the sauce thickens.

3. When the sauce is done, spoon a few tablespoons onto the bottom of a covered, ovenproof casserole and place fish skin side down on the sauce. Then spoon the remaining sauce and vegetables evenly over the fish. Cover and bake 15–20 minutes, checking and basting occasionally. Then uncover and bake another 15 minutes or until the fish is tender and nicely cooked.

*Pomegranate concentrate can be made by simply boiling down a quantity of pomegranate juice. For the amount called for in this recipe, boil 1 ½ cups of pomegranate juice down over low heat until its volume decreases by more than half and it thickens substantially.

Lamb and Rhubarb Stew

This is an unusual stew from the northeast of Iran near Mashhad that borders on Turkmenistan. It uses that central Asian wonder, rhubarb, as a souring agent to complement the earthy lamb, much as sour plums or sour cherries are used. Like many other central Asian dishes, it also relies on herbs rather than spices for much of its flavor. It's a great example of the foods that came flooding west from the various Persian conquests of the territories to its north and east. Since rhubarb is being rediscovered as a vegetable, it is often available beyond its traditional short "season," which allows this recipe to be made almost any time of the year.

4 thick steaks of a fleshy white fish, such as sea bass (or rockfish) or trout
3–4 tablespoons pomegranate syrup (also called concentrate)*
3 tablespoons light sesame or peanut oil
12 spring onions, chopped crosswise
1 cup pomegranate juice
1 teaspoon sour grape powder
1 cup orange juice (about 3–4 oranges)
1 cup tomato sauce
1 teaspoon salt
¼ teaspoon black pepper
1 teaspoon red pepper flakes
2 teaspoons sugar
2 teaspoons **advieh**
1 medium bunch fresh cilantro leaves, chopped (25–30 sprigs)

1. Preheat oven to 375°. Brush or pour 2 tablespoons of pomegranate syrup over the fish steaks. Then season with a little bit of extra salt and ground black pepper and set aside. Heat oil in a sauté pan and sauté the spring onions until they are wilted. Add the pomegranate juice, remaining pomegranate syrup, and sour grape powder and mix well.

2. Add orange juice, tomato sauce, salt, black pepper, red pepper, sugar, advieh, and cilantro and mix well. Cook for 5–8 minutes or until the liquid starts to evaporate and the sauce thickens.

3. When the sauce is done, spoon a few tablespoons onto the bottom of a covered, ovenproof casserole and place fish skin side down on the sauce. Then spoon the remaining sauce and vegetables evenly over the fish. Cover and bake 15–20 minutes, checking and basting occasionally. Then uncover and bake another 15 minutes or until the fish is tender and nicely cooked.

Stuffed Peppers

Vegetable Dishes and Salads

Just as with their meats, Iranians tend to slow cook their vegetables in stews and casseroles, as we see in **Okra Koresh** and **Orange Sweet Potatoes with Sour Plums**. They are also grilled, skewered separately as side dishes for kebab meals, and stuffed with meat and rice or simply rice and seasoned with black pepper, sweet lime juice, and a variety of herbs, as in **Stuffed Tomatoes** and **Iranian Stuffed Peppers**. Iranians also have a rich tradition of salads using tomatoes and cucumbers either individually or in combination, as in **Shiraz Tomato Salad** and **Cucumber Salad with Mint**. Another way of eating vegetables that is Persian in origin but which has spread to the Caspian and Caucasus is to bake them in egg-based casseroles called kuku, which are essentially omelets eaten at any time of the day, as in **Kuku with Green Peas and Pistachio Nuts**.

Okra Koresh

In this wonderful way to prepare okra, the turmeric jumps right out and wraps this dish in a warm, buttery blanket that is cut by the occasional sharpness of the lime juice. Delicious with **Lamb in a Pomegranate-Cardamom Sauce (*Fesenjan*)** or some other roasted meat or matched with other strong main-dish vegetables on a vegetarian table.

1 pound okra, washed, caps and tails removed, and cut crosswise
2 tablespoons peanut oil
2 medium onions, peeled, sliced lengthwise, and separated into crescents
1 teaspoon garlic, peeled and diced
1 cup tomato sauce
½ cup water
3 tablespoons lime juice
1 teaspoon salt
½ teaspoon ground black pepper
1 tablespoon ground turmeric

1. Heat oil in a sauté pan and sauté onions until they begin to soften and color. Then add garlic and cook until it swells and begins to become

light tan or golden. Add tomato sauce, water, and lime juice and cook to heat liquid.

2. When sauce is hot, add salt, pepper, and turmeric and stir well to mix. Then add the okra and when hot, cook covered for 10 minutes, stirring occasionally. Then uncover and cook another 5–10 minutes or until okra is done. Serve with rice.

Shiraz Tomato Salad

A wonderful, simple, and quick-to-make salad, with the mint and lime juice offering a real Persian twist to the usual tomato-based salad. This salad has to be served immediately after making to get the full spectrum of flavor of the dish. If allowed to sit, the mint dominates the lime and the vegetables give off too much liquid. But it is really delicious served cold, so I recommend refrigerating all of the ingredients for a few hours before preparation.

4 medium tomatoes, chopped
1 medium onion, peeled, sliced, and separated into crescents
¼ cup fresh lime juice (about 1–2 limes)
2 tablespoons almond or other nut oil
2 tablespoons fresh mint, diced
1 teaspoon salt
½ teaspoon black pepper
2 small Asian cucumbers or ½ of a large Western one, peeled and seeded (optional)

1. In a mixing bowl, combine chilled chopped tomatoes and onions with the fresh mint, salt, and pepper and mix well. If using cucumbers, peel and finely chop the chilled cucumbers and add them to the salad and mix well.

2. Whisk the lime juice together with the small amount of oil, pour it over the vegetables and spices, mix a few turns, and serve immediately.

Stuffed Tomatoes with Tarragon and Lime

The rice for this stuffing is so flavorful that these tomatoes seem like they are stuffed with a little piece of heaven! The rice blends flavors of tomato, tarragon, lime juice, and sugar for delicious results, and the tomato becomes just tender enough after a short time in the oven that it is a savory and complementary container. Serve with roast meat, spicy kebabs, or other vegetable dishes for the foundations of a wonderful meal.

4 large and firm tomatoes
3 cups cooked basmati rice, cooled
2 tablespoons light sesame or peanut oil
2 medium onions, finely chopped
¼ cup water or vegetable broth
I teaspoon salt
½ teaspoon ground black pepper
3 teaspoons tomato paste
3 tablespoons lime juice (2–3 limes)
I teaspoon sugar
I small bunch fresh cilantro leaves, chopped (15–20 sprigs)
5 spring onions, finely chopped
⅓ cup tarragon, finely chopped

1. Preheat oven to 350°. Cut a small circle at the tops of the tomatoes, reserve the top for a lid, and scoop out the insides, taking care not to make the outer layer thin. Discard the tomato meat. Sprinkle a small amount of salt inside the tomatoes and set aside.

2. Heat oil in a medium sauté pan and sauté onions 2–3 minutes or until they soften and start to become golden. Add water, salt, pepper, and tomato paste and cook 3–5 minutes until the liquid starts to evaporate and the mixture thickens.

3. Then add lime juice, sugar, cilantro, spring onions, and tarragon and sauté until the herbs are cooked. Add the rice one cup at a time and fold into the vegetable and herb mixture. Depending on the size of the tomatoes, you may only need to use 2 cups of rice instead of 3.

4. Fill the tomatoes with the mix. Fill them so they are firm but not packed, and close the tops loosely. Spray or oil a baking dish large enough to accommodate the tomatoes, and add 3 tablespoons of water to the dish. Place the tomatoes in the dish and bake 15–20 minutes.

Cucumber Salad with Mint

This is a light, slightly spicy salad to help clear the palate after a rich, flavorful dinner. The cucumbers and onions are marinated in a vinegary dressing that is just slightly sweetened by some chopped fresh mint—a delightful combination!

l medium to large cucumber, peeled, seeded, and chopped
l medium onion, peeled and very finely diced
l tablespoon fresh mint leaves, chopped
l teaspoon salt
½ teaspoon black pepper
l teaspoon black peppercorns, lightly cracked
2 tablespoons white vinegar
2 tablespoons lime juice
⅛ teaspoon ground sumac

Combine cucumber, onion, and mint with salt, pepper, and white vinegar and mix well. Refrigerate for at least 30 minutes. Just before serving, stir the salad and sprinkle sumac over it.

Orange Sweet Potatoes and Sour Plums

This dish is sort of like a curried, sweet potato pie made into a stew. It blends a complement of "sweet" spices with those traditionally used in curries to accent the flavor of the sweet potatoes and dried sour plums. The secret, if there is one, is cooking the sweet potatoes enough to get them to contribute their unique flavor without overcooking them into a mash. Makes a nice side dish on either an omnivore or vegetarian table.

4 cups sweet potatoes, peeled and chopped (2–3 sweet potatoes)
3 tablespoons butter
l medium onion, peeled and sliced
l tablespoons garlic, peeled and diced
l teaspoon salt
¼ teaspoon ground black pepper
l ½ cups orange juice
l teaspoon ground coriander
½ teaspoon ground cardamom

1 teaspoon ground cumin
1 teaspoon cinnamon
1 teaspoon turmeric
1 teaspoon ground ginger
¼ teaspoon ground cloves
1 cup dried sour plums, pitted and chopped very finely

1. Boil 4 cups of water in a small saucepan, and when it reaches a full, rolling boil, add the dried sour plums and cook for 2–3 minutes. Then remove from heat and let them sit for an additional 5 minutes or so. Then drain and let dry and cool completely. This parboiling loosens the fruit from its pit and makes it easy to remove the pits with just your hands. I usually do this the day before cooking a recipe that needs pitted sour plums.

2. Heat butter in a large sauté pan and sauté onion for 2–3 minutes until it softens and starts to color. Then add the garlic and cook another 2–3 minutes or until it starts to swell and color. Add salt and black pepper and stir well. Add orange juice and cook to heat the juice.

3. When the juice is hot, add the ground coriander, cardamom, cumin, cinnamon, turmeric, ginger, and cloves and stir well. When the spices are integrated, add the sweet potato and cook 2–3 minutes to warm the vegetable. Then cook covered for 10–15 minutes, stirring occasionally, or until the squash starts to soften.

4. When squash is almost done, gently fold dried plums into the pan and cook another 3–5 minutes to warm the plums and serve immediately.

Beet and Yogurt Salad

This salad and others like it are eaten all over the Muslim world from the Maghreb through the Levant. Vegetables are paired with drained yogurt or yogurt cheese called "laban." In other parts of western Asia and even into southern Russia, similar salads are flavored with sour cream instead of yogurt. This dish probably originates on the Saudi peninsula and was adopted in Iran and spread throughout western Asia during the Umayyad or Abbasid Dynasties.

2–3 beets, rinsed and baked in aluminum foil until tender at 350° (30–45 minutes)
1 small onion, very finely diced
⅛ cup olive oil
⅛ cup fresh lemon juice
1 small bunch chopped fresh cilantro (15–20 sprigs)
1 cup **Chaka** (see Afghan Sauces, Spice Mixtures, and Condiments)
½ teaspoon salt
½ teaspoon ground black pepper

1. Set up the yogurt to drain while preparing the salad. When the beets have cooled enough to handle, unwrap them and peel the skin off by hand. If they are cooked enough, the skin should just slip off into your hands. Slice the beets into thin strips and combine with the diced onions. Chill in the refrigerator until the vegetables are cold.

2. Remove vegetables from the refrigerator and set aside. In a mixing bowl, combine oil, lemon juice, cilantro, and drained yogurt and mix well. Add salt and pepper and mix again. Pour over vegetables, mix, and serve in a bowl, or for a more traditional presentation, arrange vegetables on a plate and pour the yogurt dressing over all.

Iranian Stuffed Peppers

Another wonderful stuffed vegetable recipe that will stand on its own for a light meal or as the centerpiece on either a vegetarian or omnivore table. The flavors of sweet lime, mint, and cilantro combine with the tomato and pepper to make this a sweet but slightly spicy recipe that is sure to please both you and your guests.

4 medium red peppers, cored and defleshed
3 cups cooked basmati rice, cooled
2 tablespoons light sesame or peanut oil
2 medium onions, finely chopped
1 cup water or vegetable broth
1 teaspoon salt
½ teaspoon ground black pepper
1 tablespoon tomato paste
¼ cup plus 2 tablespoons fresh lime juice
2 teaspoons sugar
¼ cup pistachio nuts, finely chopped

Iranian Girl Smiling

1 small bunch fresh cilantro leaves, chopped (15–20 sprigs)
⅓ cup fresh mint, finely chopped
½ cup spring onions, finely chopped
½ cup tomato sauce

1. Sprinkle some salt inside the peppers and set aside. Heat oil in a medium sauté pan and sauté onions for 2–3 minutes or until they soften and start to color. Add water, salt, pepper, and tomato paste. Cook until the water starts to evaporate and the mixture thickens.

2. Add ¼ cup lime juice, 2 teaspoons sugar, pistachio nuts, cilantro, mint, and spring onions and sauté until the herbs wilt. Fold in the rice, cup by cup, taking care not to smash it.

3. Fill the peppers loosely with the rice and herb mix, and place the tops of the peppers back on. In a large saucepan, combine ½ cup water and tomato sauce with the remaining lime juice and sugar and cook for 2–3 minutes until warm. Place the peppers side by side in the pan and cook covered 20–30 minutes, basting occasionally until they are cooked.

Rice and Grain Dishes, Breads

Rice and other grain dishes are enjoyed in a wide variety of ways in Iran and range from simple pilafs to very complex layered dishes that are the living predecessors of South Asia's biryanis. One of my favorite techniques used by the Iranians—the coloring of part of a rice dish, simply for the beauty of the presentation—is highlighted in two of the rice recipes. The first recipe offered is the flavorful but simple **Rice with Herbs**, which flavors the rice with bunches of cilantro and dill. The second rice dish, **Rice with Sour Cherries**, is more complex but is deliciously tart and sweet and flavored with sour cherries, cinnamon, and nutmeg. The bread recipes offered here are everyday staples enjoyed in Iran. **Barbari Bread** is a delicious bread flavored with sesame seeds, and **Sweet Walnut Rolls** are made from ground walnuts flavored with vanilla.

Rice with Herbs

This is a tasty, *green* way to prepare rice, with the fresh herbs balancing the onions to provide lots of flavor in each bite. It is great matched with a flavorful kebab or a sourer dish like the **Sour Beef with Vegetables**. Leftovers (if you have any) can even be used to stuff peppers or tomatoes for the next day's meal.

1 cup uncooked basmati rice
2 tablespoons unsalted butter
1 medium onion, peeled, sliced, and separated into crescents
1 small bunch cilantro leaves, chopped (15–20 sprigs)
¼ cup fresh dill leaves, diced
¼ cup spring onions, diced
1 teaspoon salt
½ teaspoon ground black pepper
¼ teaspoon saffron (dissolved in extra water below)
2 cups plus 2 tablespoons water

1. Heat butter in a large sauté pan and add the onion slices. Sauté until the onion starts to soften and color. Then add the cilantro, dill, and spring onions and continue to cook until the herbs are cooked. Add salt and pepper and stir well. Heat water and dissolve the saffron into it.

2. Add boiling water and mix well. Add the rice and bring back to a boil. Then reduce heat and cook covered on low heat for 15–20 minutes or until the rice is done.

Rice with Sour Cherries

This is a recipe that is a sweet and sour feast fit for a king. The cherries and spices make the dish delicious, and the sprinkled saffron-colored rice over the top of the pilaf makes it beautiful to behold as well. Adding color to rice just for the sake of decoration is an ancient Persian culinary art, and many different vegetable dyes can be used to yield different colors including beet juice (purple), leek juice (light green), or onion peels (light brown). Feel free to experiment with different colors as the mood strikes you.

1 cup uncooked basmati rice
2 tablespoons butter
1 large onion, peeled, sliced, and separated into crescents
½ teaspoon ground cinnamon
¼ teaspoon ground nutmeg
1 teaspoon salt
¼ cup water or sour cherry nectar
1 teaspoon sugar
¼ teaspoon ground black pepper
2 tablespoons slivered almonds
2 tablespoons pistachio nuts, finely chopped
1 ½ cups sour cherries, drained, rinsed, and drained again
2 cups boiling water
¼ teaspoon saffron, dissolved into 2 tablespoons hot water

1. Heat butter in a large 3-quart saucepan. When hot, add sliced onions and sauté until they soften and start to color. Add cinnamon, nutmeg, salt, sugar, and pepper and stir well. Cook for 2–3 minutes to warm the spices and then add the nuts and water or nectar and stir well. Cook a few minutes to warm the liquid and then stir in the cherries, taking care not to smash them. Cook for 3–5 minutes.

2. Add uncooked rice in a thin layer on top of cherry and onion mixture. Cook covered for 2–3 minutes just to steam rice. Then, place pot of boiling water right on the side of the cooking pot and pour the boiling water by increments into the pot. Pour at several different places to ensure even distribution of the water. Cover and cook on low flame for 45 minutes to 1 hour until done. Check mixture every 15 minutes or so, but do not stir.

3. When done, skim about 4 tablespoons of rice off of the top and place into a bowl. Pour the dissolved saffron over the rice and stir to mix and set aside. Place a large, round serving dish over the mouth of the large saucepan and quickly invert the pot contents onto the plate. This method allows the flavor and juices of the fruit and vegetables to flow down into the rice and spread more evenly around.

4. Take saffron-infused rice and stir lightly. If necessary, drain excess water out of the rice. Sprinkle colored grains of rice over the pilaf and serve.

Rice with Barberries

For a more tart taste, try this dish, which flavors the rice with barberries and hints of cumin and cinnamon and also colors the rice for its beauty in the bowl. This simple pilaf goes well with any roast meat or kebab but works best with chicken or other fowl.

2 cups basmati or long-grain rice, cooked and cooled
3 tablespoons butter
½ cup barberries (if dried, soak in warm water before use)
1 tablespoon sugar
2 medium onions, peeled and diced
1 teaspoon salt
½ teaspoon ground black pepper
¼ teaspoon cinnamon
½ teaspoon cumin
½ teaspoon saffron, dissolved in 2 tablespoons hot water

1. Melt butter in a medium sauté pan and sauté barberries and sugar for 3–5 minutes. Add diced onions and continue to cook until the onions turn translucent and start to color.

2. While cooking the onions, dissolve the saffron in the water and add about ⅓ of the rice to the mixture. Mix rice, lifting rather than stirring so as not to crush it, until the rice is colored evenly.

3. Combine colored and uncolored rice in the sauté pan with the barberries and onions and mix well. Cook until rice is well heated and serve.

Iranian Barbari Bread

A basic bread flavored lightly with sesame seeds that is enjoyed as an everyday bread with meals, dips, and a wide variety of pickles and snacks.

1 cup lukewarm water
1 tablespoon active dry yeast
1 teaspoon salt
2 teaspoons sugar

2 tablespoons peanut or other vegetable oil (not olive oil)
3–3 ½ cups all-purpose white flour
3 tablespoons sesame seeds
2 tablespoons butter, melted

1. Dissolve the yeast in the warm water. Add the salt, sugar, and oil and stir. Cover and set aside for 10–15 minutes to allow yeast to activate. Then add flour a little at a time, mixing until you have manageable dough. Knead for 3–5 minutes, then place in an oiled bowl, cover, and allow dough to rise in a warm area for 1 hour.

2. Knead the dough for another 3–5 minutes then divide into two pieces. Work and stretch the dough into long oblong shapes about ½ inch thick. Place them on oiled or sprayed baking sheets. With a dull knife, cut three stripes into the surface of the bread. Brush with melted butter and sprinkle sesame seeds over the surface of the bread.

3. Cover with a clean towel and let rise in a warm place for 30–45 minutes. Bake 20–30 minutes or until coloring nicely and turning golden around the edges. Serve immediately.

Sweet Walnut Rolls

These are delicious sweet rolls or cookies that, in classical Persian manner, are enjoyed before or even during a meal instead of as a dessert, where we in the West would find them more familiar.

6 egg yolks
1 teaspoon vanilla
4 tablespoons sugar
4 tablespoons butter, melted and cooled or softened at room temperature
½ teaspoon cinnamon, nutmeg, or other spice (optional)
1 ⅓ cups walnuts, finely ground

1. In a medium mixing bowl, mix egg yolks, sugar, vanilla, and butter and beat well until the mix is quite thick. Add crushed walnuts and mix well. Take small portions with a teaspoon, scoop up a heaping round, and place it on a greased or sprayed baking sheet.

2. Bake in the oven at 300° for 15–20 minutes.

Desserts and Beverages

This section delivers a nice selection of Iranian desserts and a beverage called **doogh**, which is yogurt mixed with mint and black pepper that is a standard in Iran. The desserts range from the complex, like **Iranian Baklava** with its paper-thin pastry filled with almonds and flavored with ground cardamom and sweet rosewater to **Sweet Almond Rolls** to the simple but beloved **Date and Walnut Stuffed Pastry (Ranginak)**, whose rounds of cinnamon- and sugar-sweetened dough are stuffed with dates and nuts, baked, and then given a light dusting of fine sugar to finish.

Iranian Baklava

This is a baklava made with thin sheets of dough that are thicker than the filo used in Greek and Turkish baklava more familiar to most Westerners. The filling is also almond-based instead of walnut-based and has the unmistakable Persian touch of rosewater that permeates the desserts of the region from Armenia to northern India.

½ cup milk
½ teaspoon baking powder
2 tablespoons peanut or other vegetable oil
2 egg yolks
I cup flour
2 cups almonds
3 cups sugar
I tablespoon ground cardamom
3 tablespoons unsalted butter, melted
½ cup rosewater

1. Mix milk, baking powder, oil, and egg yolks until they froth and thicken. Add flour gradually while mixing until a dough of good texture emerges. Knead the dough well for 3–5 minutes. Set aside in a warm place for 2–3 hours. Meanwhile, peel and grind almonds. Add I cup of sugar and ground cardamom and mix well for filling.

2. Take a small amount of dough (about the size of a golf ball), flour board or counter, and roll the ball as thinly as possible. Peel dough

off counter or use a dull knife to loosen and place in the bottom of a small-to-medium buttered or sprayed baking dish. Allow dough to overlap the dish slightly. Roll out two more pastry balls and place them over the first layer in the baking dish.

3. Add the almond spice mix on top of the sheets and press down to flatten. Cover with 3 more dough sheets and seal the edges of dough together by pressing with your fingers. With a very sharp knife, cut stuffed pastry into squares or diamonds and brush with melted butter.

4. Add remaining sugar to ½ cup of hot water and bring to boil. Stir constantly to dissolve sugar and form a syrup. Add rosewater and continue boiling for 2–3 minutes. Keep this syrup warm.

5. Place baking dish into a preheated 300° oven. Bake for 15–20 minutes, then remove and pour about ⅓ of the syrup evenly over the pastry. Return to the oven and bake for another 15–20 minutes or until the pastry starts to color and turn golden. Remove from the oven and pour the next third of the syrup evenly over the pastry. Allow baklava to cool for about 15–20 minutes and pour remaining syrup over the pastry. Let rest for at least ½ hour and then serve.

Iranian Girls Touring Persepolis

Pastries with Cardamom and Almonds

These delicious pastries are brimming with a sweet and strong mixture of almonds and cardamom and are best served still warm from the oven. Easy to make and delightful to eat, this simple dessert is a good example of holiday home cooking that is beloved by all Iranians.

2 medium egg yolks
I teaspoon baking powder
½ cup yogurt
½ cup butter, melted
I cup flour
I cup almonds, peeled and ground
I cup sugar
I tablespoon ground cardamom powder

1. Separate eggs and set egg whites aside if baking the pastries. Mix egg yolks with baking powder, yogurt, and butter until frothy and thickened. Add flour gradually while stirring the mix until you have manageable dough. Knead for 3–5 minutes and then cover and set aside in a warm place for I–2 hours.

2. Mix ground almonds with ½ cup sugar and ground cardamom. Mix well and set aside. Divide dough into 2–4 pieces and roll out onto a floured surface until ¼ inch thick. Cut circles in the dough about 4 inches in diameter and spoon some of the almond-spice mix into the center of the circle. Fold circle in half and seal edges by pressing them together with your fingers.

3. Traditionally, these pastries are fried in hot oil until colored and then rolled in sugar, but if you wish, you can brush egg whites onto the surface of the pastries and sprinkle some sugar over them and bake for I5–20 minutes at 350°. No matter how you cook them, cool them slightly and then serve warm.

Date and Walnut Stuffed Pastry (Ranginak)

This is a dish that reminds many Iranians traveling abroad of home. It is a great example of a home-cooked dessert that a mother or a grandmother would make, and varies a great deal by region. The students I have met all have a hankering for this easy-to-prepare dish, and it also is one of the first dishes they learn to prepare while living away from home.

2 cups wheat flour
1 cup butter, melted
2 cups pitted dates
½ cup sugar
½ cup walnuts, shelled and separated
1 teaspoon ground cinnamon
½ teaspoon ground cardamom
1 tablespoon ground pistachio nuts

1. In a medium mixing bowl, combine the melted butter with the flour by adding flour bit by bit and mixing it in. Continue until you have manageable dough. Add sugar, cinnamon, and cardamom to flour and mix well.

2. Divide the dough in half and roll it out until it is ¼ inch thick. Insert a piece or two of walnuts inside each date and place the dates on the flour-mix. Continue covering with dates until evenly covered. Then roll out second half of dough and place over the dates as a cover. Seal edges of the pastry with your fingers and sprinkle ground pistachio nuts over the top.

3. Cook in preheated 325° oven for 15–20 minutes or until the dough starts to color and become golden.

Saffron Rice Pudding

This is another variation on a theme of rice- and milk-based puddings that are enjoyed all across Asia. The Iranian version is a bit more complex than some of the others encountered and combines the flavors of both rosewater and cinnamon with saffron and a sprinkling of ground nuts. I think it's best when served only slightly chilled and not cold.

1 cup uncooked basmati or other long-grain rice
4 cups water
2 cups sugar
2 teaspoons saffron, dissolved in 3 tablespoons hot water
¼ cup butter, melted

¼ cup rosewater
I teaspoon cinnamon
¼ cup almonds, slivered
2 tablespoons pistachios, ground

1. Rinse the rice well, drain, and bring to a boil in a medium saucepan. Cover and cook gently for 15–20 minutes or until the rice is tender. Add the sugar and cook, stirring constantly, until the mixture thickens. Dissolve the saffron in hot water and add to the rice mixture. Melt the butter and stir in. Stir in the rosewater and the cinnamon. Continue stirring over a medium or low heat until the mixture becomes quite thick.

2. Pour the mixture in a bowl. Sprinkle with pistachios and then with almonds. Set aside to cool and then refrigerate before serving.

Yogurt Drink with Mint and Black Pepper (Doogh)

No chapter on Iranian Food is complete without a *doogh* recipe. I'm lucky enough to have a wonderful Persian market near my home and can buy this sour but delicious drink on my way home from work. If you are lacking a Persian market near your home, this recipe will allow you to prepare *doogh* at home.

2 ½ cups water (more or less depending on thickness desired)
I cup yogurt
I teaspoon salt
I teaspoon dried mint
½ teaspoon ground black pepper

Beat the yogurt until smooth. Add mint, salt, and black pepper and mix well again. Add water to yogurt gradually and mix as you add. The quantity of water can be adjusted to obtain the desired thickness of the drink. Cool in the refrigerator for several hours and mix again before serving. If you have seltzer canisters at home, you can carbonate this drink as they often do in Iran.

Appetizers and Condiments

From herbed potato patties to a pistachio-flavored omelet to pickled onions, dips, and jams, this chapter gives a nice introduction to the incredible breadth of Iranian appetizers and condiments. For a light start to a meal, the **Yogurt and Spinach Dip** or the **Iranian Eggplant Dip** along with the minty **Pickled Onions** go wonderfully with a simple bread. For a heartier start, try the **Herbed Potato Patties with Lamb or Beef** or the **Kuku with Pistachios and Peas**, which also make great snacks or light meals all by themselves. To sweeten or offset a spicy or hot kebab or roast meat, try one of the delicious fruit jams offered here with sour cherries or oranges.

Herbed Potato Patties with Lamb or Beef

Delicious, lighter than expected, and with a sweet airiness that only the combination of tarragon and mint can offer, these herbed potato patties are a delicious way to begin a large meal, have a snack, or to be the centerpiece of a light meal with a few condiments.

Potato Pancakes
1 pound of potatoes, peeled, cooked, and mashed
3 eggs, beaten
1 ½ teaspoons salt
½ teaspoon ground black pepper
¼ cup fresh parsley, finely chopped

Filling
3 tablespoons unsalted butter
2 medium onions, peeled and finely diced
1 tablespoon garlic, peeled and finely diced
½ pound ground beef or lamb
1 teaspoon salt
½ teaspoon ground black pepper
½ cup beef broth
¼ cup fresh tarragon, finely chopped
¼ cup mint, finely chopped
2 tablespoons tomato paste
Peanut or vegetable oil to fry patties

1. Peel potatoes and boil in water until tender. Drain and mash them well. Add beaten eggs, salt, pepper, and chopped parsley and mix well. Set aside to cool.

2. In a sauté pan, melt butter and sauté onions until they start to turn translucent and color. Add garlic and continue to cook until it swells and colors as well. Add ground meat and cook until meat begins to brown. Add salt, black pepper, and beef broth and mix well. When the broth warms up, add the tomato paste, chopped tarragon, and mint and mix well. Set aside to cool.

3. When both the potatoes and the meat filling have cooled enough to work with by hand, take a handful of mashed potatoes and shape them into a ball. Then make a hole in the middle and fill with the meat-mix. Collapse the sides to cover the meat or cover by adding a bit more potato-mix and shape into a disc. Repeat until both mixes are used up. Fry both sides of the discs in cooking oil over medium heat until golden. Drain on paper, cool a bit, and serve with a condiment like cucumbers in yogurt.

Kuku with Green Peas and Pistachios

This is another delicious egg casserole flavored with vegetables and nuts from western Asia. Taking all of about 15 minutes to prepare (and another 15 minutes to bake), this is an easy-to-prepare, anytime meal. Delicious for breakfast, lunch, dinner, or in between, this kuku is best served right out of the oven when it is piping hot!

3 tablespoons butter
1 large onion, peeled and finely diced
1 tablespoon garlic, peeled and diced
2 hot, dried, red chili peppers
1 teaspoon salt
¼ teaspoon ground black pepper
¼ cup pistachio nuts, finely diced
1 cup fresh or frozen green peas

4 eggs, beaten
1 tablespoon yogurt
1 teaspoon sugar
¼ teaspoon ground turmeric

1. Preheat oven to 375°. On the stovetop, melt butter in an ovenproof, covered casserole and sauté onions over medium-low heat until they soften and start to color. Add garlic and sauté until the garlic swells and starts to color as well. Then add salt, pepper, chili peppers and pistachio nuts and cook 2–3 minutes until everything is well mixed and warm. Add peas and cook to warm once more.

2. Combine yogurt, sugar, and turmeric with the beaten eggs and beat again until all ingredients are well integrated. Pour egg-spice mixture into the casserole with the onions and pistachios and stir well until everything is blended. Cover and bake for 15–20 minutes.

3. When done, loosen the edges of the omelet by running a knife around the edge of the casserole. Serve in casserole, or place a serving plate over the mouth of the casserole dish and quickly invert. Then cover the bottom of the omelet with another serving plate and invert again so the puffy, baked side faces upward.

Yogurt and Spinach Dip

Spinach, whole milk yogurt, and a touch of sumac and maybe some fenugreek make this a delicious, mild, and cooling dip to serve with freshly baked flatbread or naan. It makes a great appetizer when served in that way and can also be used as a condiment for other appetizers like the **Herbed Potato Patties with Lamb or Beef**.

3 tablespoons peanut or vegetable oil
2 onions, peeled and finely diced
2 tablespoons garlic, peeled and finely diced
2 large bunches fresh spinach, rinsed and spun dry (at least 1 pound)
1 pound whole milk yogurt (about half a large container)
1 ½ teaspoons salt
1 teaspoon ground black pepper
¼ teaspoon sumac plus a bit more for garnish
1 teaspoon dried fenugreek leaves (optional)

1. Heat oil in a large saucepan and sauté the onions until they start to turn translucent and color. Add the garlic and cook until it swells and starts to color as well. Add rinsed spinach and mix well. When spinach warms, cover and cook, stirring often, until the spinach wilts and

becomes tender. Cook 5–8 minutes or until the spinach is completely cooked. Remove from heat and chill until cold. When the vegetables are sufficiently cooled, mix them in a food processor until they are well blended.

2. In a large mixing bowl, combine yogurt, salt, pepper, sumac, and fenugreek (if using) and whisk until the yogurt liquefies. Add spinach and onion mixture to yogurt and mix until blended. Serve.

Pickled Onions

A wonderful, minty, and slightly sour pickled onion that is delicious as an appetizer with flatbread, a sourdough, or crispy crusts. Simple to make and authentically Iranian, these pickled onions will set the stage for a great West Asian meal.

I pound pearl onions (all one color or a mix)
½ cup garlic, peeled and diced
2 tablespoons dried mint
3 teaspoons granulated sugar
2 teaspoons salt
I cup white vinegar

1. Peel and rinse onions well, and strain to remove water. In a small bowl mix garlic, mint, 2 teaspoons of sugar, and salt together until well blended. In a separate small bowl, mix vinegar and remaining sugar together.

2. Place a layer of onions in a clean, sterilized jar. Add a layer of garlic-mint mix. Repeat until the jar is full. Pour in vinegar and sugar mix to the top of the jar, and place the lid on tightly.*

3. Store in a cool, dry place for 2–3 months.

*If more vinegar is needed to cover the onions, mix I teaspoon sugar to I cup vinegar.

Iranian Eggplant Dip

Another great dip to enjoy while waiting for the fesenjan or kebabs. This is Iran's version of the Arab eggplant dip, baba ghanoush. This version of the dish is from the Caspian region in northern Iran, and the prominence of the eggs is the regional variation.

1 large Western or 8 small aubergine eggplants
2 medium tomatoes
2 tablespoons garlic, peeled and finely diced
4 tablespoons peanut or other vegetable oil
1 ½ teaspoons salt
1 teaspoon ground black pepper
4 eggs, beaten

1. Bake the eggplant(s) in a preheated 325° oven until softened (about 20–30 minutes for small eggplants, about 45 minutes for a single large Western one). When done, remove from the oven to cool.

2. When sufficiently cooled to handle, peel the eggplant and remove the top and bottom as well. Blend lightly in a food processor with the tomatoes until mixed but not completely liquefied.

3. In a medium sauté pan, heat oil and sauté garlic over medium heat until the garlic starts to swell and barely color. Add the eggplant and tomato mixture and mix well. When eggplant heats, add the salt and pepper and continue to cook until liquid has mostly evaporated— about 5–8 minutes.

4. Cook eggs halfway with remaining cooking oil in a separate small sauté pan. Turn into the pan with the eggplant-tomato mix and blend well. Cook for 1–2 more minutes and serve with bread or rice.

Orange Jam

Another way to mix flavors at a meal is to serve a sweet fruit jam to help offset the spiciness of roasts or kebabs or to enjoy with a sweet roll before or after a meal. This recipe offers an option of using rosewater for a mellower jam, or orange blossom water for a full blast of sweet citrus flavor.

1 pound orange slices, seeds and peel remnants removed
2 cups sugar
Water to cover
2 tablespoons lime juice

2 tablespoons rosewater (or orange blossom water)

1. Wash orange slices and place in a large saucepan. Add sugar and mix well. Let sit for 1–2 hours until the sugar has drawn some juice from the orange slices.

2. Barely cover slices with water and bring to a boil over high heat. Add the lime juice and the rosewater or the orange blossom water and cook for about 30 minutes, stirring often and skimming foam from the top. When mixture becomes very thick, the jam is done. Remove from heat to let cool and then spoon into clean, sealable jars. Serve with meat dishes to offset spiciness or as one of several condiments on a bountiful table.

Sour Cherry Jam

Another Iranian favorite is this jam of sour cherries to eat with kebabs or roasts or to eat with bread before or after a meal.

1 pound sour cherries, rinsed and drained
2 cups sugar
Water to cover
1 tablespoon lime juice
1 teaspoon vanilla extract

1. Place cherries in a large saucepan. Add sugar and mix well. Let sit for 1–2 hours until the sugar has drawn some juice from the fruit.

2. Barely cover cherries with water and bring to a boil over high heat. Add the lime juice and the vanilla extract and cook for about 30 minutes, stirring often and skimming foam from the top. When mixture becomes very thick, the jam is done. Remove from heat to let cool and then spoon into clean, sealable jars. Serve with meat dishes to offset spiciness or as one of several condiments on a bountiful table.

Sauces and Spice Mixtures

No meal is complete without a few sauces and Iran's ubiquitous spice mixture **advieh** to bring a blast of sweet and spicy flavors to bear on meat and vegetable dishes. As sauces go, the ones offered here feature lime, tomato, and a little tamarind to spice up meat, fish, and vegetable dishes. Strongly flavored but not overbearing, these sauces can bring out the best in whatever you're serving.

Lime Sauce for Fish and Shellfish

Ahh...finally, a delicious sauce for Iranian fish and shellfish dishes that also works nicely for chicken and fowl dishes! Here the fresh lime juice is sweetened and offset by the mint and cilantro and then the bitterness is toned down by the saffron. Best if made at least 1 hour before serving.

½ cup fresh lime juice
¼ cup olive oil
1 small bunch fresh cilantro, chopped (15–20 sprigs)
1 tablespoon fresh mint, chopped
½ teaspoon saffron
½ teaspoon salt
¼ teaspoon ground black pepper

In a medium mixing bowl, combine the lime juice and the olive oil and whisk until blended and slightly thickened. Add the cilantro and the mint and mix again. Then add the saffron, salt, and pepper and mix again. Set aside to let the flavors blend and then use to flavor your favorite Iranian fish dish!

Iranian Tomato-Lime Sauce

This sauce is most commonly used in vegetable dishes to add flavor to beans or okra, but it can also be used as a sauce for stuffed vegetables or kebabs or to offer a bit of flavorful zing to anything on your plate.

1 tablespoon butter
2 teaspoons garlic, peeled and diced
2 cups tomato sauce
3 tablespoons lime juice
1 tablespoon ground turmeric
2 teaspoons granulated sugar
½ teaspoon salt
½ teaspoon pepper
1 small bunch chopped fresh cilantro (15–20 sprigs)

In a medium saucepan, heat the butter, add the garlic, and cook until the garlic swells and starts to color. Add the tomato sauce and cook until well warmed. Add the lime juice, turmeric, sugar, salt and pepper and mix well. Cook 3–5 minutes. Add fresh cilantro and stir until leaves are wilted. Cook another 3–5 minutes and serve or set aside for use in another recipe.

Tamarind Sauce

Variations on this wonderful sauce are used from Iran and Azerbaijan to Afghanistan and Pakistan to flavor vegetables and meats. Particularly delicious on potatoes and eggplants, but it works with almost any meat or vegetable.

I tablespoon butter
2 teaspoons garlic, peeled and chopped
2 cups tomato sauce
2–3 teaspoons tamarind concentrate
I teaspoon salt
½ teaspoon ground black pepper
2 teaspoons dried ground coriander
I small bunch chopped fresh cilantro (15–20 sprigs)

1. In a medium saucepan, heat the butter, add the garlic, and cook until the garlic swells and starts to color. Add the tomato sauce and cook until well warmed. Add the tamarind concentrate and cook for 5–8 minutes over low heat, stirring often.

2. Add salt, pepper, and ground coriander and mix well. Add fresh cilantro and stir until the leaves are fully wilted. Cook another 3–5 minutes and serve or set aside for use in another dish.

Advieh

If you plan on cooking a lot of Iranian food, you may want to have a spice mixture called *advieh* on hand to use by the teaspoonful rather than having to put smaller amounts of many different spices in. *Advieh* is sort of like an Iranian *garam masala*—there are more recipes than there are chefs, and the recipes vary (sometimes substantially) according to what is being prepared. The difference between *advieh* and *garam masala* is that *advieh* is usually the centerpiece of the Iranian dish and not an addition to an already complex array of flavors.

1 tablespoon ground cinnamon
½ teaspoon ground cardamom
½ teaspoon ground nutmeg
½ teaspoon ground cumin
½ teaspoon ground black pepper
¼ teaspoon ground coriander
¼ teaspoon dried Persian lime powder

Combine ground spices in a grinder and blend briefly to mix. If you have whole dried limes instead of lime powder, you will have to crush them first before grinding. Mix well and store in a sealable container.

Kabul by Air

Afghanistan

Main spices and flavors: tamarind, coriander, cilantro, fennel, mint, bay leaf, saffron, sumac, sour grapes, sour plums, cumin, dill, garlic, onion, turmeric, cardamom, black cardamom, sweet basil, cinnamon, ginger, cloves, nutmeg, mace, chili peppers, tomato, potato

Souring agents: white vinegar, lemons, sour grapes, cider vinegar, oranges

From the time of the Persian emperor, Darius the Great in 500 BCE, the Afghan people have, at least from time to time, been engaged in resistance against foreign powers bent on conquering them. Even when outsider tyrants succeeded in bringing down one or more of the most powerful tribes, revolution percolated in the mountains and countryside and fed rebellion against the foreign invaders. An uneasy history has plagued the proud peoples of Afghanistan: Persians, Alexander, Greeks, Buddhists, Huns, Arabs, and the Uzbek Tamerlane all seized the reins of Afghan power at one time or another. It wasn't until 1747 and the foundation of modern Afghanistan that Afghans have held power for extended periods of time in their own country, and even then they continued to be plagued by usurping Persians, British, and Russians. This history of conflict and resistance means that over the millennia, Afghan culture has been influenced by a wide variety of foreign cultures.

The effect of all of this blending of cultures on Afghan cuisine has produced a merger of both western Asian, which is still heavily influenced by European food and the cuisines of the Levant states, with southern Asian cooking or cuisines of the Indian subcontinent. From the West, we still see a wide variety of familiar spices—fennel, bay leaf, mint, and saffron—but these are often used in concert with southern and eastern Asian spices such as cardamom, cinnamon, or ginger rather than as main flavors.

Once again the Persian influence is strongly felt in the combination of fresh and dried fruits with meat dishes, in the use of sour grapes as a "souring agent" in a wide variety of foods, and in sumac as a spicy garnish to sauces and skewered meats. Another much-generalized trend that Afghan food has in common with southern and eastern Asian cuisines is the eating of smaller portions of animal protein at most meals. Kebabs may seem like a lot of meat, but most of this is in fact in the presentation instead of on the portion scale. Part of this trend away from meat has to do with the cost of meat, but part of this is also due to simple cultural preference.

The recipes offered below give a good overview of the complex flavors that prevail in Afghan cuisine. In meats, they range from the gentle **Afghan Chicken Kebab** and **Lamb Chops Afghan Style** with dashes of cinnamon and black pepper working with the flavors of the meats to slightly accent them, to the sharp **Lamb with Lemons and Pine Nuts** with its spicy trio of cardamom, coriander, and cinnamon adding their pungent flavors to a lemon-pepper sauce. The vegetable recipes offered are not shy cousins to their meaty relatives; in fact, some of them—most notably, **Tamarind-Ginger Potatoes** and **Spicy Eggplant with Mint**—may be even more spicy than most of the meat dishes. Afghan vegetable dishes aren't just about bold flavors, though; sometimes they gently coax diners into submission, as with **Sautéed Quinces,** where nutmeg and cinnamon work in concert with basil to bring a unique flavor to a fruit that is much underappreciated in the West, or **Sweet and Spicy Squash** where a sweet, baked butternut squash absorbs a sweet and spicy tomato sauce seasoned with ginger and garlic to magnificent results.

Meat Dishes

Chicken, quail, and semidomesticated or wild fowl are the most affordable and frequently eaten meats in Afghanistan. Lamb is adored but eaten less frequently or in smaller portions than chicken, primarily because of its expense. Mutton is eaten more frequently than lamb but less so than fowl. Some older people, having grown accustomed to mutton's sharper flavor, prefer it to the younger, gentler lamb. Beef is eaten more rarely, as cows are more prized for their milk, and in modern Islamic Afghanistan, pork is very hard to come by at all. Meat is usually eaten in chunks of varying size—either in stews, pilafs, or on skewers—instead of in chop form or other on-the-bone cuts. Ground meats formed into meatballs and kebabs are also frequently enjoyed.

Although type of meat and styles of preparation vary, meats are almost always heartily spiced, with cinnamon and black pepper forming one *leit motif* and mint coupled with coriander forming the other. Unlike other cuisines, however, the spices don't overpower the meat, but rather simply enhance it. Although the recipes offered below use a large litany of spices, the focus of the diner's attention will still tend to be on the chicken or lamb and not on the sauce that accompanies it.

Chicken Kebab with Cinnamon and Black Pepper

This wonderful dish couples chicken with cinnamon and black pepper with delicious results! It is delicately spiced and works well with one of the more flavorful Afghan pilafs, such as **Sour Plums and Oranges Pilaf** or **Carrots and Raisins Pilaf**. If you would like to venture a bit further afield, try it with the Tajik **Pilaf of Chicken, Fennel, and Citrus**. Serving the kebabs with **Afghan Cilantro Sauce** adds a touch of spicy and intense flavor that changes the taste of the whole dish. So go ahead, try this two-for-one recipe and enjoy!

2 chicken breasts cut into bite-size pieces
2 medium yellow onions, roughly chopped
10 cherry tomatoes, whole
2 teaspoons ground black pepper

Afghan Kebabs

2 teaspoons ground cinnamon
½ teaspoon ground turmeric
2 teaspoons salt
4 tablespoons white vinegar

1. Mix 1 onion and *half* of the pepper, cinnamon, turmeric, and salt together in a sealable, 1-gallon plastic bag. Add the vinegar and chicken and mix well. Marinate for several hours at room temperature or in the refrigerator overnight, turning several times.

2. When ready to cook, remove the chicken and string 5 or 6 cubes of chicken on each metal skewer. String the tomatoes and chunks of onions on their own skewers. Sprinkle the other half of the spices over the kebabs and grill or cook in a broiler oven for 5–8 minutes per side. Serve hot with **Afghan Cilantro Sauce** and Afghan bread.

Meatballs with Garlic and Mint

This wonderful recipe was the first Afghan dish I ever ate. Over the years, I've reconstructed the recipe until, I believe, it's just right. Mint is combined with coriander and black pepper, with tasty results. I love lamb and use it preferentially to beef, but the recipe works well with beef meatballs as well. Serve with plain basmati rice or **Saffron Rice** with plenty of **Yogurt with Garlic and Mint** available for a blast of additional spiciness.

2 medium yellow onions, peeled and roughly chopped
1 medium tomato, rinsed and roughly chopped
1 pound ground lamb or beef
2 teaspoons garlic, finely chopped
2 teaspoons ground coriander
1 small bunch fresh cilantro leaves, chopped (10–15 sprigs)
1 ½ tablespoons dried mint
2 teaspoons lemon juice
1 teaspoon salt
1 teaspoon ground black pepper

1. In a food processor, combine all of the ingredients except the meat and blend lightly so that the vegetables are chopped but still have their form. Then add the meat and blend again until the vegetables

and herbs are well integrated with the meat. Transfer into a bowl and chill for several hours to firm the mixture up.

2. Preheat broiler on highest setting. Remove from refrigerator and roll the meatballs about 2 inches in diameter. Place on a baking sheet that has been oiled or sprayed.

3. Cook about 6 inches from the flame for 5 minutes on each side. If meat still feels soft to the touch, cook another few minutes, but do not let the meatballs burn.

Chicken with Apricots in a Lemon-Pepper Sauce

This recipe unites chicken, apricots, and a host of spices in a lemony-pepper sauce. The apricots offer their flavor to the sauce blend as well as provide discrete blasts of apricot flavor when eaten along with the chicken. It is both spicy and slightly sweet at the same time and is an example of the Persian influence on Afghan cooking with its coupling of meat with dried fruits. With plain basmati rice or with a simple pilaf like **Caramelized Onion Pilaf**, the dish really shines.

2 chicken breasts cut into bite-size pieces
¼ cup dried apricots, quartered and soaked in warm water for 1 hour
2 tablespoons peanut oil
1 medium yellow onion, peeled, sliced, and separated into crescents
zest of 2 lemons, very finely chopped
2 teaspoons garlic, peeled and diced
3 hot, dried, red chili peppers
¼ cup brown raisins
1½ cups water (enough to just cover)
1 teaspoon salt (more if desired)
½ teaspoon ground coriander
1 teaspoon ground black pepper
1 teaspoon ground cardamom
1 teaspoon cumin
1 teaspoon cinnamon
1/2 teaspoon turmeric
2 teaspoons sugar
2 teaspoons lemon juice
½ cup pistachio nuts, chopped
3 tablespoons plain yogurt

1. Heat oil in a sauté pan over high heat. Add chicken and cook, stirring quickly, to sear the chicken and preserve its juices. When the chicken is just starting to color, remove from the oil with a slotted spoon and set aside. Lower heat to medium and add onions. When onions have just started to soften and color, add garlic, chili peppers and half of the lemon zest and stir well to mix. Cook for 3–5 minutes.

2. Add ½ cup water, drained apricots, and brown raisins and cook to heat. Add salt, coriander, pepper, cardamom, cumin, cinnamon and turmeric. Stir to coat apricots with the warm spices. Cook for another minute or two and add the remaining water and stir again.

3. When the stew is well heated, add chicken and lemon juice and the remaining lemon zest and stir. Add chopped pistachio nuts and cook covered over low heat for 10–15 minutes, stirring occasionally. Uncover and cook until chicken is done and liquid has evaporated enough to form a sauce. Add yogurt and heat. Serve with rice or bread.

Lamb with Lemons and Pine Nuts

This stew is like no other you've ever tasted! During cooking, the ingredients meld together to form something heavenly and something much more than just the sum of its parts. Added in the last five minutes of cooking, the lemon zest contrasts nicely with the mellowness of the lamb stewed in the pantheon of spices, including cardamom, cinnamon, nutmeg, and pepper. Serve with plain basmati rice or with a big piece of Afghan bread to help mop up this stew.

½ pound stew lamb, cut into bite-size pieces
2 tablespoons peanut oil
2 medium yellow onions, peeled, sliced, and separated into crescents
2 teaspoons garlic, peeled and diced
½ teaspoon turmeric
¼ teaspoon ground cardamom
3 hot, dried, red chili peppers
1 nutmeg corm, grated
½ teaspoon cinnamon
1 cup beef stock
1 teaspoon salt
¾ teaspoon ground black pepper

¼ teaspoon cayenne pepper
2 small-to-medium tomatoes, chopped
1 cup tomato sauce
2 cups spinach
½ cup plain yogurt
Zest from 1 lemon, finely chopped
¼ cup dry roasted pine nuts

1. Heat oil in a large saucepan and sear lamb over high heat until it firms up and starts to color around the edges. When done, remove from the pan and set aside. Lower heat and add the onions; sauté them for 3–5 minutes or until they begin to soften and color. Then add the garlic and sauté it for 2–3 minutes. Put in the turmeric, cardamom, chopped chili peppers, nutmeg, and cinnamon and sauté the mixture for 1–2 minutes more, being careful not to burn the onions or garlic.

2. Add the beef stock and stir well, scraping the bottom of the pan to free up all of the little bits of meat and spices clinging to the pan. When broth is hot, add the salt, red and black pepper, and tomatoes and stir. When the tomatoes have warmed, add the lamb back into the stew and stir well. When the lamb has heated, add the tomato sauce and bring the stew to a low boil.

3. When stew is hot, lower heat to medium-low and cook covered for 30–40 minutes or until lamb starts to become tender. Stir often to make sure that the stew doesn't burn. If necessary, turn heat down to low and continue to cook.

4. After lamb has started to become tender, uncover and cook over medium heat to reduce the liquid in the stew. After about 5 minutes stir in the spinach and cook until spinach wilts. Then add lemon zest and pine nuts and cook another 5 minutes. Then add ½ cup yogurt, stirred in a little bit at a time. Cook to warm the yogurt and serve with flat bread like naan or with rice.

Lamb Chops with Cloves and Black Pepper

This recipe is an example of how Afghans prepare chops or other on-the-bone roast meats. The secret is in the rub, which in this case is an **Afghan Char Masala**. I use enough masala to coat the meat without overpowering it; you may wish to add more to accent the flavor of the rub. My rule of thumb in rubbing meat (as opposed to crusting it) is to be able to see the meat beneath the rub right after the rub is applied. Tread lightly—you can always add more, but you will have a hard time taking the flavor away. However you go about it, this is a tasty dish that is exotic but conservative enough to lend a bit of zing to a traditional Western table.

4 lamb chops (the thicker the better) (pork may also be used, but most Afghans wouldn't eat them)
1 teaspoon salt
½ teaspoon chili pepper
2 teaspoons Afghan Char Masala
¼ cup beef broth (or more as needed)

1. Wash and dry chops and trim off the excess fat, leaving just a bit to ensure moistness. Using a fork pierce the chops on both sides in several places. Sprinkle salt and ground chili powder over both sides of the chops.

2. Sprinkle the Afghan *Char Masala* all over the meat and rub into the flesh. Use as much as needed to cover chops well on both sides, and place in a lightly oiled ovenproof pan or dish and refrigerate several hours before cooking.

3. Preheat oven to 375°. Pour a small amount of beef broth to just cover the bottom of the dish and place in the oven. Cooking times will vary according to whether the chops have been boned or not. For chops with the bone in them, cook about 20 minutes on each side, gently turning them with a spatula to leave the crust intact. For chops without the bone, cooking times are approximately halved. When chops are done, transfer them to a serving platter, garnish with chopped cilantro, and serve.

Vegetable Dishes and Salads

With the exception of the potatoes and tomatoes, the vegetable dishes that Afghans eat most are in the gourd family and include eggplants, squashes, and pumpkins of almost every sort, but primarily butternut squashes, kabocha pumpkins, and zucchini. Most squash dishes and most vegetable dishes in general are cooked in a tomato-based sauce, but don't let that put you off thinking that the recipes will be too similar; rather, the tomato works with the seasonings and the taste of each main vegetable to produce a wide variety of different tastes without overpowering the flavor. Potatoes are eaten in a wide variety of ways, but the one I chose for this book, **Tamarind-Ginger Potatoes**, is the most uniquely flavorful and offers blasts of intense tamarind and ginger with each bite. Afghans also use several fruits like vegetables but especially love the quince for this—the fruit that, by its flavor (not its genetic relationship), is the chewier and lemonier cousin to the Granny Smith apple. Try the **Sautéed Quinces** to see how this fruit goes undercover as a vegetable!

Zucchini in Sour Tomato Sauce

This is a rustic dish of zucchini and tomatoes that is very simple to prepare. The flavors come as much from the freshness of the vegetables as from lemon juice and spices. It goes well with kebab as a side or served over rice like a thick sauce. Prepare with the juiciest tomatoes you can find for a really authentic taste. If you like the taste of the sauce, a similar one can be used to prepare other vegetables as well.

1 tablespoon peanut oil
1 medium red onion, peeled and diced
3 teaspoons garlic, peeled and diced
2 medium tomatoes, washed and chopped
4 ounces tomato sauce
1 heaping tablespoon ground coriander
½ teaspoon ground cumin
2 medium zucchini, washed, quartered, and cut into ½-inch chunks
2 teaspoons lemon juice
½ teaspoon salt (more to taste)
½ teaspoon ground black pepper
Pinch of sour grape powder (no more than ¼ teaspoon)

1. Heat the oil in a sauté pan and add the onion. Stir until the onion starts to soften. Add the garlic and sauté for a few minutes. Then add the tomatoes and cook 3 minutes before adding the tomato sauce, coriander, cumin, lime juice, salt, pepper, and sour grape powder.

2. Add the zucchini and lower heat. Cook covered for 5 minutes until the zucchini starts to soften. Uncover and continue cooking about 5 minutes or until zucchini is done.

Afghan Chickpea and Onion Salad

Although similar in name to its northern Tajik cousin, this dish shows how foods and ingredients have been selected and prepared differently by neighboring cultures. Instead of cinnamon and marigold petals to season the chickpeas, this Afghan recipe opts for cumin and dill as the main spices and adds a dollop of yogurt to smooth the apple cider vinegar. The overall effect is of a slightly sweet salad with a blast of spicy onions every now and again. The dish is excellent with kebabs or as a cooling accompaniment to any western, central, or southwestern Asian meat dish.

1 cup chickpeas, precooked
½ medium red onion, peeled, sliced, and very finely diced
2 tablespoons apple cider vinegar
½ teaspoon ground cumin
¼ cup (tightly packed) fresh dill, finely chopped
½ teaspoon salt
¼ teaspoon pepper
2 tablespoons plain yogurt

Combine chickpeas, onions, and apple cider vinegar and stir. Add the cumin, dill, salt, pepper, and yogurt and refrigerate for at least 1 hour prior to serving to allow the dill to sweeten the dish. Stir well prior to serving.

Tamarind-Ginger Potatoes

This incredibly flavorful potato dish is both sour and spicy at the same time. The tamarind water provides the sourness and the chili peppers lend their heat while ginger brightens the composition and fennel sweetens it. It's a bold and robust flavor that needs to be coupled with a hearty marinated kebab or an on-the-bone chop or roast such as **Uzbek Shish Kebabs**, **Azeri Lamb or Pork Chops with Sour Cherry Sauce**, or even a grilled-to-perfection Western New York strip steak.

3 medium potatoes, parboiled, cooled, and chopped
2 teaspoons tamarind concentrate, dissolved into 1 cup hot water
2 tablespoons butter
1 medium yellow onion, peeled, sliced, and separated into crescents
1 tablespoon sugar
1 teaspoon garlic, peeled and diced
2 teaspoons grated ginger
2 hot, dried, red chili peppers, finely diced
1 teaspoon ground fennel
½ teaspoon ground black pepper
½ teaspoon salt
2 tablespoons drained plain yogurt (*chaka*)
2 tablespoons beef broth (more if desired)

1. When potatoes are completely cool, chop them into bite-size pieces.

2. Heat butter in a sauté pan over medium heat. Add onion and 1 teaspoon of the sugar and cook until the onion starts to soften. Lower heat and cook over very low heat, stirring infrequently, until the onion is nicely caramelized, about 20–30 minutes.

3. Add the ginger, garlic, and chili peppers and stir well. Stir the tamarind water vigorously to dissolve any remaining paste and add it to the mixture. Stir and add the remaining sugar.

4. When the tamarind water has heated, add the fennel, black pepper, and salt. Stir well, add yogurt and cook 5 minutes over medium heat or until tamarind water forms a sauce. Add the potatoes.

5. Stir the potatoes, lifting rather than mixing to avoid breaking the potatoes too much. Cover and cook 5 minutes. If potatoes have absorbed too much sauce and the sauce is too thick or too sour, add 2 tablespoons of beef broth and stir to thin and sweeten.

Spicy Eggplant with Mint

This dish is full of surprise flavors! Like Georgian **Sweet and Sour Eggplant with Pomegranate Sauce**, it may help convince the staunchest eggplant haters out there to give the often overcooked vegetable another chance. Here, the baked eggplant blends with a creamy tomato sauce that is flavored with mint, vinegar, and coriander and kicked up with a couple of chili peppers for a unique taste experience. I find the flavor extremely potent and recommend serving it with other vegetable or meat dishes so that it will not overpower diners' palates.

1 medium purple eggplant
1 cup tomato sauce
½ cup drained plain yogurt (*chaka*)
1 teaspoon white vinegar
1-2 teaspoons crushed dried mint
½ teaspoon salt (more to taste)
¼ teaspoon ground black pepper
½ teaspoon ground coriander
3 tablespoons undrained plain yogurt
¼ cup beef broth
2 hot, dried, red chili peppers

1. Slice the eggplant crosswise into ½-inch slices. Place onto sprayed or oiled baking sheet and bake in 375° oven for 15–20 minutes or until nearly, but not quite, done. Remove from oven and let them cool.

2. Pour the tomato sauce into a sauté pan and heat. Add drained yogurt (*chaka*) and white vinegar as the sauce heats. When hot, add salt, pepper, chili, coriander, and mint. Cook 2–3 minutes, add the beef broth and the undrained yogurt, and simmer over low heat for 15 minutes to give the flavors a chance to blend.

3. Cut the cooled eggplant into bite-size pieces and add it to the tomato sauce; mix well, lifting more than stirring to allow the eggplant to keep its form. Sauté for 2–3 minutes until eggplant is warmed. Cover and cook another 5 minutes until eggplant is done. It's best to serve as soon as possible after cooking. The squash will absorb a great deal of the sauce.

Sautéed Quinces

Afghanis love quinces, and so they should with their lemony-apple flavor and spicy-sweet fragrance! They also love to cook with quinces and treat them like vegetables, adding them to stews as well as serving them sliced as an accompaniment to kebabs and roast meats. This recipe allows diners to directly enjoy the flavor of quinces in a buttery medley of sweet spices, with lemon zest offering a sharp accent. It is a delicate dish and works wonderfully with **Afghan Chicken Kebab** or **Meatballs with Garlic and Mint**.

3 medium quinces, peeled, cored, and diced
2 tablespoons butter
1 medium onion, peeled, sliced, and separated into crescents
1 medium tomato, chopped
10 pitted dried sour plums
Zest of 1 lemon, very finely chopped
¼ cup water
1 teaspoon dried basil leaves, crumbled
½ teaspoon ground cinnamon
½ medium nutmeg corm, grated
⅛ teaspoon ground cloves
½ teaspoon salt
1 teaspoon sugar
¼ teaspoon ground black pepper

1. Melt butter in a sauté pan and add onion. Cook over medium heat until the onion starts to soften. Add the tomato, sour plum meat, and lemon zest and cook another 3–5 minutes.

2. Add water and basil and heat. Then add cinnamon, nutmeg, and cloves and stir. Add the salt, sugar, and pepper and stir again.

3. Add quinces and cook covered for 10 minutes. Uncover and stir and recover if necessary to facilitate cooking. After about 15 minutes they should be nicely done. Stir again and serve.

Sweet and Spicy Squash

As tasty as it is, I don't think that butternut squash has ever been more flavorful than in this recipe. This is my take on Afghan Sweet Pumpkin or *Kadu Bouranee*, with the yogurt sauce omitted. I felt that the yogurt didn't add to the already remarkable flavor of the baked squash in the sweet and spicy tomato sauce and that in this case simpler was better. Watch your guests' eyes light up when they bite into this wonderful dish!

½ medium butternut squash, peeled and chopped into bite-size pieces
I batch **Sweet Afghan Tomato Sauce** (see Afghan Sauces and Spice Mixtures)

1. Place chopped squash on an oiled or sprayed baking sheet and bake at 350° for 30–45 minutes or until the squash has partially cooked. When done, remove from heat and set aside.

2. Add cooled squash and mix well with the thickened tomato sauce. Cook for 3–5 minutes or until the squash has absorbed most of the tomato sauce. It's best to serve as soon as possible after cooking.

Rice and Grain Dishes, Breads

Three wonderful pilafs followed by a classic everyday bread await to introduce you to the range of flavors and dishes available in Afghani cooking. From the simple (**Pilaf with Caramelized Onions and Cinnamon**) to the complex (**Sour Plum and Orange Pilaf**) to the classic Afghani yellow rice (**Carrot and Raisin Pilaf**), these pilafs will accent any meat or vegetable dish and can also serve as anchors for a complex, multicourse Afghan meal or buffet.

Pilaf with Caramelized Onions and Cinnamon

This simple pilaf gets its depth of flavor from the caramelized onions more so than from the added spices, so be careful not to burn the onions! The cinnamon, mace, and pepper help make the dish delicious and make it work so well as part of so many other meals. Pair it with **Chicken with Apricots** or **Lamb Chops Afghan Style** for the basis of a great meal.

I cup uncooked basmati rice
2 cups boiling water
2 tablespoons butter
2 medium yellow onions, thinly sliced into crescents
2 teaspoons sugar
¼ teaspoon ground cinnamon
I bay leaf, ground

2 whole cloves, ground
⅛ teaspoon mace
½ teaspoon ground black pepper
I teaspoon salt

1. Heat the butter in a sauté pan on medium and add the onions and stir briefly. Add sugar and stir. Lower heat and caramelize onions. Stir only often enough to stop the onions from burning. Soak rice in enough water to completely cover it in a bowl.

2. Grind the cinnamon, bay leaf, cloves, and mace together until finely ground.

3. After about 20–30 minutes or when onions have caramelized, add the ground spices. Cook 5 minutes stirring frequently. Drain rice.

4. Add uncooked rice in a thin layer on top of onion mixture. Place pot of boiling water right on the side of the cooking pot and pour the boiling water by increments into the pot. Pour at several different places to ensure even distribution of the water. Cover and cook on low flame for 45 minutes to I hour until done. Check mixture every 15 minutes or so, but do not stir.

5. When done, spoon rice and onion mixture into two separate bowls and have diners layer the meat mixture over the rice. Alternatively, you can use the method I prefer and place a large, round serving dish over the mouth of the pot and quickly invert the pot contents onto the plate. This second method allows the flavor and juices of the onions to flow down into the rice and spread more evenly around.

Sour Plum and Orange Pilaf

This is one of my favorite Afghan pilafs using the wonderful sour plums found throughout western, southwestern, and central Asian cuisine. The sour plums add depth and breadth to the flavor so highlighted by citrus, not unlike a solid bass line in a classical symphony. Afghans also use similar rice-plum mixtures to stuff onions, peppers, and quinces.

½ cup sour plum meat
2 tablespoons butter
I medium red onion, peeled, sliced, and separated into crescents

2 teaspoons garlic, peeled and chopped
Zest of 2 medium oranges, very finely chopped
½ cup orange juice
½ cup almonds, thinly sliced
1 teaspoon ground fennel
1 teaspoon ground cardamom
½ teaspoon ground cinnamon
2 teaspoons sugar
1 teaspoon salt
¼ teaspoon ground black pepper
1 cup uncooked basmati rice
2 cups boiling water

1. Place 1 cup of sour red plums with pits in a saucepan of boiling water and bring back to a boil. Cook over high heat for about 8–10 minutes and remove plums to cool. When they are cool enough to handle, separate the meat from the pits with your fingers or a utensil. One cup of pitted plums will yield about ½ cup of plum meat. (I usually boil the plums one day and pit them the next. To me it seems easier to do with a long interval of time in between the two events.)

2. Soak rice in enough water to cover it in a bowl. Heat the butter in a sauté pan on medium and add the onions and stir briefly. Cook until onions start to soften. Add garlic and the orange zest, and stir again. Stir in half the orange juice and add the plum meat and almonds, and cook.

3. Grind the fennel, cardamom, cinnamon, and pepper until finely ground. Add to the onion and nut mixture along with the sugar and the salt. Stir in the rest of the orange juice and cook for 3–5 minutes. Drain rice.

4. Add uncooked rice in an even layer on top of onion mixture. Place pot of boiling water right on the side of the cooking pot and pour the boiling water by increments into the pot. Pour at several different places to ensure even distribution of the water. Cover and cook on low flame for 45 minutes or until done. Check mixture every 15 minutes or so, but do not stir.

5. When done, spoon rice and onion mixture into two separate bowls and have diners layer the meat mixture over the rice. Alternatively, you can use the method I prefer and place a large, round serving dish over the mouth of the pot and quickly invert the pot contents onto

the plate. This second method allows the flavor and juices of the onions to flow down into the rice and spread more evenly around.

Carrot and Raisin Pilaf

This delicious pilaf is a vegetarian version of the famous Afghan *Q'aubili* pilaf. I have omitted the lamb from it to allow the flavor of the vegetables to shine and to allow it to be combined with more dishes. The carrots and raisins lend a sweetness that brightens the **Afghan Char Masala**, don't overpower, and that complements many spicier dishes nicely.

1 cup uncooked basmati rice
2 cups boiling water
2 tablespoons soybean or peanut oil
2 medium onions, chopped
2 cups carrots, julienned
½ cup black seedless raisins
¼ cup beef broth
1 teaspoon salt
2 teaspoons sugar
2 teaspoons **Afghan Char Masala**
⅛ teaspoon saffron

1. Soak rice in enough water to cover it in a bowl. Heat oil in a large sauté pan and add the chopped onions. Sauté them until they begin to soften, then add the carrots and cook gently until they start to get tender. Add the raisins and cook until they begin to swell up. Add the beef broth to moisten the mix. After raisins are cooking, add salt, sugar, and Afghan *Char Masala* and stir.

2. In a small saucepan, bring the water to a boil and when it is hot, remove from the heat and dissolve the saffron into it. When the raisins are done, stir once more and use a spoon or spatula to flatten the layer of carrots and onions. Drain rice.

3. Add rice in a single layer over the onion-carrot mix, cover, and let it steam for a few minutes. Then, place pot of boiling water on the side of the cooking pot and pour the boiling water by increments into the pot. Pour at several different places to ensure even distribution of the water. Cover and cook on low flame for 45 minutes or more or until done. Check mixture every 15 minutes or so, but do not stir.

4. When done, spoon rice and onion mixture into two separate bowls and have diners layer the meat mixture over the rice. Alternatively, you can use the method I prefer and place a large, round serving dish over the mouth of the pot and quickly invert the pot contents onto the plate. This second method allows the flavor and juices of the onions to flow down into the rice and spread more evenly around.

Afghan Naan

These small oval breads are baked in a tandoor, the stove of the region, which is sometimes buried in the ground. As with Georgian *lavash* and *shoti*, it is possible to use an all-metal wok turned upside down in the oven as a surface to "slap" dough on. Likewise, one can use the recommended method of baking on ungreased baking sheets for a delicious taste of Afghanistan.

I ½ cups water, warm
I package dry, active yeast
I tablespoon sugar
4 cups flour
¼ cup corn oil
I tablespoon salt
I egg yolk, mixed with 2 tablespoons milk
I tablespoon black cumin or caraway seeds

1. Mix warm water, yeast, and sugar together and set aside to activate for about 10 minutes. Add 1 teaspoon of flour to the yeast mixture, mix well, and set aside for another 5 minutes.

2. Add remaining flour to a large mixing bowl, indent the center to form a well, and add the yeast mixture and oil to the flour and mix well. When mixed enough to handle with your hands, knead the dough for about 5 minutes and then place it back in the bowl, cover, and let rest for 1–1 ½ hours.

3. Punch down the dough, divide into 8 equal parts, and roll each part into a ball. Shape each ball into a long oval about 7–8 inches long and ½-inch thick and place on an ungreased cookie sheet. Take a fork and lightly trace lines or crisscrosses and brush with egg yolk and milk mixture. Sprinkle with black cumin or caraway seeds and bake in a 350° preheated oven for 20–25 minutes.

Desserts and Beverages

Two easy-to-prepare Afghan desserts can be found in the **Rose and Cardamom Pudding** and the **Cardamom Cookies** and two more complex but wonderful sweets await in the **Elephant Ears** and the lemony Afghan take on baklava. All add up to great new tastes to grace your globalized table.

Rose and Cardamom Pudding

Another wonderful variation on a theme here with the sweetness of rosewater and cardamom blended with ground pistachio nuts in a wonderful whole-milk pudding. Easy to make and elegantly delicious at the end of a spicy or hot meal.

2 cups whole milk
½ cup sugar
4 tablespoons corn starch
2 teaspoons ground cardamom
½ teaspoon rose water
1 tablespoon ground pistachio nuts

Mix whole milk with sugar, cornstarch and cardamom and rosewater in a sauce pan. Bring it to a boil, stirring constantly. When the mix comes to a boil, remove from the stove, and put into shallow serving dishes. Refrigerate and serve with finely chopped pistachios sprinkled on top.

Cardamom Cookies

These little cookies deliver a blast of sweet cardamom flavor as they melt in your mouth. A delicious taste of Afghanistan that brings a new flavor to the Western dessert table.

1 ½ cups white flour
½ cup sugar
1 tablespoon ground cardamom
½ cup melted butter, slightly cooled
¼ cup milk, warm
¼ cup ground pistachio nuts

Preheat the oven to 350°. Mix the white flour with the sugar and ground cardamom. Add the butter and milk and mix well. Make the dough into 2-inch round balls and put them on a cookie sheet and bake for 15 minutes, or until lightly browned. Sprinkle finely ground pistachios on top of the cookies while they are still hot.

Elephant Ears

These pastries are not as foreign as they may seem at first glance. In fact, they remind me of the fried funnel cakes dusted with powdered sugar and ground nuts that grace many a fall festival in the Western world. In the Afghan version, the basic pastry is made of dough instead of a liquid that is rapidly poured into very hot oil. These lovely pastries grace Afghan tables particularly during celebrations and holidays

Pastries
3 eggs
1 tablespoon sugar
¼ teaspoon salt
2 tablespoon vegetable oil
1 cup milk
3 ¾ cups white flour, sifted

1 cup corn or vegetable oil (for frying)

Syrup
1 cup sugar
½ cup water
1 cup powdered sugar (no need to use all)
1 teaspoon ground cardamom
⅓ cup ground pistachio nuts

1. Beat eggs, then add and beat together sugar, salt, oil, and milk. Add sifted flour to beaten mixture, and mix well. When dough is mixed enough to handle with your hands, knead for 5–8 minutes. Then on a floured surface, roll out small sections of dough into circles no more than ¼ inch thick (thinner is better). Circles can be as large as your sauté pan can accommodate. Pinch the dough lightly, especially around the edges, to crenulate the surface of the pastry.

2.   Heat oil in a large sauté pan or skillet and fry the pastries one at a time (for large pastries) or several at a time for small pastries over medium heat. When the pastries become firm on one side, flip them and cook on the other side. When done, remove from the oil and drain on paper towels.

3.   When all of the pastries are cooked, mix the syrup by combining the water and sugar bit by bit in a small saucepan and mixing well over low heat until all of the sugar is dissolved. Lower heat and cook for about another 5 minutes, stirring constantly, until the syrup thickens. When syrup is done, let it cool (and thicken a bit more) and pour dribbles of it over the pastry and dust at once with generous amounts of powdered sugar, cardamom, and pistachios. Set aside to dry and then serve.

Afghan Baklava

This baklava is yet another variation on a theme that is enjoyed around the region. The Afghan version is spicy by comparison to some and very lemony. Otherwise, its construction and ingredients will be fairly familiar.

Filo dough as needed
2 sticks unsalted butter, melted
2 teaspoons ground cinnamon
2 teaspoons ground cardamom
1 cup peeled and ground almonds
1 cup water
1 ½ cups sugar
1 ½ teaspoons lemon juice
⅓ cup ground pistachio nuts

1.   Preheat the oven to 375°. Brush a baking pan small enough to easily be covered by a single sheet of filo lightly with butter. Combine the cinnamon and cardamom and mix until blended. Lay two layers of filo over the pan and brush with melted butter. Add another two layers of filo and brush again. Next, sprinkle a thin layer of ground almonds and a small amount of the cinnamon and cardamom mixture. Cover with two layers of filo that are brushed with butter.

2.   Repeat these layers until the pan is filled. Top with two layers of filo that are brushed with butter and bake in preheated oven until the filo is golden, about 30–40 minutes.

3. To make the syrup, combine water with sugar and lemon juice in a small saucepan. Bring the mix to a boil, turn down the heat, and simmer for 5 minutes. Stir constantly as the syrup thickens.

4. Remove baklava from oven and cool for about 5 minutes. Then with a very sharp knife cut diagonal lines across the pastry, first in one direction and then perpendicular to form diamond-shaped pieces.

5. While the baklava is still warm, drizzle about ⅓ of the syrup over it. Wait 5 minutes until most of that syrup is absorbed and pour a bit more. Likewise wait until that is absorbed and if desired, pour a bit more. To finish, sprinkle with ground pistachio nuts and serve.

Appetizers and Condiments

A couple of wonderful pastries and a delicious, elegantly simple dip for bread await you in the next section and offer an introduction to Afghan appetizers and condiments. Two savory pastries are offered—one filled with potatoes and lamb or beef and the other filled with a delicious sweet and spicy butternut squash mixture. Last up is a simple yogurt-based dip to enjoy with flatbread.

The Traditional Way to Cook Samsas

Pastries Filled with Savory Potatoes and Lamb

These delicious pastries are reminiscent of India's samosas but are easier to wrap! The flavors of spring onions, cayenne, cumin, and coriander mix with the potatoes and lamb for a spicy, delicious treat, any time. Can also be enjoyed as a snack or even a light meal.

Dough
1 ½ cups warm water
1 teaspoon sugar
1 package dry, active yeast
3 ½ cups flour
3 tablespoons corn or other vegetable oil

Filling
2 large potatoes
1 ½ teaspoons salt
1 teaspoon ground coriander
½ teaspoon cayenne pepper
1 medium bunch chopped cilantro (20–25 sprigs)
4 green onions, chopped

3 tablespoons butter
½ pound ground lamb or beef
1 teaspoon freshly ground black pepper
1 teaspoon salt
1 teaspoon ground cumin
1 egg, beaten

Corn or other vegetable oil for frying pastries

1. Combine the warm water, sugar, and yeast in a medium bowl and mix well. Set aside and let activate for 10 minutes or until it begins to froth.

2. In a large mixing bowl, place the flour, indent the surface, add the corn oil and yeast mixture, and mix well. When the dough is mixed well enough to handle with your hands, knead it for 5 minutes. Set aside in a warm, quiet place for 1 hour or so until it has doubled in bulk.

3. Boil potatoes in their skin until soft. Peel and mash. Add salt, coriander, cayenne pepper, cilantro, and green onions and mix. Brown ground beef with pepper, salt, and cumin. Mix ground beef with mashed potatoes and beaten egg. Let cool.

4. Punch down the dough and divide into four equal pieces. Form each piece into a ball, and on a floured surface roll the dough out until it is about ¼ inch thick. Cut into 4–5-inch squares.

5. Place a few spoonfuls of filling along the middle of the wrapper and fold over into a triangle. Seal edges with your fingers and then crimp with the tines of a fork.

6. Heat oil and fry the pastries until golden on both sides, about 4–5 minutes. Drain on paper towels and serve.

Tricorners Filled with Sweet and Spicy Squash

Tricorner pastries of every type, filled with meat, potatoes, squash, or other vegetables like leeks, are very popular in Afghanistan where they are served at cafes as snacks with a glass of tea. This filling is like a portable version of the **Sweet and Spicy Squash** offered in the vegetable section. Delicious, surprisingly sweet, and flavorful—an interesting variation on ordinary pastries.

Dough
1 ½ cups warm water
1 teaspoon sugar
1 package dry, active yeast
3 ½ cups flour
2 tablespoons corn or other mild vegetable oil

Filling
1 butternut squash or other squash or pumpkin, peeled and chopped
3 tablespoons butter
1 large red onion, peeled and finely diced
2 teaspoons garlic, peeled and diced
2 teaspoons ginger, peeled and diced
2 medium tomatoes
1 teaspoon salt

189

½ teaspoon ground black pepper
2 teaspoons ground coriander
2 tablespoons sugar

1. Combine the warm water, sugar, and yeast in a medium bowl and mix well. Set aside and let activate for 10 minutes or until it begins to froth.

2. In a large mixing bowl, place the flour, indent the surface, add the corn oil and yeast mixture, and mix well. When the dough is mixed well enough to handle with your hands, knead it for 5 minutes. Set aside in a warm, quiet place for 1 hour or so until it has doubled in bulk.

3. Place the chopped squash on a greased or sprayed baking sheet and bake in a preheated 350° oven for 30–40 minutes or until partially cooked. Remove and cool.

4. Heat butter in a sauté pan and sauté the onion until it starts to become translucent and color around the edges. Add the garlic and ginger and cook another 3–5 minutes or until the garlic swells and begins to color. Add the tomatoes, salt, pepper, and coriander and continue to cook until the tomatoes soften and lose their form. Add sugar and mix well. Add the squash and cook until the squash begins to break down into smaller pieces. Remove from heat and let cool.

5. Punch down dough and divide into 6 equal pieces. Roll each piece into a ball and on a floured surface roll each one out until about ¼ inch thick. Cut into 4–5-inch squares and place several spoonfuls of filling mixture along the center of the pastry. Fold over into a triangle and seal the edges with your fingers. Then take the tines of a fork and seal edges again.

6. Brush with the mixture of egg white and milk, place on a sprayed baking sheet, and bake in a preheated 350° oven for 30–40 minutes until golden. Cool slightly and serve.

Yogurt and Mint Dip

This is the simplest dip of its type in the region. You will recognize it instantly, but notice that it has been pared down to its bones, missing spinach, sumac, spring onions, coriander, and any of the other ingredients that cultures of this region add to their dips. Enjoy with flatbread.

2 cups plain yogurt, slightly drained
2 teaspoons crushed garlic
½ teaspoon salt
3 teaspoons dried mint

Mix the yogurt with the garlic and salt. Add dried mint and mix well. Let sit to infuse flavor for at least 30 minutes, mix again, and serve.

Sauces, Spice Mixtures, and Condiments

Two sauces, an important ingredient in many dishes, and two spice rubs can be found in the following pages. The first is **Afghan Cilantro Sauce**, which is a common addition to the Afghan table. It is spiced with cumin and chili peppers and made sour by a blast of white vinegar or lemon juice and is used as a last-minute flavoring for kebabs and roast meat dishes. Next is the **Sweet Tomato Sauce** used to flavor vegetables such as squash, eggplant, or potatoes. Following these is a recipe for *Chaka*, Afghanistan's drained yogurt used in so many dishes.

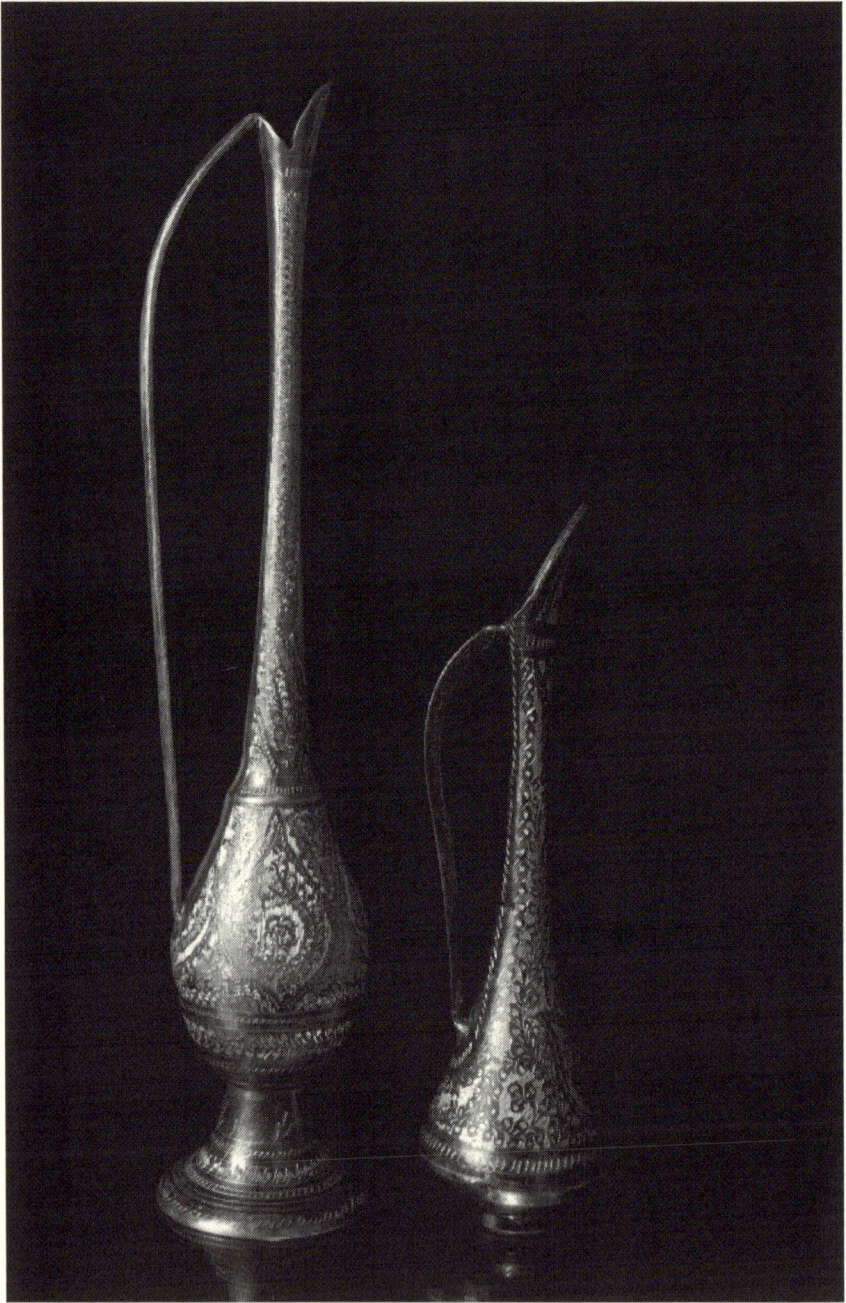

Antique Afghan Pitchers

Afghan Cilantro Sauce

This is Afghanistan's version of Georgia's **Garlic and Walnut Sauce (Garo)**. It has several of the same ingredients, but it is the differences that matter most to the taste. Substituting cumin for the trio of coriander, fenugreek, and turmeric dramatically changes the sauce's flavor. As usual, several different versions of the sauce exist and, as you can imagine, using vinegar instead of lemon juice produces a sauce more bitter than sour. However you prepare it, the sauce is a standard on the Afghan table and is found at almost every kebab meal.

1 medium bunch fresh cilantro leaves (20–25 sprigs)
¼ cup white vinegar or lemon juice
½ cup walnuts, diced
1 teaspoon ground cumin
3 hot, dried, red chili peppers
1 teaspoon garlic, peeled
½ teaspoon ground black pepper
1 teaspoon salt

1. In a blender, combine the cilantro and vinegar or lemon juice. When the cilantro and vinegar or lemon juice has become a smooth paste, add walnuts, cumin, chili peppers, and garlic and blend again until the walnuts are integrated. (If necessary, add a bit more water or lemon juice to blend the walnuts.) Then add pepper and salt and blend well so that spices are well distributed throughout the puree.

2. Pour the puree from the blender into a saucepan and heat. Cook over low to medium heat for 3–5 minutes. Serve hot or at room temperature.

Sweet Afghan Tomato Sauce

This is the secret sauce behind that wondrous Afghan dish, **Sweet and Spicy Squash** or *Kadu Bouranee*. It is easy to prepare, sweet, and lightly spicy all at the same time and brings out the natural sweetness of the butternut squash or any other sweet vegetable nicely. Also works well with eggplants, zucchini, and potatoes.

1 cup water
4 ounces tomato sauce
1 teaspoon garlic, peeled and diced
1 teaspoon ginger, peeled and finely chopped
1 teaspoon ground coriander
½ teaspoon ground black peppercorns
½ teaspoon salt
¼ cup sugar

Heat tomato sauce and water in a sauté pan. When hot add garlic, ginger, and coriander and stir well. Then add salt, pepper, and sugar and stir until the sugar is completely dissolved. Cook to reduce the sauce a bit and make it thicker. Set aside or use in another recipe.

Drained Yogurt (Chaka)

Drained or dried yogurt is an important ingredient in Afghan cooking particularly and in western Asian cooking in general. It brings a powerful blast of soured milk flavor to recipes without changing the consistency of sauces, stews, and curries. If you are exploring the cuisine or cooking it on a regular basis, it is best to make a good-size batch of it and store it in the refrigerator until needed.

I make mine in my automatic drip coffee maker by simply placing the yogurt in a paper coffee filter and letting it drip into an empty carafe. If you use this method, make sure the coffee maker is really clean or your *chaka* will have a coffee flavor.

2 cups plain whole-milk yogurt
1 paper coffee filter
1 automatic drip coffee maker

Spoon the yogurt into the filter-lined coffee maker and position the filter over the carafe. The yogurt will drain over the course of 2–3 hours and become more condensed. When drained, place remaining *chaka* into a sealable container and refrigerate until use.

Afghan Char Masala

This is Afghanistan's own five-spice powder and is used as a rub for meats, to flavor rice dishes, and even to add a zing to food already on the table. Like every other masala or five-spice powder in Asia, there is no one recipe but rather a series of recipes that vary between regions and chefs and are even adapted to different foods they season.

I tablespoon black peppercorns
I tablespoon cumin seed
I tablespoon ground cinnamon
I tablespoon seeds from black cardamom pods
2 teaspoons whole cloves

Grind all whole spices together in a spice grinder. Add previously ground spices and grind again to mix. Store in an airtight container until use. Makes about ⅓ cup.

Masala for Meat and Fish

Missing the sweetness of the cloves and cinnamon of the **Afghan Char Masala**, this masala lends an unmistakable Southwest Asian flare to meats and fish. Rub on 2–3 hours before cooking and it will make roasts and kebabs bloom with flavor.

2 tablespoons black peppercorns
3 tablespoons black cumin seeds
I tablespoon ground turmeric
I tablespoon ground cardamom
I tablespoon ground coriander

Grind all whole spices together in a spice grinder. Add previously ground spices and grind again to mix. Store in an airtight container until use.

Kutwal Lake in northwestern Pakistan

Pakistan

Main spices and flavors: tamarind, coriander, cilantro, fennel, mint, mustard, bay leaf, saffron, fenugreek, cumin, garlic, onion, turmeric, cardamom, black cardamom, curry leaves, cinnamon, ginger, coconuts, cloves, nutmeg, mace, chili peppers, tomato, potato

Souring agents: lemons, limes, white vinegar, rice vinegar

Although the history of Pakistan as a nation began only about 70 years ago, the area has been inhabited for millennia and shows evidence of human habitation that reaches back to the Neolithic period over ten thousand years ago. Some of the earliest human agricultural settlements are also known from the Indus Valley that rose and fell more than four thousand years ago. The great Vedic civilizations followed those of the Indus Valley and gave way to the Persian Achaemenid Dynasty in the fifth century BCE and Alexander the Great's empire just a couple of hundred years later. Alexander's sway over the region fell finally to the Indo-Greek kingdom founded by Demetrius of Bactria from about 184 BCE onwards.

In the seventh century, the Sindh, Multan, and southern Punjab were conquered by the Arab General Muhammad bin Qasim who set up what would be the first in a succession of Muslim empires that ruled the region for almost ten centuries. Toward the end of the last Muslim empire, the rule of law broke down and Afghan and Sikh warlords dominated large portions of the territory. The British East India Company took over in the mid-eighteenth century and held sway until Indian independence and the partition of East and West Pakistan in 1947.

Pakistani cooking is a unique blend of the cuisines of India, western and central Asia, and the Levant states of the Middle East.

Foods eaten and methods of preparation also vary from one region to another. The cuisine in Sindh and the Punjab can be very hot and spicy, as with the **Vegetable Curry with Tamarind and Fenugreek**, **Tomato with Black Pepper and Cloves**, and **Spicy Pakistani Potatoes** offered here. This food has a great deal in common with the cuisine of northern India, while food in the North-West Frontier Province, Baluchistan, and northern areas on the other hand is more akin to dishes found in Afghanistan, central Asia, and Iran and include lots of skewered and grilled meats and kebabs such as the stuffed **Pakistani Beef or Lamb Kebabs** and **Chicken Tikka**.

The Middle Eastern influence on Pakistani cuisine is seen sparingly, usually in the particular combination of herbs and spices, but is evident in such dishes as **Rice with Pine Nuts and Garlic** and **Rice with Mint and Red Peppers**.

Interestingly, because of its tropical seacoast and active role in modern and historical trade, Pakistani cookery also incorporates elements of Southeast Asian and Pacific cuisines, such as the use of coconuts and mangoes in **Butternut Squash in Coconut Cream** and **Mango and Tomato Salad with Lime Dressing**.

Meat Dishes

Like the Afghans and central Asians and to a lesser extent the Iranians, the Pakistanis love to grill meat and serve it in all shapes and sizes. The loaf-type kebabs are common, as in the **Pakistani Beef or Lamb Kebab** stuffed with coriander, mint, and ginger; also common are "dry" kebabs in which marinated meat is skewered on metal blades that look like unsharpened swords. Like the Indians, they also bake meats by seasoning whole cuts or steaks and then layering them in a casserole with lots of vegetables in a spicy sauce, as in the mild but flavorful **Chicken with Lime and Cumin** or the fiery **Baked Fish with Cinnamon and Ginger**.

Kebabs Stuffed with Ginger and Mint

This dish is a Pakistani take on stuffed ground-meat kebabs. The filling gives a blast of ginger and mint to the already flavorful meat. An absolutely delicious kebab that can be served with rice or flatbread and a salad for a wonderful meal. Interesting to compare this spicy kebab with the filled sweet kebab eaten in Bangladesh.

1 pound ground beef or lamb
½ cup lentils
1 teaspoon cumin seeds
Seeds from 4 black cardamom corms
12 black peppercorns
1 teaspoon coriander seeds
1 3-inch piece of cinnamon, ground
6 hot, dried, red chili peppers
2 teaspoons garlic, peeled and diced
1 tablespoon ginger, peeled and grated
1 tablespoon plain yogurt
1 egg, beaten
1 teaspoon salt

Filling
1 small bunch fresh cilantro leaves, finely chopped
1 tablespoon grated ginger
1 small bunch mint leaves, finely chopped
1 large onion

1. In a medium saucepan, heat 4 cups of water, and when it is boiling, add the washed lentils and cook for 30 minutes or until the lentils start to soften. When they are done, drain and set aside to cool. Grind

together the cumin seeds, cardamom seeds, peppercorns, coriander seeds, cinnamon, and red chili peppers until you have a fine powder.

2. In a food processor, combine meat, garlic, ginger, yogurt, beaten egg, and salt. Add the ground spices and cooled lentils and grind until all ingredients are well mixed. Let meat rest in the refrigerator for at least an hour to give the flavors a chance to blend.

3. Chop cilantro, mint, onion, and ginger, mix well, and set aside. Roll meatballs or loaf-shaped kebabs out of the meat and indent the top with your fingers to create a well for the filling. Fill the kebabs with the herb and onion paste and reseal the hole with your fingers. Finish by rolling each one back into a meatball or loaf-shaped kebab.

4. Put kebabs on a greased or oiled baking sheet and place 4–6 inches beneath a preheated broiler for 5–7 minutes per side. Be careful not to overcook.

Baked Chicken with Lime and Black Cumin

This is a delicious and easy way to prepare chicken that is eaten all across Pakistan in one form or another. The dominant flavors are lime, ginger, cinnamon, and black cumin. It's delicious with a simple rice dish or pilaf, such as **Rice with Pine Nuts and Garlic** or **Rice with Red Peppers and Mint**.

2–3 chicken breasts, rinsed and dried
1 tablespoon grated ginger
2 teaspoons garlic, peeled and diced
1 cup **Drained Yogurt (Chaka)** (see Afghan Sauces and Spice Mixtures)
1 egg, beaten
1 teaspoon salt
½ teaspoon ground black pepper
2 cloves, ground
½ teaspoon ground cinnamon
1 teaspoon ground black cumin (roast lightly before grinding)
1 large pinch saffron
2 tablespoons lime juice

1. Drained Yogurt (Chaka) takes a couple of hours to make, so have some on hand or prepare it well before starting the rest of the recipe. Pierce

chicken in several places with a fork or knife and set aside. Combine ginger, garlic, *chaka*, egg, salt, pepper, cloves, cinnamon, roasted and ground black cumin, saffron, and lime juice in a bowl and mix well. Pour into a sealable gallon-size plastic bag or onto a plate. Add chicken and marinate for several hours at room temperature, turning meat occasionally and spooning the marinade over the meat.

2. Preheat oven to 350° and turn chicken and marinade out into an ovenproof casserole dish. Bake 20–25 minutes in preheated oven and then remove from oven. Cover and let sit for 5 minutes before serving. Garnish with onion rings, mint, and lemon slices. Serve with rice and a salad for a delicious meal.

Meatballs with Coriander and Cinnamon

Although the official status of Kashmir remains in dispute between Pakistan and India, this recipe is an example of the tiny meatballs eaten throughout the subcontinent. These are sweetly spicy and use an array of spices such as cinnamon, nutmeg, and cloves that we in the West associate most with desserts, and just a little bit of chili peppers to add to the interest. Great with rice and a vegetable dish like **Vegetable Curry with Tamarind and Fenugreek**.

1 pound ground lamb
1 tablespoon grated ginger
1 tablespoon ground cumin seeds
1 tablespoon ground coriander seeds
¼ teaspoon ground cloves
¼ teaspoon ground cinnamon
½ corm nutmeg, grated
¼ teaspoon ground black pepper
½ teaspoon cayenne pepper
1 ½ teaspoons salt
5 tablespoons plain yogurt
4 tablespoons peanut oil
2-inch stick cinnamon
5 whole cardamom pods
2 bay leaves
6 whole cloves
1 cup water

1. Combine the lamb, ginger, cumin, coriander, ground cloves, ground cinnamon, grated nutmeg, black pepper, cayenne, salt, and 3 tablespoons of the yogurt in a bowl. Mix well and set aside for at least an hour to allow for the flavors to infuse the meat.

2. Wet your hands with cold water and form small meatballs about 1 ½ inches in diameter. Heat the oil in a large sauté pan and when hot, put in the cinnamon stick, cardamom pods, bay leaves, and whole cloves. Stir for 2–3 minutes to warm the spices and allow them to infuse the oil with their flavors.

3. Now put in the meatballs and sauté them on medium-high heat until they are lightly browned on all sides. Then, combine the remaining yogurt with the water and pour this over the meatballs and bring to a boil. Cover, lower heat, and simmer for about 15 minutes, turning the meatballs when half that time has elapsed. When meatballs are done, remove them and place them in a bowl.

4. Continue to reduce sauce (use just a touch of cornstarch if necessary to thicken it) until it is thick and flavorful. Remove whole spices and pour sauce over meatballs and serve with rice.

Skewered Chicken with Ginger, Lemons, and Spices (Tikka)

This is a wonderful chicken shish kebab that is eaten all around the Indian subcontinent. After you taste it, you'll understand why the dish is so widespread—it is simply delicious. Hot chili peppers blend with garlic, cumin, cinnamon, and other spices, and a blast of lemon juice lightens and brightens the flavor.

3 chicken breasts cut into bite-size pieces
1 tablespoon grated ginger
2 teaspoons garlic, peeled and diced
1 cup plain yogurt
1 teaspoon red chili powder
½ teaspoon turmeric powder
1 teaspoon salt
½ teaspoon ground black pepper
1 teaspoon cumin

1 teaspoon coriander
½ teaspoon **Pakistani *Garam Masala***
3 tablespoons lemon juice
1 tablespoon peanut oil

1. Combine all of the ingredients (except the chicken) in a bowl and whisk together into a mixture. Take half of this mixture and set it aside for later. Use the other half to marinate the chicken pieces for about 3–4 hours.

2. After the chicken is done marinating, place it on skewers (without rinsing or wiping marinade off). Grill outside or under a broiler until chicken colors on the edges, 10–15 minutes, turning when about half that time has elapsed. When chicken is done, remove from heat and place skewers on a serving plate.

3. While chicken is cooking, heat the reserved marinade up in a small saucepan and cook until the mixture reduces and thickens a bit. If necessary, sprinkle just a bit of cornstarch into the sauce to aid thickening. Pour sauce over the chicken or serve separately and allow diners to spoon it over their meals on their own. Serve with rice or on flatbread with tomatoes and onions for garnish.

Baked Fish with Cinnamon and Ginger

In this recipe, the cinnamon and cloves from the *garam masala* mingle with the ginger and garlic and bring out the best in this lemony fish dish. Once again the spices that we combine with sugar in the West are accented here with black pepper and chilies to yield a different aspect of the flavor that we are generally unaccustomed to tasting. This dish goes well with plain rice or a simple pilaf and a vegetable dish like **Vegetable Curry with Tamarind and Fenugreek** or **Tomatoes with Black Pepper and Cloves**.

4 steaks of firm white fish, such as sea bass (or rockfish), cod, or carp
2 tablespoons mustard oil
2 medium onions, peeled, sliced, and separated into crescents
1 ½ teaspoons salt
1 teaspoon ground black pepper
Juice and zest of 1 lemon, finely chopped

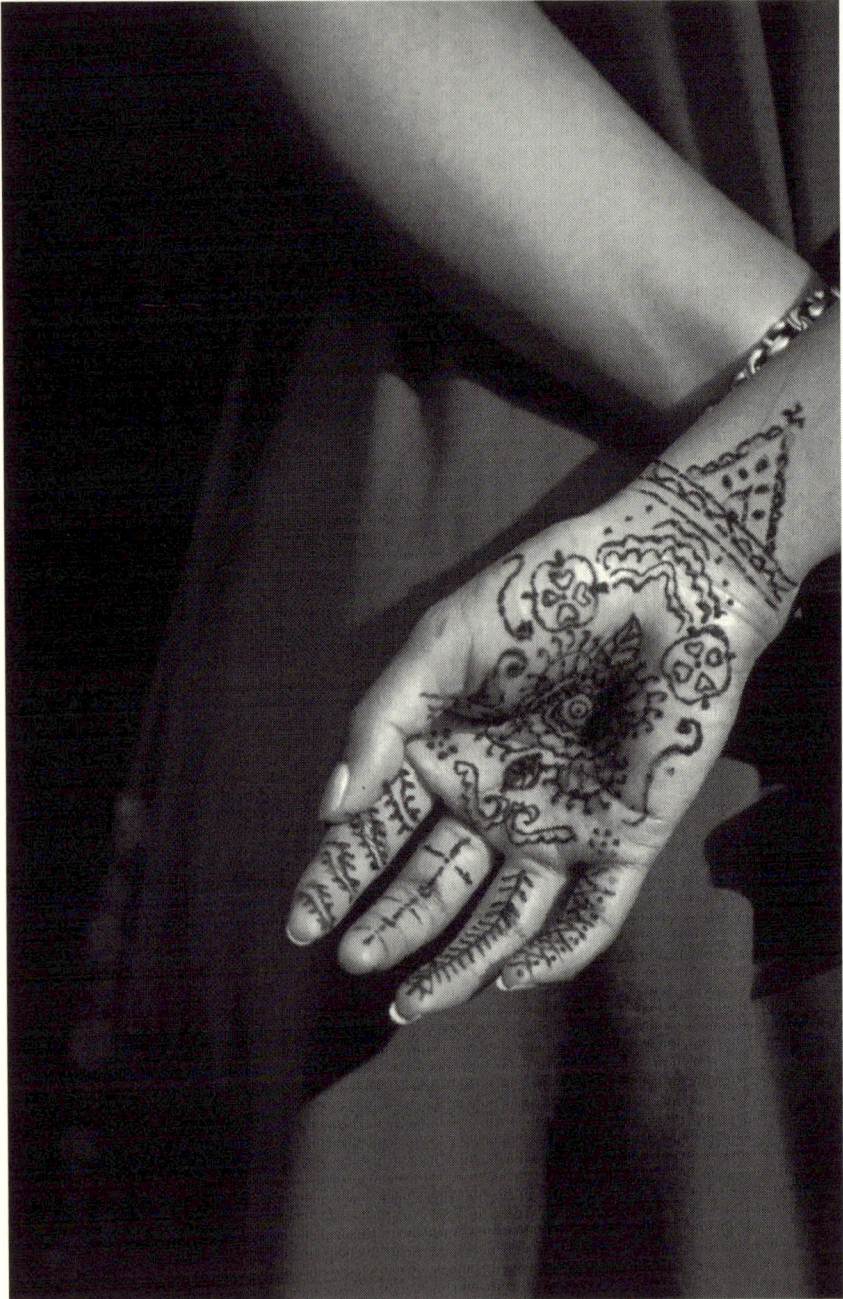

Henna Decorations on a Girl's Hands

1 tablespoon garlic, peeled and diced
1 tablespoon grated ginger
¼ cup water or chicken broth
6 hot, dried, red chili peppers, finely diced
1 teaspoon **Pakistani *Garam Masala***
½ cup plain yogurt

1. Place the fish skin side down in a buttered or oiled casserole dish. Sprinkle with lemon juice, ½ teaspoon salt, and ½ teaspoon ground black pepper and set aside for at least 1 hour.

2. Preheat oven to 375° and heat mustard oil in a sauté pan. When the oil is hot add the sliced onions and sauté until they start to soften and color. Add the garlic and sauté until it swells and colors, and then add the ginger and continue to cook, adding water or chicken broth to moisten the mix.

3. Add the diced chili peppers and the remaining salt, pepper, lemon zest and cook for 3–5 minutes to blend and warm the chilies. Add *garam masala* and mix well. Then add the yogurt and cook to warm the yogurt. When yogurt is hot, pour entire mixture over the fish, cover, and bake in the preheated oven for 15–20 minutes. Uncover and cook another 10–15 minutes and serve with rice and vegetables.

Vegetable Dishes and Salads

The Pakistani take on vegetables is widely varied and ranges from complex curries like the **Vegetable Curry with Tamarind and Fenugreek** to the simple but elegant **Mushroom and Tomato Bahji with Ginger and Fennel** or the **Tomatoes with Black Pepper and Cloves** offered here. There is a whole range of spiciness and heat offered in the vegetables as well. Not to be missed are the heavenly salads that really help to cool the spice-stressed palate. In fact, one of my favorite salads of all time is a Pakistani dish: the **Pakistani Mixed Bean Salad**, which will convince even dyed-in-the-wool bean haters to give them another try.

Vegetable Curry with Tamarind and Fenugreek

This wondrous vegetable stew is so flavorful and so delicious that you'll be going back for seconds or perhaps even thirds. It is spicy and a bit hot and is a tasty way to prepare these vegetables. If you like the curry, try the recipe on other vegetables as well—that's what Pakistani cooks would do!

2 medium potatoes, well washed and chopped
1 cup cauliflower florets
2 tablespoons peanut oil
2 cups okra, washed, trimmed, and sliced crosswise
¼ cup pigeon peas
1 small Chinese eggplant, chopped crosswise
2 cups hot water
1 teaspoon salt
½ teaspoon ground black pepper
4 fresh green chili peppers, diced
¼ teaspoon ground turmeric
1 teaspoon tamarind concentrate
1 teaspoon mustard seeds
1 teaspoon cumin seeds
1 teaspoon onion seeds
1 teaspoon fenugreek seeds
¼ teaspoon asafetida
1 medium bunch fresh cilantro leaves, chopped (25–30 sprigs)

1. Heat oil in a deep saucepan and sauté potatoes and cauliflower for 5 minutes, stirring often. Then add the okra and cook another 2–3 minutes. Lastly, add the peas and the eggplant and cook another 5 minutes. Add the hot water, salt, red and black pepper, turmeric and tamarind and stir gently to mix.

2. Grind the seeds together into a fine powder and add to the curry. Stir and cook covered for 10 minutes or until the cauliflower and potatoes are done. Finish with the addition of asafetida and cilantro. Serve with rice.

Mushroom and Tomato Bhaji with Ginger and Fennel

A *bhaji* is a type of stew or curry of sliced, diced, or shredded vegetables sautéed in a small amount of oil with turmeric as the main flavor and coloring. Also important to the definition of a *bhaji* is the short cooking time, which Western cooks especially are going to love. I use the all-purpose king-oyster mushrooms for this recipe, because their strong texture holds up well to stewing and the mushrooms keep their form nicely, but feel free to experiment with other types if you prefer.

¾ pound king-oyster mushrooms, well washed and sliced
1 tablespoon mustard oil
1 teaspoon yellow mustard seeds
1 teaspoon fennel seeds
1 tablespoon grated ginger
1 tablespoon lemon juice
4 tomatoes, diced
½ medium onion, diced
1 teaspoon salt
¼ teaspoon ground black pepper
½ teaspoon ground turmeric

1. Heat the oil in a sauté pan over medium heat, add the mustard and the fennel seeds, and sauté 2–3 minutes until they just pop. Keep a lid nearby to cover the pan to keep the seeds from flying out. Then add the grated ginger, lemon juice, and water and stir well. Add the diced tomatoes and onions and cook 5–8 minutes until the liquid from the tomatoes starts to evaporate. Add the salt and pepper and turmeric and stir well to mix.

2. Add the mushrooms and cook covered for 2 minutes, stirring occasionally, until mushrooms start to give off their liquid. Then cook uncovered, stirring often, until the liquid from the mushrooms dissolves and they are tender. Serve hot with rice.

Mango and Tomato Salad with Lime Dressing

This is a nice cooling slightly sweet salad to serve on a table with spicy meats and vegetables. It helps cool and clear the palate after a flavorful meal. To get the full range of flavors, it has to be served and enjoyed right after preparation, or the fruits and vegetables will juice, so refrigerate all ingredients before preparing.

1 ripe mango, peeled, pitted, and sliced
1 firm tomato, finely chopped
1 red onion, peeled and diced
½ medium red pepper, cored and thinly sliced
1 teaspoon salt
2 teaspoons brown sugar
1 tablespoon lime juice

Refrigerate all ingredients for at least 2 hours before preparing. Slice and chop all of the vegetables and fruits and pour off any accumulated excess juices. Combine the fruit and vegetable slices in a bowl. Add salt, brown sugar, and lime juice and mix well. Serve immediately.

Butternut Squash in Coconut Cream

An interesting recipe that is reminiscent of the coconut cream vegetables in Burma, Indonesia, and Malaysia. Since Pakistan is such a varied climate, dishes from the south include a fair amount of coconut and other subtropical ingredients. The sweetness of the dish provides a nice balance in a meal with other spicy or sour entrees. If there's a secret, it's to not overcook the squash.

1 medium butternut squash, peeled and chopped
2 tablespoons peanut or light sesame oil
1 teaspoon black mustard seeds
1 medium onion, peeled, sliced, and separated into crescents
1 medium tomato, chopped
1 teaspoon ground turmeric
1 cup coconut cream
1 cup water
1 teaspoon salt
1 small bunch fresh cilantro leaves, chopped (15–20 sprigs)

1. Heat oil in a sauté pan and sauté mustard seeds until they pop. You may wish to cover them to keep most of them in the pan and to protect yourself as well. Add sliced onion and sauté until softened

and colored. Add chopped tomato and turmeric and cook briefly, about 2–3 minutes.

2. Then add the chopped butternut squash, salt, and water. Stir well and cook covered for 3–5 minutes until the squash starts to soften. Add coconut cream. Cover and cook until squash is still firm but tender. Stir in chopped cilantro and serve.

Pakistani Mixed Bean Salad

This is a mild salad to end a spicy meal with. It's moderately spicy when first made and mellows a lot after sitting for a while. I like to prepare it in the morning or by noon before an evening meal and let it rest in the refrigerator for several hours. I recommend taking it out at least one hour before serving as it is best served only slightly chilled, not cold.

I cup northern white beans or butter beans, drained
I cup chick peas, drained
I medium onion, peeled and chopped
½ medium red pepper, cored and finely chopped
I medium tomato, chopped
2 green chili peppers, diced
¼ cup white vinegar
¼ cup grapeseed oil
I tablespoon sugar
I teaspoon salt
½ teaspoon ground black pepper
I small bunch fresh cilantro leaves, chopped (15–20 sprigs)

1. Combine beans, onion, red pepper, tomato, and chili peppers into a large bowl. Then whisk together vinegar, oil, sugar, salt, and pepper and when well blended, pour over the bean mixture. Mix well.

2. Cover and refrigerate for at least 3 hours. Just before serving, fold in fresh chopped cilantro leaves and stir gently.

Tomatoes with Black Pepper and Cloves

If you really love tomatoes and want to feature them in a main dish, here is the recipe for you. This is a delicious, spicy, and slightly hot way to prepare the New World's gift to Asian cuisine. In this curry, the red peppers, cumin, and coriander provide the spicy curry base, while the turmeric and black cardamom richen and deepen the flavor and a bit of *garam masala* sweetens the mix just before serving. Works well with spicy grilled meats and roasts as well as other vegetable dishes.

4 medium tomatoes, chopped
2 medium potatoes, parboiled or cooked in the microwave and cooled
3 tablespoons light sesame or peanut oil
I large onion, peeled, sliced, and separated into crescents
2 teaspoons grated ginger
I teaspoon garlic, peeled and chopped
I teaspoon salt
10 black peppercorns, crushed
6 whole cloves, crushed
6 hot, dried, red chili peppers
Seeds from 2 black cardamom pods, crushed
¼ teaspoon cumin seeds
¼ cup water or vegetable broth
I teaspoon ground coriander
¼ teaspoon ground turmeric
½ teaspoon **Pakistani *Garam Masala***

1. Heat oil in a sauté pan and sauté the onion until it softens and starts to color. Add the ginger and the garlic and sauté until the garlic starts to swell and color. Add salt and stir well. Grind together the whole spices: peppercorns, cloves, chili peppers, black cardamom seeds, and cumin seeds. When ground, add them to the onions, mix well, and cook 2–3 minutes.

2. Add the water or vegetable broth and then the coriander, turmeric, and chili peppers and stir well. Add the chopped tomatoes and stir. Cook 2–3 minutes to heat, then lower heat and cook uncovered for 10 minutes, stirring occasionally, until tomatoes are softened. Add the *garam masala* and stir well. Cook for another 5 minutes until the liquid evaporates a bit and the sauce thickens.

3. Chop the cooled potatoes and add them to the curry, folding them in so as not to smash them. Cook for 3–5 minutes to warm the potatoes, and when they are hot, serve immediately.

Spicy Pakistani Potatoes

This is a wonderful way to prepare potatoes that is spicy and silky smooth at the same time. Black mustard seeds have a gentler, earthier flavor than their lighter cousins, and when coupled with freshly ground turmeric, the results are wonderful for tempering the heat of the red chili peppers in this dish. Delicious by itself or when coupled with a kebab or roasted meat dish.

4 medium potatoes, parboiled or incompletely cooked in the microwave and cooled
1 tablespoon butter
1 teaspoon black mustard seeds
1 teaspoon ground turmeric
½ teaspoon red chili powder
1 teaspoon salt
½ cup vegetable broth or water
2 medium onions, peeled, sliced, and separated into crescents

1. Chop the cooled potatoes and set aside. Heat the butter in a sauté pan and fry the mustard seeds until they pop. Add the turmeric powder, red chili powder, and salt and stir. Cook for 2–3 minutes to blend and warm spices.

2. Add the onions and continue frying on low heat until the onions are soft and golden. Add the broth and cook to warm. Then add the potatoes and mix well, lifting rather than stirring so as not to break the potatoes. Cook 3–5 minutes or until the potatoes are done.

Rice and Grain Dishes, Breads

This section offers a couple of pilafs, a tahari rice dish that is common throughout the north of the subcontinent all the way to Nepal and Burma, and two breads—an everyday Pakistani flatbread and a holiday or celebratory sweet roll. The first pilaf, **Rice with Pine Nuts and Garlic**, has roots in Saudi Arabia and is eaten today throughout the Levant. The second pilaf is more Persian and blends mint and red peppers. The next rice dish is cooked more like a stew and the rice picks up the flavor of the spices and vegetables cooked with it. A recipe for **Pakistani Naan** follows, as does a recipe for a delicious little pastry sweetened with *garam masala* and ground nuts.

Rice with Pine Nuts and Garlic

This tasty way to cook rice actually has roots that stretch back to Saudi Arabia. The garlic is the main flavor, so this works well with roasts and kebabs of all types, and the pine nuts add a bit of crunch and nutty flavor. The Pakistanis, however, make an addition to the traditional flavor by adding fresh cilantro to the recipe to sweeten and brighten it a bit.

1 cup uncooked basmati rice
3 tablespoons butter
1 medium onion, peeled and diced
2 tablespoons garlic, peeled and diced
½ cup of pine nuts, lightly roasted
1 cup chicken stock
1 cup water
1 medium bunch fresh cilantro, chopped (25–30 sprigs)

1. Melt the butter in a saucepan and sauté the onion until it softens and starts to become golden. Then add the garlic and pine nuts and continue to sauté until the garlic swells and begins to color as well. Add rice and stir well. Cook 3–5 minutes to warm the rice.

2. Add chicken stock and water and bring to a near boil over high heat. When nearly boiling, reduce heat to low and cook covered for 15–20 minutes or until the rice is done. Let rice sit, covered until needed.

Rice with Mint and Red Peppers

This is a nice, delicately flavored pilaf with overtones of mint and lemon that will accent any of the roast meat or kebab recipes offered here. Alternatively, serve it with the vegetable curries, stews, or casseroles that grace vegetarian tables.

1 cup uncooked basmati rice
3 tablespoons butter

1 onion, peeled and finely diced
1 teaspoon garlic, peeled and minced
1 medium red bell pepper, cored and thinly sliced
3 tablespoons fresh mint, chopped
Zest and juice from 2 medium lemons, finely chopped
½ teaspoon ground coriander
1 teaspoon salt
2 cups water

1. Heat butter in a saucepan and sauté onion until it starts to soften and color. Then add garlic and red bell pepper and continue to sauté for 2–3 minutes. Add mint and mix well. Then add lemon zest, juice, and ground coriander, stir well, and cook for 2–3 minutes.

2. Add rice and salt and cook for about 3 minutes to warm the rice. Then add water and bring to a near boil over high heat. When nearly boiling, lower heat to the lowest setting, cover, and cook for 15–20 minutes or until rice is done. When done, just let rice sit covered until needed.

Tahari Rice

This type of stewed rice called tahari is eaten all across the north of the subcontinent from Pakistan through Nepal and even into western Burma. A bit more of a mélange than a central Asian pilaf, these rice dishes cook soaked rice with a variety of vegetables and spices, allowing for the rice to absorb the flavors infused into the mix. A delicious alternative to plain rice or even a pilaf.

1 medium onion, peeled and diced
3 tablespoons peanut or other vegetable oil
2 teaspoons garlic, peeled and diced
2 teaspoons ginger, peeled and grated
3 green chili peppers
1 large tomato
2 ½ cups water (more if needed)
1 teaspoon salt
10 whole black peppercorns, crushed
½ teaspoon ground cumin
½ teaspoon ground turmeric
6 cloves, ground

Seeds from 3 cardamom pods, crushed or ground
1 cinnamon stick
2–3 medium potatoes, peeled and chopped
1 cup basmati or other long-grain rice, soaked for at least 1 hour and drained

1.   In a large saucepan, heat the oil and sauté the onion until it starts to become transparent and color around the edges. Add the garlic, ginger, and chili peppers and cook another 3–5 minutes or until the garlic starts to swell and color. Add the diced tomato and cook for 5 minutes or until the tomato starts to break down. Add 1 cup of water and mix well.

2.   Add salt, pepper, cumin, turmeric, cloves, cardamom, and cinnamon and mix well. Cover and cook over low heat until the spices start to infuse their flavors. Add chopped potatoes and another ½ cup of water, and cover and cook for about 15–20 minutes, stirring occasionally, or until the potato starts to soften.

3.   Add in the presoaked rice and the remaining 1 cup of water. Cover and cook over medium heat until the rice is hot. Then lower the heat to low and cook another 15–20 minutes or until the rice is soft. When done, remove from the heat and let rest for 5 minutes before serving.

Pakistani Naan

This flatbread differs from the ones encountered in Georgia, Azerbaijan, and Afghanistan by the addition of yogurt and baking soda into the dough. This gives the dough a puffy consistency that resists crusting and crackling, and a slight sour tang that is missing from the other flatbreads. Another difference is the use of poppy seeds or caraway seeds instead of sesame seeds to coat the surface of the bread, as is favored in some of the other recipes.

4 cups all-purpose flour
1 teaspoon baking powder
½ teaspoon baking soda
1 teaspoon salt
1 egg, beaten
½ cup plain yogurt, lightly drained

3 tablespoons butter or ghee melted
I cup warm milk
I tablespoon poppy seeds or caraway seeds

1. Sift flour, baking powder, baking soda, and salt together in a large mixing bowl. Stir in egg, yogurt, and 2 tablespoons of the butter. Gradually stir in enough milk to make a smooth dough. If dough reaches a good consistency before all of the milk is used, that's okay; there is no need to use all of the milk. Knead for 3–5 minutes, cover, and allow to rest in a warm place for I ½–2 hours.

2. Preheat oven to 400°. Punch down dough and knead for another 2–3 minutes. Then divide the dough into about 8 evenly sized pieces and roll them out on a floured surface until they are ovals about 6–8 inches long

3. Place on a greased or oiled baking sheet, brush lightly with butter, and then sprinkle with poppy seeds or caraway seeds. Bake for about 10 minutes or until the bread starts to color a light golden brown, especially around the edges. Let cool for about five minutes and serve.

Sweet Nut Rolls

These "nut rolls" are more like cookies than rolls and might be enjoyed today as a break for the palate in a long, highly spiced, or hot multicourse meal as they have been for centuries of subcontinental dining. In the West, they would be more likely enjoyed as a dessert, and have them that way if it suits your habits, but understand that especially in times past, many cultures enjoyed sweet breaks to offset spice and try them as part of a main meal for an authentic slice of an ancient meal.

Pastry
¼ cup warm water
I cup sugar
2 teaspoons dry, active yeast
I cup warm or room-temperature milk
3 cups white flour
I teaspoon salt
I teaspoon baking powder

Filling
Peeled and ground pistachio nuts
I cup ground cashew nuts
2 teaspoons *garam masala*
2 teaspoons rosewater
3 tablespoons butter or ghee, melted

1. In a small mixing bowl, combine the warm water, I teaspoon sugar, and yeast and mix well. Set aside in a warm quiet place for about 10 minutes and allow yeast to activate. In a large mixing bowl, add the flour, salt, and baking powder, mix well, and indent the top to form a bowl.

2. Mix together the milk and half the remaining sugar and add it to the flour mixture, blending well. Add the yeast mixture and blend again. When the mixture is blended well enough to handle, knead for about 5 minutes and then set aside for about 15 minutes in a warm, quiet place.

3. Combine ground pistachios, ground cashews, *garam masala*, remaining ½ cup of sugar, rosewater, and butter or ghee and mix together. Mix mixture into the dough and mix just enough to blend the nuts with the dough. Take handfuls of dough and roll them into golf balls. Then flatten them so that they are between ½ inch and I inch thick. Place them on a sprayed baking sheet. Cover and set aside for about 30 minutes in a warm place.

4. Uncover the baking sheet, pierce each roll with a fork several times, and bake in a preheated 350° oven for about 12–15 minutes or until the rolls are golden around the edges. Let cool slightly and serve.

Desserts and Beverages

Pastry in Sweet Milk and Rosewater (Ras Malai)

This is Pakistan's version of *gulab jamun*, which you may have experienced in an Indian restaurant. Pakistanis enjoy their pastries in a sweet milk-based sauce flavored with black cardamom and rosewater instead of sugary syrup, as enjoyed elsewhere on the subcontinent.

Pastry

1 cup powdered milk
1 egg, beaten
1 teaspoon vegetable oil
¼ teaspoon baking powder

Sauce

3 cups whole milk
¼ cup sugar
Seeds of 4 black cardamom pods, ground
½ teaspoon rosewater
1 tablespoon pistachio nuts, finely diced

1. In a medium saucepan, mix milk, sugar, and ground black cardamom together and heat to a boil. Reduce heat and cook at a steady simmer until about half of the milk is evaporated. Remove from heat and let cool until the mixture is just warm to the touch.

2. Mix the ingredients for the dough together and form into small, oval, slightly flattened balls.

3. Reheat the milk and when it just starts to boil, reduce heat to a steady simmer and add the balls of dough. After they swell up, cook for 10 minutes. Spoon pastries into serving bowls or dishes. Add rosewater to spiced milk and spoon over pastries, which should not be swimming in sauce. Garnish with diced pistachios and serve.

Sweet Milk Squares with Cardamom

This is one of the delightfully sweet desserts you might see in the refrigerators of Indo-Pakistani markets. It is made from powdered milk and sugar syrup flavored with cardamom, saffron, and a touch of sliced almonds. A sweet way to end a spicy, flavorful meal.

3 cups powdered milk
2 tablespoons butter or ghee, melted
2 tablespoons warm milk
1 cup water
½ cup sugar
1 teaspoon ground cardamom
½ teaspoon saffron
Finely chopped almonds

1. Mix powdered milk with melted butter or ghee and warm milk, blend thoroughly, and set aside. In a small saucepan, heat the water to boiling and then reduce heat to a steady simmer and slowly stir in sugar to make a syrup. When sugar is completely dissolved, reduce heat and cook for at least 5 minutes until the syrup thickens.

2. Add ground cardamom and saffron and mix well. Cook for another 2–3 minutes to infuse the flavors and add the powdered milk a bit at a time and mix well. Brush a baking pan with butter and pour/place the mixture into the dish. Sprinkle chopped almonds over the dessert and let set for about 20–30 minutes or until the dessert holds its form. Cut into squares or diamonds and serve.

Pineapple Custard

This is an unusual offering from the south that showcases some of Pakistan's use of tropical fruits and flavors. Here the pineapple is ground in a food processor and mixed with egg, milk, and custard powder and then garnished with whipped cream and chopped nuts for a delicious treat.

1 medium to large pineapple, peeled, eyes removed, and chopped (alternately use canned pineapple)
1 ½ cups milk
¼ cup sugar
1 egg, beaten
2 tablespoons custard powder
1 pint heavy cream, whipped with ⅛ cup sugar (garnish)
¼ cup mixed almonds and pistachios, finely chopped (garnish)

1. In a food processor, grind pineapple until it becomes a pasty puree. Transfer pineapple and its liquid to a medium saucepan and cook over a low flame for 10 minutes to warm.

2. In a small mixing bowl, whisk together the milk, sugar, egg, and custard powder until well mixed. Combine this mixture with the pineapple in the saucepan and stir constantly over low flame until the custard thickens.

3. Remove from flame and pour into a serving dish and let cool before refrigerating. Before serving, garnish with whipped cream and chopped nuts if desired.

Spiced Tea

This is a delicious spicy tea that can be made as sweet or sour as you wish. Although not authentic, the milk can be omitted and it makes a great iced tea as well.

4 tablespoons or 4 teabags Darjeeling tea
3 cups water
1 teaspoon ginger, peeled and grated.
Seeds from 4 cardamom pods
3 cloves
1 teaspoon black cumin seeds
2 whole black peppercorns
Small piece of cinnamon (1 inch long)
Sugar to taste
Whole milk as desired, warmed

1. Place water in a medium saucepan and begin to heat. Grind together the cardamom seeds, cloves, black cumin seeds, and peppercorns. Add ground spices to the water and mix well. Add grated ginger and cinnamon stick and mix again. Bring to a boil and then reduce heat to a steady simmer and cook for 2–3 minutes.

2. Remove from heat, add loose tea, and stir or steep teabags for 2–3 minutes or until desired strength of tea is achieved.

3. Strain the tea into a serving pot or into cups or glasses and add sugar and milk if desired and serve. Without the milk it makes a great iced tea in hot weather.

Sweet Coffee with Cinnamon and Cardamom

In Pakistani shops, you can often see this beverage being made as the cook artfully pours the spiced coffee back and forth between hot pans to aerate and thicken the brew. With the grace of a gymnast doing floor exercises, the coffee flows like silk from pan to pan. The coffee is steeped in a spiced mixture of milk and water and is delicious hot or cold.

3 cups water
3 cups milk

1 3-inch cinnamon stick
Seeds from 5 cardamom pods, ground
6 tablespoons sugar
3 tablespoons coffee

1. In a saucepan, combine water, milk, cinnamon, cardamom pods, and sugar and bring it to a boil. Cook for about 5 minutes and then remove from heat and cover to let the spices infuse into the thinned milk for at least 30 minutes.

2. Remove the cinnamon stick from the milk mixture, pour the mixture into a blender, and blend for 3–5 minutes, removing the cover of the blender to really aerate the mixture.

3. Return to a saucepan and bring back to a boil. After boiling, lower heat to a steady simmer and add coffee. Stir for 3–4 minutes until the coffee is done. Strain and serve.

Appetizers and Condiments

Three great appetizers to nibble on before a large meal, a classic dip, and some pickles and chutneys to either add flavor to a curry or kebab or to enjoy all by themselves with Pakistan's slightly sourdough flatbread await you in the next section. **Potato Kebabs with Pomegranates** and **Chicken Kebabs with Feta Cheese** are two ground meat or vegetable kebabs that are traditionally fried but can be baked for a Pakistani taste sensation. The **Spicy Noodles with Coconut and Curry Leaves** offer a uniquely Pakistani blending of central Asian and Southeast Asian flavors, and the **Spicy Yogurt with Cucumbers (*Raita*)**, which, despite its name, will cool down your palate afterwards. Two chutneys (tomato and cucumber) and a mustardy mango pickle end the section and can be enjoyed alone or used to lend flavor to other dishes.

Potato Kebabs with Pomegranates

These unusual vegetable kebabs are made hot by the addition of all the peppers, spicy by the cumin, and a bit sweet and sour by the pomegranates. Not a common dish, but a welcome one when encountered, this dish showcases the Persian love of pomegranates and the legacy left on Pakistani cooking by successive Persian empires. Serve with a selection of pickles and chutneys.

8 medium-large red potatoes, peeled, boiled, and mashed
4 tablespoons unsalted butter
4 green chili peppers, finely diced
1 medium bunch fresh cilantro, diced (20–25 sprigs)
2 teaspoons salt
¼ teaspoon ground black pepper
¼ teaspoon red chili powder
2 teaspoons ground cumin
½ cup pomegranate seeds, dried
1 egg, beaten
¼ cup peanut or other vegetable oil to fry (if not broiling)

Samosas and Rice

1. Melt butter in a medium sauté pan and sauté the green chili peppers and the diced cilantro for 3–5 minutes. Add the salt, black pepper, red pepper, cumin, and pomegranate seeds and sauté another 2–3 minutes. Remove from heat and let cool.

2. Mix beaten egg with mashed potatoes and then add seasonings and blend well until flavorings are mixed evenly throughout. Form into

tiny loaflike kebabs about 3–4 inches long and 1–2 inches in diameter, place on a plate, and cool for at least ½ hour before cooking.

3. If frying (as is the authentic cooking method), heat oil over a medium flame in a medium sauté pan, add the kebabs, and cook for about 5 minutes for each side. Drain, let cool, and then serve. If broiling, place kebabs on a sprayed baking sheet and cook 5–8 minutes per side under a preheated broiler flame. Serve immediately if broiled.

Chicken Kebabs with Feta Cheese

These kebabs are spicy and flavorful and offer a little blast of sour feta cheese when you bite through the breaded or floured crust—kind of like Pakistani poppers! A great example of mixed ground meat and vegetable kebabs. Makes a great light meal as well as a starter or a snack. Serve with pickles and chutneys or a sweet and sour tomato sauce for an authentic treat.

3 medium red potatoes, peeled, boiled, and mashed
1 cup chicken breast or other white meat, cooked and diced or ground
½ cup crumbled whole milk feta cheese
2 eggs beaten (separately)
3 green chili peppers, finely diced
1 ½ teaspoons salt
1 teaspoon ground black pepper
2 teaspoons ground coriander
1 medium bunch fresh cilantro, diced (20–25 sprigs)
1 cup plain, fine ground bread crumbs or a rice or lentil flour for coating kebabs
¼ cup peanut or vegetable oil for frying (more as needed)

1. In a large mixing bowl, combine the mashed potatoes, chicken breast, and crumbled feta cheese and mix well. Add one of the beaten eggs, the green chili peppers, salt, pepper, coriander, and cilantro and mix again until all ingredients are well blended.

2. Form into balls about the size of a golf ball or a loaflike kebab. Dip quickly into the second beaten egg and then roll in the flour or breadcrumbs. Dip in egg mixture again and back into the bread crumbs once more. Give a gentle shake of the ball or kebab to knock loose excess crumbs or flour and place on a plate. Chill for at least 30 minutes before cooking.

3. Heat oil in a medium to large sauté pan and fry quickly in hot oil until golden. Drain on paper and serve with pickles, chutneys, or a sweet and sour tomato sauce.

Spicy Noodles with Curry Leaves and Coconut

2–3 servings oriental egg noodles, depending on the number of diners
3 tablespoons peanut or light sesame oil
I teaspoon mustard seeds
2 onions, peeled and diced
8 curry leaves, sliced or diced
4 green chili peppers, diced
2 cups sprouted mung beans, lentils, or other chana (purchased or prepared beforehand)
½ red pepper, cored, defleshed, and diced
2 cups beef, chicken, or vegetable broth
2 cups water
I teaspoon salt
½ teaspoon ground black pepper
½–I teaspoon red chili powder
I teaspoon **Pakistani *Garam Masala*** or **Tandoori *Masala*** (see Pakistani Sauces and Spice Mixtures)
2 teaspoons lemon juice
I small bunch fresh cilantro, diced (15–20 sprigs)
2 tablespoons roasted peanuts
¼ cup coconut, grated (for garnish)

1. Heat oil in a large saucepan, add mustard seeds, and cover tightly when seeds begin to pop. Add diced onions and cook until they start to become transparent and color around the edges. Add the diced curry, green chili peppers, bean sprouts, and sweet red peppers and mix well. Cook for 3–5 minutes, stirring often, until the bean sprouts start to soften.

2. Add broth and water and heat. Add salt, black pepper, red chili powder, and one of the *masalas* and stir well. Add lemon juice, cilantro, and roasted peanuts and stir again. Bring broth to a boil and then reduce heat to a steady simmer and let cook for 5 minutes to blend flavors.

3. Turn heat off, remove pot from burner, and add egg noodles. Cover and let sit 3–5 minutes depending on the width of the noodles. At least once during that time, take a fork and separate the noodles a bit. When noodles have softened to the desired degree, serve in a big tureen or spoon into individual bowls and top each bowl with a bit of grated coconut. Serve with small dishes of extra coconut and ground roasted peanuts for diners to use as desired.

Spicy Yogurt with Cucumbers (Raita)

Here is the Pakistani take on the cooling yogurt dish that is served with spicy meat dishes that we've seen on the journey from western Asia to southern Asia. You'll notice that it's a bit more robust than some of the other dishes we've encountered and makes a great dip for bread or snack on its own.

2 cups plain yogurt
3 Asian cucumbers or 1 Western cucumber, peeled, seeded, and chopped
1 medium tomato, diced
3 teaspoons garlic, peeled and diced
1 teaspoon ground cumin
½ teaspoon sweet paprika
½ teaspoon salt
½ teaspoon ground black pepper
1 small bunch fresh cilantro leaves, chopped (15–20 sprigs)

In a mixing bowl, combine all of the ingredients and stir just enough to mix everything together but not so much as to thin the consistency of the yogurt. Chill for several hours before serving, pouring off any collected water. Before serving, stir again, transfer to a serving bowl, and garnish with a bit more chopped cilantro if desired.

Cucumber Chutney

Here's a cooling, spicy, and sour chutney that will clear even the most overburdened of palates during a complex multicourse meal. The natural cooling effect of the cucumbers combines with the malt vinegar and the ginger to provide a blast of sour flavor that is made lighter and a bit sweeter by the added cilantro.

3 Asian cucumbers or 1 Western cucumber, peeled, seeded, and very finely sliced
¼ cup malt vinegar
½ teaspoon salt (more if desired)
1 teaspoon ginger, peeled and grated
1 green chili pepper, diced
1 tablespoon fresh cilantro, diced

In a mixing bowl, combine finely sliced cucumbers with malt vinegar. Add salt, grated ginger, diced chili pepper, and diced cilantro and mix well. Let sit in a refrigerator for at least 1 hour. Remove from refrigerator and serve lightly chilled. If desired make double or triple batches and store in a sealed jar. Will keep for several months.

Mango Pickle

This is a nice Pakistani mango pickle that has strong mustard and fenugreek overtones that blend with the mango. It differs from Indian mango pickle in having less chili powder and a broader array of supporting spices. After blending, let it sit for a week or two before serving. Best served cold, and make sure to stir well before serving.

3 unripe, firm green mangoes
1 tablespoon salt
⅓ cup peanut oil
1 tablespoon mustard seeds
1 tablespoon fenugreek seeds
1 tablespoon red chili powder
1 teaspoon ground turmeric
½ teaspoon asafetida
2 teaspoons coriander seeds
2 teaspoons cumin seeds
1 teaspoon onion seeds
1 tablespoon garlic, peeled and diced or ground
¼ cup tomato sauce

1. Wash mangoes, wipe dry, and chop into pieces, including the skin. Add salt to the mangoes, mix well, cover, and let them sit in a warm, place overnight.

2. Grind all of the remaining spices together, first grinding the whole seeds then adding the powdered spices. In a medium sauté pan, heat the peanut oil and add all of the spices. Cook 2–3 minutes to blend the flavors and then remove from flame, and when the spice mixture is cooled, add in the mango and salt mixture and the garlic and tomato sauce and mix.

3. Store in a sterilized, sealable jar until needed. Refrigerate or cover with a thin layer of oil or water and store at room temperature until needed. Refrigerate once opened.

Tomato Chutney

This is a great chutney that can be prepared like a sauce or more like a chunky salsa depending on your mood and need for it at the table. I like it as a chunky salsa better and have written it that way. If the sauce preparation intrigues you, please warm up the food processor and pulse away.

3 medium ripe or just overripe tomatoes
1 red onion, peeled and roughly diced
3–4 green chili peppers, diced
1 teaspoon cumin seeds
½ teaspoon salt (more if desired)
½ teaspoon red chili powder
1 tablespoon fresh mint, diced or 1 teaspoon dried mint
1 teaspoon ground coriander
½–1 cup tomato sauce
2–3 tablespoons lemon juice
1 medium bunch fresh cilantro leaves, chopped (20–25 sprigs)

In a medium mixing bowl, combine all the ingredients except the tomato sauce, lemon juice, and cilantro leaves and mix well. Add the tomato sauce, lemon juice, and cilantro leaves and mix again. Let sit for at least 1 hour to blend the flavors. Mix again before serving, if desired, and serve lightly chilled. As with cucumber chutney, multiple batches can be made beforehand and stored for several weeks or months.

Sauces and Spice Mixtures

Two Pakistani sauces that are similar to two Georgian sauces start this section. **Spicy Cilantro Sauce** is related to Georgia's **Garlic and Walnut Sauce (Garo)** and Afghanistan's **Cilantro Sauce**; and **Sour Plum Sauce—Pakistani Style** is a lot like Georgia's **Sour Plum Sauce (*Tkemali*).** The cultural connections—whether through successive Persian empires, through the Abbasid dynasty, or though simple trade of goods and services—are obvious and show the links of each nation with central Asia as well. Rounding out the section are a **Pakistani *Garam Masala***, which is simpler than its Indian cousin and a very complex **Tandoori Spice Mix** that can be mixed with yogurt for a great marinade or rubbed directly on meat and fish for a great flavor.

Spicy Cilantro Sauce

This is Pakistan's cilantro-based sauce for flavoring meats and vegetables that is related to **Afghan Cilantro Sauce** and Georgia's **Garlic-Walnut Sauce (*Garo*)**.

2 medium onions, peeled and roughly chopped
1 teaspoon ginger, peeled and grated
1 teaspoon garlic, peeled and diced
2 cups plain yogurt
¼ cup lemon juice or rice vinegar
1 tablespoon sugar
1 teaspoon black pepper
2 tablespoons ground cumin
2 tablespoons ground coriander
½ teaspoon ground turmeric
½ teaspoon chili powder
1 teaspoon **Pakistani *Garam Masala*** (see Pakistani Sauces and Spice Mixtures)
1 medium bunch fresh cilantro leaves, chopped (20–25 sprigs)

1. In a blender, combine chopped onions, ginger, and garlic with yogurt and lemon juice or rice vinegar and blend until smooth. Add remaining spices and blend again until smooth. Add fresh cilantro leaves and blend one last time.

2. Turn into a medium saucepan and heat over medium heat. Cook for 8–10 minutes, stirring often. Lower heat to low and cook another 10 minutes, stirring occasionally. Serve, or let cool slightly before serving.

Sour Plum Sauce—Pakistani Style

Like Georgia's *Tkemali*, this is a plum sauce using the sour dried plums of central Asia that is used as a condiment for kebabs and roast meats. Much simpler than the Georgian sauce, in this sauce the sour plums are accented only with a bit of black pepper, some chili powder, and salt. The vinegar and sugar is really there to help balance the natural flavor of the plums.

½ pound dried sour plums
2 cups water
2 tablespoons vinegar
1 teaspoon salt
½ teaspoon ground black pepper
½ teaspoon red chili powder
2 tablespoons sugar

1. In a medium saucepan, cover the plums with water by at least 2 inches. Bring to a boil and then reduce heat to low and simmer for about 5 minutes. Remove plums from the pan and set aside for at least 2 hours or overnight. When ready, work the plums with your fingers or slice to remove the pit. Chop pitted plums and set aside.

2. Bring the water and vinegar to a boil and add the salt, black pepper, chili powder, and sugar to the water and mix well. Add the chopped plums and bring back to a boil. Then reduce the heat and cook on a steady simmer until the plums soften, about 20–30 minutes.

3. Reduce heat and cook on low another 10 minutes, stirring often until done. Remove from heat and spoon into a serving bowl. Let cool to room temperature and serve.

Pakistani Garam Masala

This is Pakistan's simpler *garam masala* that features the delicate black cardamom from Nepal instead of the bolder green cardamom and is accented by lots of black pepper, cloves, and cumin. Powerful but not particularly sweet, this *garam masala* can be used as an afterthought and added to already complex curries, or it can be a main flavor in a noodle dish or used as a meat rub for a bold and flavorful change.

1 tablespoon black peppercorns
4 tablespoons cumin seeds
1 teaspoon ground cloves
Seeds from 6 black cardamom pods

Grind the whole spices together and then add the ground cloves and grind briefly once more to mix. Store in a sealable jar until needed.

Tandoori Masala

This mixture is one of the secrets to Pakistani tandoori cooking. Mixed with partially drained chaka yogurt to form a marinade, these spices impart a broad and delicious range of flavors to the meat that is then seared in by the tandoori oven's ultra high heat. Use for tandoori cooking or as a spice rub directly on meat or for a flavoring for rice, noodles, or a vegetable dish.

2 tablespoons cumin seeds
2 teaspoons coriander seeds
2 cinnamon sticks
1 teaspoon ground cloves
1 teaspoon red chili powder
1 teaspoon ground ginger
1 teaspoon ground turmeric
1 teaspoon garlic powder
1 teaspoon ground mace
1 teaspoon salt

Over low heat, dry roast the cumin, coriander, and cinnamon on the stovetop until they begin to smoke lightly. Cool and grind these spices and mix with the already ground spices and salt. Store in an airtight jar.

A Crowded Waterway in Bangladesh

Bangladesh

Main spices and flavors: tamarind, sesame, coriander, cilantro, fennel, mint, mustard, bay leaf, fenugreek, cumin, garlic, onion, turmeric, cardamom, cinnamon, ginger, coconuts, cloves, nutmeg, mace, chili peppers, tomato, potato

Souring agents: lemons, limes, white vinegar

Bangladesh has a special place in my heart. I have been there many times and am in love with the country and the people and their endless ingenuity in making the best of their home on a semihospitable flood plain. In slightly less than forty years since independence, the country has gone from sweeping famine to a country of bustling cities with a rapidly growing middle class—and this development and rising prosperity is due principally to the industriousness and works of ordinary Bangladeshi citizens. The cities are permeated with a feeling that almost anything can happen—sort of what I imagine the American Wild West was like back in the mid-1800s. The countryside, on the other hand, is peaceful and moves to a slower rhythm that is all but gone from the West—women cooking and raising children and men fishing or farming in accord with daily and seasonal cycles.

When visiting Bangladesh, I was often up before dawn, listening for that first human sound that separated night from day—the revving up of a gas-powered generator for the cleric's microphone and morning prayers. Then across our camp on the Gangetic Delta, his voice would echo, rising and falling and calling the faithful to their morning devotion. At more exciting times, we would race with river dolphins in the Brahmaputra, try to outrun an incoming cyclone, or surreptitiously try to make our way through the streets during a general strike. Nighttime in Bangladesh is a wild time. The cities glow with incandescent light as people bustle from place to place. Even in the best neighborhoods, cats mewl, dogs bark, and birds of all kinds take noisily to stands of trees to proclaim their territories.

The ancestors of modern Bangladeshis are a blend of the indigenous tribes that inhabited the area in prehistory: Tibetan and Burmese peoples who came over the Himalayas into the country, Dravidians from southern India, and the Indo-Aryans from northwestern India. In addition, Iranians, Arabs, and Turks also settled in the area in the late Middle Ages, bringing Islam with them as they came. Long before that time, however, Bangladesh was first a Vedic Kingdom beginning in antiquity, and later it came under Hindu stewardship, which lasted until the mid-eighth century. During these successive states, Bangladeshi rulers were amongst some of the most powerful on the subcontinent, and their empires extended well beyond the borders of the modern state and across the Delhi plateau and into what is now Pakistan. Some histories say that these kings even kept Alexander at bay with only the threat of reprisal by a strong, well-trained, and prolific military.

The Buddhist Pala Empire ruled from the mid-eighth century until the dawn of the twelfth century and created a period of stability and prosperity with the building of major public works, including temples and palaces at that time. The Palas were also responsible for spreading Buddhism to Tibet, Bhutan, Burma, Malaysia, and Indonesia as their traders and merchants bought and sold goods along the land and sea routes of the Great Silk Road.

Islam made its first appearance in Bangladesh rather late, with the arrival of Sufi Muslims in the twelfth century. The Pala kingdom had all but disintegrated by this time and was replaced by a rapid series of sultans of Turkic, Bangladeshi, or Afghan origin who remained independent from Delhi despite attempts to rein them in. It was during this time that the country began to be known as "the land of the rebels" or *Bulgapur*. During the late fifteenth century, the Portuguese arrived and peacefully—at first—set up trading businesses and religious missions in coastal towns and cities. The Mughals of Delhi reasserted control in the late sixteenth century, and their rule continued until the mid-eighteenth century when the British East India Company gained control. Continued protest and rebellion from the Bangladeshis and brutal repression caused the British government to take control of the area in the mid-nineteenth century, and they held sway until Indian Independence and partition one hundred years later.

Bangladeshi food bears the marks of all of these civilizations. Although it is superficially similar to Indian and some Pakistani food, generally speaking, it is much more delicate and subtle in flavor with a tendency towards sweet rather than sour. Bangladeshi cookery also tends to be less hot than other subcontinent cuisines; much of this is due to the addition of chili peppers or chili powder towards the end of cooking or just before serving, more as an afterthought instead of a main idea. Many recipes also often call for spices to be dissolved in water before cooking which has a tendency to dampen the flavor a bit as well.

Shared with the Afghans and the Mughals are the love of fruit and nuts in meat and rice dishes, as in **Lamb Rezala**, **Shrimp and Coconut Curry**, **Kebab with Raisins and Mint**, and **Chicken and Pineapple Curry**. The hallmark Mughal dish—biryani, the layered rice with fruit, nuts, meat, and vegetables—is still a national favorite as well.

Meat Dishes

Curries and kebabs and kebabs and curries—that's how the Bangladeshis prepare meats. Well, most meat anyway. Occasionally, they do also grill and bake fish or cook casseroles, but for the most part, if it walks on four legs, swims, scurries, or flies, the Bangladeshis will probably slow cook it in a wonderful, rich but delicately flavored sauce. Offered here is **Lamb Rezala** in which buttery lamb cooks slowly in a spice-laden sauce rich with nuts and chili peppers. Also in the next few pages is a recipe for a minty-sweet kebab stuffed with paneer—a South Asian cheese—and the delicious **Chicken with Pineapple** blending sweet, spicy, and hot flavors together in one great dish. As far as fish and shellfish go, there are two recipes here: one featuring shrimp in a chili-laden sweet coconut cream sauce, and the other with fish marinated in vinegar and black pepper and then baked with a host of sweet and spicy vegetables to blend the flavors.

Lamb Rezala

Rezala is a type of Bangladeshi curry that is both smooth and spicy at the same time. Traditionally, it was reserved for celebrations because the addition of nuts and sometimes raisins made it expensive, but as more Bangladeshis begin to prosper, the dish becomes a more frequent visitor to the everyday table. It is a delicately flavored dish, and the flavors change as you eat it. At first it seems mildly sour because of the addition of yogurt, then the almonds and poppy seeds become apparent, and then the full complement of spices comes into view as the unusual curry disappears from the bowl. Serve with plain or mildly spiced basmati rice.

1 pound stew lamb or beef, cut into bite-size pieces
1 tablespoon mustard oil
2 tablespoons corn or vegetable oil
1 medium onion, peeled and finely diced
1 teaspoon garlic, peeled and finely diced
2 teaspoons grated ginger
1 cup water
½ teaspoon ground turmeric
½ teaspoon ground ginger
¼ teaspoon ground chili powder
1 teaspoon ground coriander
½ teaspoon salt
¼ teaspoon ground black pepper
1 bay leaf

½ cup plain yogurt
2 teaspoons palm sugar, crumbled
2 teaspoons poppy seeds, lightly roasted
½ cup almonds, thinly sliced and lightly roasted
2 teaspoons white vinegar
6 hot, dried, red chili peppers, diced

1. Heat the oil in a large saucepan and when hot, add the lamb or beef cubes and sear the meat to preserve the juices. Cook 2–3 minutes or until the meat just starts to brown, and then lower the heat and remove the meat from the pan with a slotted spoon and set aside.

2. Add the onion to the oil and stir well. Cook over medium heat until the onion starts to soften, then add the garlic and grated ginger and cook 2–3 minutes. Dissolve the turmeric, ground ginger, chili powder, and coriander in 1 cup water and add to the onion mix. When water is hot, add the salt, pepper, and bay leaf and stir again.

3. Add the meat cubes back to the water and cook to heat, 3–5 minutes. Add the yogurt and crumbled palm sugar, poppy seeds, and sliced almonds and cook to heat yogurt. When the curry is hot, cover and cook over low heat for 30–45 minutes or until the meat softens and becomes tender. Stir often to prevent sticking and burning. If the liquid evaporates too much, add a bit more water, but not too much. This curry has only a light sauce and should be much more solid than liquid.

4. When the meat is done, add the chili peppers and the white vinegar, cook 2-3 more minutes, and serve.

Shrimp and Coconut Curry

This dish is a wonderful combination of subtle flavors in a gentle coconut base. It is very Bangladeshi and democratic in that no one of the flavors can be said to really dominate the mix. The dish can be made with almost any type of fish or shellfish and is very tasty when made with a fleshy river fish.

1 pound shrimp or fish steaks
1–1 ½ cups coconut cream (the more you add the sweeter the recipe gets)

I medium onion, peeled and chopped
2 tablespoons soybean or peanut oil
½ teaspoon ground turmeric
I teaspoon ground chili powder
I teaspoon ground coriander
½ teaspoon ground ginger
I ½ cups water
I teaspoon grated ginger
¼ teaspoon ground cardamom
½ teaspoon ground cinnamon
½ teaspoon salt
¼ teaspoon ground black pepper
¼ teaspoon ground cumin
2 teaspoons lemon juice
I teaspoon palm sugar, crumbled
4 hot, dried, red chili peppers, diced

1. Heat oil in a sauté pan and when it is hot, add onion and sauté over medium heat until the onion softens and starts to become translucent. Dissolve turmeric, chili powder, coriander, and ground ginger in I ½ cups water and add it to the onions. Stir well and cook to heat the water. When the water is hot, add the grated ginger and stir well. Cook for 3–5 minutes.

2. Add the cardamom, cinnamon, salt, black pepper, and cumin and stir well. Add the lemon juice and palm sugar and stir again. Cook until the liquid evaporates to form a thick sauce. Add the coconut cream and stir well to mix. Cook until the coconut cream thickens and the sauce becomes very flavorful.

3. Add diced chili peppers and stir well, then add the shrimp and stir again. Cook 3–4 minutes or until the shrimp become opaque and pinkish and start to curl up. Serve immediately. If using fish steaks, lengthen the cooking time accordingly to 10 – 20 minutes depending on the thickness of the steak.

Kebab with Raisins and Mint

So far, there have been several different types of kebabs as we've journeyed across western and southern Asia, but this is one of the most interesting.

This kebab is so flavorful! The meat spiced with coriander, cumin, and other spices is complemented by a delicate, sweet filling of raisins and mint that offer a taste explosion when eaten. It's an unusual combination of flavors—and perhaps not to the liking of those that find sweet-flavored meats too much of a challenge. But to those more adventurous souls, it's a treat. It's best to prepare the meat a day ahead of time or in the morning and let the spices infuse the meat before cooking.

Meat
1 pound ground beef or lamb
Seeds from 5 cardamom pods
1 stick cinnamon
5 cloves
4 hot, dried, red chili peppers
1 teaspoon salt
½ teaspoon black pepper
2 teaspoons sugar
2 bay leaves
1 tablespoon cumin seeds
1 tablespoon coriander seeds
Zest and juice from 1 lemon
1 small yellow onion, coarsely chopped
2 teaspoons grated ginger

Filling
¼ cup mint leaves, finely chopped
2 tablespoons sugar
Juice of 1 lemon
½ cup raisins
½ cup paneer, crumbled (a South Asian cheese)
1 small onion, diced

1. In a spice grinder, grind cardamom seeds, cinnamon, cloves, chili peppers, salt, black pepper, sugar, bay leaf, cumin seeds, and coriander seeds and set aside.

2. In a food processor, blend onion, lemon zest and juice, and ginger until you have a smooth paste. Add ground spices from step 1 and blend again. Add meat and blend until the paste is evenly distributed throughout the meat. Turn into a bowl and set aside in the refrigerator

for several hours or overnight for the spices to impart their flavor to the meat.

3. In a food processor or blender, mix together the onion, paneer, raisins, and mint for the filling; set aside. About I hour before cooking, remove spiced meat from the refrigerator and roll into meatballs. With your thumb, make a deep hole in the top of the meatball that runs to the center. Put I teaspoon of filling into the hole, making sure that it gets all the way to the bottom. Reseal the hole with your fingers and shape the meat back into a ball or into a kebab-style loaf.

4. Grill on an oiled or sprayed baking sheet under preheated broiler for 3–5 minutes per side or until cooked. Be careful turning so as to not break the meat up.

Chicken and Pineapple Curry

This dish is a delicate balance between sweet, hot, and spicy with each bite starting as an earthy chicken curry and finishing with either a hint or blast of sweet pineapple. It's a dish of average heat so it should please diners who shy away from dishes with too much red pepper. Serve with plain or lightly flavored rice for the foundations of a wonderful meal.

3–4 chicken breasts, cut into bite-size pieces
3 tablespoons peanut oil
I medium onion, peeled, sliced, and separated into crescents
I tablespoon grated ginger
I teaspoon ground turmeric
I teaspoon chili powder
½ cup water or chicken broth
2 teaspoons ground coriander
½ teaspoon ground cinnamon
Seeds from 3 cardamom pods, crushed
2 whole cloves, crushed
I bay leaf
I teaspoon salt
½ teaspoon ground black pepper
I teaspoon sugar
I cup finely chopped pineapple

1. Heat peanut oil in a sauté pan and over high heat sauté the chicken pieces until they become firm and opaque, 3–5 minutes or until done.

2. Add the onion slices and sauté onion until it softens and starts to color. Add grated ginger, turmeric, and chili powder and stir well. Then add the water or chicken broth to moisten the spices and heat until the sauce is warmed.

3. Add coriander, cinnamon, cardamom seeds, whole cloves, bay leaf, salt, and pepper and stir well. Add sugar and stir. Then add cooked chicken and cook to heat, 5–8 minutes. Once heated, add pineapple and stir well. Cook to heat until pineapple is hot and then serve.

Bangladeshi Family in a Houseboat

Curried Fish with Mangoes

This is another sweet and spicy dish that has just a hint of sourness to it from the rich and diverse cuisine of Bangladesh. Here, fish partially cooks in the vinegar marinade and then is covered by a rich blanket of curried vegetables and baked to perfection. Serve with plain rice or a spiced rice such as **Rice and Peas with Cinnamon and Cumin** or **Sri Lankan Spiced Rice**.

239

1 pound fleshy white fish, such as carp or cod, cut into steaks
1 teaspoon salt
2 teaspoons black peppercorns, cracked or crushed
2 tablespoons white vinegar

Curried vegetables
1 small onion, peeled and diced
3 tablespoons peanut oil
1 teaspoon garlic, peeled and diced
1 teaspoon turmeric
½ teaspoon chili powder
1 teaspoon ground ginger
1 teaspoon ground coriander
1 teaspoon salt
½ teaspoon ground black pepper
1 teaspoon sugar
¼ cup chicken, fish, or vegetable broth
½ cup long beans or string beans cut into 1-inch lengths
1 cup green papaya or green mango, peeled and chopped
1 cup butternut or acorn squash, peeled and chopped

1. Preheat oven to 375°. Salt and pepper fish steaks and arrange in a sprayed or oiled coverable casserole and sprinkle white vinegar over them and set aside.

2. Heat oil in a sauté pan and sauté onion until it softens and starts to color. Add garlic and cook until it swells and starts to color. Then add turmeric, chili powder, ginger, coriander, salt, and pepper and sugar and stir well to mix. Cook 2–3 minutes to warm the spices. Add a bit of broth to moisten, add squash and beans, and cook to heat, 2–3 minutes. Then add mangoes and cook to warm. Lower heat and cook covered for 8–10 minutes, stirring occasionally, or until squash and beans are partially cooked.

3. Evenly spoon curried vegetables over the fish, cover, and cook another 15 minutes. Then uncover and cook another 10. Serve with rice.

Vegetable Dishes and Salads

Once again, Bangladeshis tend to curry a lot of vegetables in rich flavorful sauces, as in **Potato Curry with Cardamom and Cinnamon**, **Eggplant with Panchforan**, and **Zucchini in a Spicy Tomato Sauce**. Occasionally they also cook them quickly without skimping on flavor, as in the **Tomato and Peas Bhaji with Fenugreek and Cumin** or the bright and delicious **Spinach with Fennel**.

Potato Curry with Cardamom and Cinnamon

Different from other potato curries on the subcontinent, this curry is sour, sweet, spicy, and mildly hot at the same time. Yogurt blends the mix of spices together and soothes the sourness of the sauce just enough to make the dish work. The addition of cumin seeds gives a blast of flavor that brightens up the whole recipe.

4 medium potatoes, parboiled and cooled
2 tablespoons soybean or peanut oil
½ teaspoon cumin seeds
1 bay leaf
2 teaspoons grated ginger
¼ teaspoon ground turmeric
¼ teaspoon chili powder
1 teaspoon ground cumin
1 teaspoon ground coriander
½ teaspoon ground cardamom
½ teaspoon ground cinnamon
1 cup water
2 teaspoons sugar
1 teaspoon salt
¼ teaspoon black pepper
3 tablespoons plain yogurt

1. Make a paste of the turmeric, chili powder, ground cumin, coriander, cardamom, and cinnamon using just enough water to moisten them together. Heat the oil in a sauté pan and add the cumin seeds, bay leaf, and grated ginger and cook over low heat to warm the spices, stirring constantly.

2. Raise the heat to medium and add the spice paste and 1 cup of water. Cook stirring constantly until the water heats up. Then add the sugar, salt, pepper and yogurt and cook to heat and thicken the sauce and then simmer for 5 minutes. Add the potatoes and stir, lifting rather than mixing so as not to mash the potatoes. When potatoes are hot, cover and cook over low heat for 5 minutes or until they are done. Serve.

Bangladeshi Boys Fishing

Tomato and Pea Bhaji with Fenugreek and Cumin

This dish utilizes the Bangladeshi spice mixture *panchforan*, which is like a Bangladeshi five-spice powder used in a wide variety of dishes. Here the flavors of the tomatoes and the peas blend to form a delicious complement to any South Asian meal. Serve over a simple rice to really appreciate the *panchforan* and the blend of tomatoes and peas.

2 cups tomatoes, chopped (about 4 medium tomatoes)
2 tablespoons peanut or light sesame oil

2 teaspoons **Panchforan** (see Bangladeshi Sauces and Spice Mixtures)
I small onion, finely diced
I teaspoon grated ginger
¼ teaspoon turmeric
4 hot, dried, red chili peppers, diced
I cup shelled peas
½ teaspoon salt
½ teaspoon ground black pepper
I teaspoon sugar
I small bunch cilantro leaves, chopped (10–15 sprigs)

1. Heat the oil in a sauté pan over medium heat, add *panchforan,* and stir for a minute to warm the spices. Add the onion, ginger, turmeric and chili peppers and stir again.

2. Add the tomatoes and the peas and stir. When the vegetables have warmed, cover and cook, stirring occasionally for 5–7 minutes. Add salt, pepper, sugar and cilantro leaves and stir well. Cook another 2–3 minutes and serve.

Spinach with Fennel

This is one of my favorite Asian ways of preparing spinach. It's got the rich earthiness of fenugreek leaves and the brightness of fennel and ginger in the same dish with just a bit of sourness from the asafetida.

2 medium bunches or a 12-ounce bag spinach, rinsed, drained, and spun dry
2 tablespoons butter or ghee
2 teaspoons fennel seeds
I heaping tablespoon grated ginger
3 dried red chili peppers, finely diced
¼ cup beef broth
½ teaspoon asafetida
2 teaspoons fenugreek leaves
½ teaspoon salt
¼ teaspoon black pepper

1. Heat the butter or ghee in a sauté pan and when warm add the fennel seeds and stir as the fennel swells and pops. Add grated ginger

and diced chili peppers and stir well. Add beef broth, and when that warms, add asafetida, fenugreek leaves, salt, and pepper.

2. If the mixture is very thick, add water one teaspoon at a time to thin the spice paste into more of a light sauce. Add spinach and stir to coat. Cover and cook for 3 minutes or until the spinach wilts, stirring occasionally.

3. Then cook uncovered to evaporate some of the liquid that the spinach gave off while cooking. If too much remains at the end of 3–5 minutes of uncovered cooking, simply pour it off. There should be a light, thin sauce, but the spinach shouldn't be floating in a soup.

Chickpea Curry

Hot, warm, or cool, this makes a delicious, hot, spicy side dish for any South Asian meal. The chickpeas are offset by a piquant tomato and cumin sauce with a touch of asafetida and cilantro.

2 cups chickpeas, drained, rinsed well, and drained again
2 tablespoons butter or ghee
2 green chili peppers, diced
2 teaspoons cumin seeds
1 teaspoon minced ginger
4 tablespoons beef broth
1 teaspoon chili powder
½ teaspoon asafetida
1 heaping tablespoon tomato paste
3 tablespoons plain yogurt
½ teaspoon salt
¼ teaspoons ground black pepper
1 tablespoon cilantro leaves, chopped

1. Heat the butter or ghee in a sauté pan and sauté cumin seeds and chopped chili peppers for 2–3 minutes. Add the grated ginger and sauté again. Add the beef broth to prevent the ginger from burning. When the broth is hot, add the chili powder, asafetida, and tomato paste and stir well.

2. Then add the yogurt and stir until yogurt is integrated into the sauce. Season with salt, ground black pepper, and cilantro leaves and cook

for 2–3 minutes before adding the drained chickpeas. Lower heat and cook covered until done or about 15 minutes.

Eggplant with Panchforan

This dish is very spicy without being hot and just a bit sour and is a great way to prepare eggplant. It goes well on either a vegetarian or omnivore table and works particularly well with roasted or grilled meats or a simple *bhaji* vegetable dish.

2–3 Chinese eggplants cut crosswise
2 teaspoons ground black mustard seeds
¼ teaspoon cayenne pepper
1 cup water
1 tablespoon mustard oil
2 tablespoons corn or vegetable oil
2 teaspoons **Panchforan** (see Bangladeshi Sauces and Spice Mixtures)

1 teaspoon salt
½ teaspoon black pepper
¼ teaspoon ground cardamom
1 cup plain yogurt
2 teaspoons white vinegar

1. Place cut eggplant on an oiled or sprayed baking sheet and place in a preheated 375° oven and cook 15–20 minutes. When done, set aside. Add mustard along with cayenne pepper to one cup of water.

2. Heat mustard oil in a wok or sauté pan on low heat, put in *panchforan,* and sauté 3–5 minutes until it starts to swell. Then add the black mustard-cayenne water and heat. Then add salt, pepper and cardamom and stir well. When everything is hot, add eggplant and cook for 3–5 minutes, stirring often. Lower heat and cover to cook for 5 minutes.

3. Add yogurt and cook to heat the yogurt. Cook until the eggplant is done. Just before serving add the white vinegar and stir well. Serve hot.

Zucchini in a Spicy Tomato Sauce

For me, this dish just hits the spot! I like to eat it all by itself or to serve it as part of a larger table of Bangladeshi food. It takes all of about 15 minutes to prepare and is delicious, warming, and ever so slightly spicy. With the simple substitution of vegetable stock for chicken stock, it also works well on a vegetarian table with ease.

2 zucchini, cubed
½ teaspoon turmeric
1 teaspoon salt
2 tablespoons mustard oil
¼ cup water
¼ cup vegetable stock
1 teaspoon grated ginger
1 teaspoon ground cumin
¼ teaspoon ground chili
1 teaspoon sugar
2 tomatoes, chopped
2 teaspoons tomato paste
1 medium bunch cilantro leaves, chopped (15–20 sprigs)

1. Coat the zucchini with turmeric and half of the salt and stir well. Let sit for 5–10 minutes and stir again. Heat the oil in a sauté pan and stir fry the zucchini for 5–6 minutes on medium-high heat or until it starts to crust. Then remove from pan with a slotted spoon and set aside.

2. Lower heat to medium and add the chicken or vegetable stock and water and deglaze the pan, getting all the little bits of turmeric and zucchini off the bottom. Then add ginger, cumin, chili powder, and sugar and heat, stirring for a few minutes until spices are dissolved.

3. Add tomatoes and cook until they start to break up, then add tomato paste and cook until the liquid starts to thicken into a sauce. Add chopped cilantro and stir. Then add zucchini and cook to warm them.

Rice and Grain Dishes, Breads

One pilaf with peas, cinnamon, and cumin; one highly spiced rice and split-pea dish called a *kitchuri*; and a simple Bangladeshi tahari rice stewed with spices, milk, and yogurt await you in the next few pages. Also offered are a couple of everyday breads including a **Whole Wheat *Chapati*** and a spiced ***Paratha***.

Rice and Peas with Cinnamon and Cumin

Leave it to the ever-inventive Bangladeshis to come up with such flavorful rice! It's spicy and full of cumin and cinnamon without being hot. It nicely complements the sweetly stuffed **Kebabs with Raisins and Mint** or the **Pakistani Beef or Lamb Kebabs** and can even be served with Western meats or vegetables in an East-West fusion cuisine dinner.

I cup uncooked basmati rice
2 tablespoons peanut oil
I small onion, peeled, sliced, and separated into crescents
I teaspoon salt
⅓ teaspoon ground black pepper
2 teaspoons grated ginger
I teaspoon garlic, peeled and diced
½ cup chicken or beef broth
I tablespoon ground cumin
I teaspoon ground coriander
½ teaspoon ground turmeric
½ teaspoon ground chili powder
I teaspoon ground cinnamon
Seeds from 4 cardamom pods
4 whole cloves, crushed
2 bay leaves
I cup green peas
2 cups water

1. Heat the oil in a sauté pan and sauté the onion until it softens and turns golden. Add salt, pepper, ginger, and garlic. Cook for 2–3 minutes and add the broth and cook until the sauce heats. Add cumin, coriander, turmeric, chili powder, and cinnamon and stir well.

2. Add cardamom seeds, cloves, bay leaves, and rice and stir well to mix. Cook 3–5 minutes to heat the rice, then add the green peas and water and bring to a near boil. Then lower heat and cook covered on the lowest setting for 15–20 minutes or until rice is done. Let sit covered until ready to serve.

Spiced Kitchuri

The Bangladeshis have a series of dishes that combine rice with lentils, split peas, or other legumes called *kitchuris*. These are eaten with meat and vegetables or for very young children are served mixed into yogurt during the transition to solid foods. *Kitchuris* are also commonly served as a food-medicine to nourish sick people during recovery. The *kitchuri* offered here is flavorful and a bit hot and will make an excellent pair with a beef-, lamb-, or pork-based curry.

1 cup basmati rice
½ cup mung beans or split peas
4 cups water
3 tablespoons butter
2 bay leaves
1 medium onion, peeled and diced
2 teaspoons ginger peeled and grated
1 teaspoon garlic, peeled and grated
¼ cup beef or vegetable broth
1 teaspoon ground turmeric
1 teaspoon ground chili powder
2 teaspoons ground coriander
2 teaspoons ground cumin

1. Mix the rice and beans or peas together and place in a medium saucepan with 4 cups of water. Bring to a boil and then cook for about 40–45 minutes until the water has largely boiled away and the peas or beans are tender. If necessary, stir once or twice, but don't bother the rice too much. When done, remove from heat and let sit covered.

2. In a sauté pan, melt butter and sauté the onions until they become translucent and start to color. Add the bay leaves and ginger and garlic and sauté until the garlic starts to swell and color as well. Add

the broth and the rest of the spices and stir well to blend. Cook for 3–5 minutes.

3. Drain any remaining water from the rice and peas and add them to the mixture. Lift rather than stir the rice and peas into the onions and spices. When all of the ingredients are well integrated, serve.

Rice and Onions with Nutmeg and Cumin

This is a version of a Bangladeshi tahari rice like those enjoyed in the northern areas of the subcontinent. It is resplendent with spices and flavor that goes well with roast meats and kebabs and strongly flavored vegetable dishes. Interestingly, this dish preserves the strong flavors found in most tahari rice dishes but also incorporates milk and yogurt, more like a biryani.

3 tablespoons unsalted butter
2 medium onions, peeled and diced
1 tablespoon ginger, peeled and grated
1 tablespoon garlic, peeled and grated
4 green chili peppers, diced
1 cup milk
½ cup yogurt
1 teaspoon salt
2 teaspoons cumin seeds
1 nutmeg corm, grated
Seeds from 5 cardamom pods
10 black peppercorns
¼ teaspoon mace
1 cup basmati rice
2 cups water

1. In a medium saucepan, melt butter and sauté onions until they become translucent and start to color. Then add the ginger, garlic, and diced chili peppers and sauté until the garlic swells and starts to color as well. Add the milk, yogurt, and salt and cook for 5 minutes stirring occasionally.

2. Grind the cumin seeds, cardamom seeds, and black peppercorns until you have a medium powder. Add the mace and nutmeg and grind together briefly. Add to the onion and yogurt mixture and mix well.

3. Add rice to the saucepan and mix well. Cover and let cook about five minutes stirring occasionally. Boil water in a separate saucepan.

4. Pour boiling or near-boiling water into the rice and bring to a boil. Cover and reduce heat until you have a steady simmer and let the rice cook 20–30 minutes or until done. Check the rice after a few minutes have lapsed and lower heat if necessary to prevent it from burning. When done, remove from heat and let sit covered for a few minutes before serving.

Whole Wheat Chapati

This is one of the subcontinent's great "everyday" breads eaten with many meals. This version is very simple, easy to prepare, and makes a great flatbread for appetizers, snacks, or meals. Unlike most breads, preparation of this flatbread takes no more than 30 minutes.

2 cups whole wheat flour
½ cup water
1 teaspoon salt

1. Mix flour, water, and salt together until you have a well-integrated dough. Let rest for 15–20 minutes, then separate into six balls and press flat with your fingers or roll out into 5–6-inch rounds.

2. Heat a cast iron pan or griddle until very hot and place a *chapati* on the griddle for about 1 minute. Flip and cook another minute. Stack chapatis on a plate and cover until ready to serve.

Parata

This fry-bread is eaten throughout the subcontinent as well and can be made plain or spiced according to the dishes it will be served with. By far I prefer the spiced version, but I made the spices optional for both authenticity and personal choice. If you choose to make the spiced bread, sift the spices into the flour along wit the salt and sugar.

2 cups *chapati* flour or all-purpose flour
1 teaspoon salt
1 teaspoon sugar
½ cup water or more as needed to moisten the dough
¼ cup peanut or corn oil

Spices
1 teaspoon ground cumin
1 teaspoon ground coriander
½ teaspoon chili powder

1. In a medium bowl, sift flour, salt, and sugar together. Make a well in the flour, add the water, and mix it until a dough forms. Add more water as needed to moisten dough. If it sticks to your hands, it's too moist, and a small amount of flour must be added to adjust the consistency.

2. Knead for 3–5 minutes and then let rest for about 15 minutes. Then divide into 5–6 pieces and roll out the dough into thin rounds about 8 inches in diameter.

3. Heat oil in a large sauté pan and fry the parata on one side for a minute or two, then flip and fry on the other side. Be careful not to burn the bread. Drain, stack, and cover until needed.

Desserts and Beverages

Three desserts—ranging from a simple pastry infused with cardamom syrup to a couple of classic Bangladeshi puddings, **Cinnamon and Almond Custard** and the citrusy **Lemon Curd** topped with pistachio nuts and lemon zest—are featured here. Rounding out the sweets is a mango *lassi*—a beverage that provides a cool, light finish to a long meal or serves as a quick cool-me-down drink on a hot day.

Simple Pastry with Cardamom Syrup

This very simple, buttery dessert flavored with cinnamon and cloves and bathed with a simple syrup flavored with cardamom is a delicious treat after a spicy Bangladeshi meal. It is a flat pastry bathed in syrup, variations of which are enjoyed all over the subcontinent.

1 cup butter or ghee
1 small cinnamon stick (about 1 ½ inches), very well crushed or ground
2 whole cloves, crushed or ground
1 cup all-purpose flour

Syrup

1 cup water
1 cup sugar
Seeds from 6 cardamom pods, crushed or ground

1. Heat butter in a medium sauté pan and when warm add crushed or ground spices and mix well. Cook for 5 minutes over low heat or until the spices have become aromatic and have infused their flavors into the butter.

2. Bit by bit, add the flour to the spice and butter mix and stir until well integrated. Mixture will be thick, but cook for 3–5 minutes and then spoon onto a sprayed baking sheet or into a baking pan and press to form an even, mostly smooth surface. Let cool a bit and become firm.

3. In a small saucepan, boil water and when boiling, slowly add the sugar into the water, stirring constantly, to make a syrup. Add crushed cardamom and stir until syrup is completely dissolved.

4. Prick the surface of the pastry with a fork and cut into squares or diamonds and pour the syrup over the dessert bit by bit. Pour about ¼ of the syrup evenly over the surface and then let it absorb into the pastry. Repeat until the dessert is sweetened to your taste—there is no need to use all of the syrup or to have the pastry swimming in it. Serve.

Cinnamon and Almond Custard

This is a simple custard that reminds Bangladeshis all over the world of their homeland, cuisine, and culture. Flavored with a bit of cinnamon and some chopped almonds, it's a nice, light dessert to end a meal with or an easy-to-make sweet treat for anytime.

1 liter whole milk
2 bay leaves
¼–⅓ cup sugar
¼–½ teaspoon ground cinnamon
3 eggs, beaten until frothy
2 tablespoons unsalted butter
Blanched, finely chopped almonds (optional)

1. Pour milk in a saucepan and add half of the sugar and the bay leaf. Bring to a boil and then lower the heat to achieve a steady simmer and cook the milk until it is reduced by almost half its volume. Stir often to avoid burning and a surface skin from forming. Remove from heat and cool.

2. Beat the eggs in a large bowl with a whisk until frothy. Bit by bit add the remaining sugar, stirring constantly until dissolved. Add the cinnamon and mix until dissolved as well.

3. Pour into reduced milk and cook over a low to medium heat, stirring constantly, until the mixture becomes very thick. After mixture begins to thicken, add the butter and stir until the custard is thick.

4. Pour or spoon into a serving bowl or into individual dishes and set aside to cool. After the custard has cooled a bit and the surface is firm, sprinkle with chopped almonds. Serve at room temperature or with a very slight chill.

Lemon Curd

A sweet, lemony pudding topped with ground pistachios and lemon zest is a great, light way to end a meal. Served cold, it is also a cooling dessert after a dinner or lunch of complex flavors and serves to cleanse the palate and refresh as well. One of my favorites!

3 large eggs, whisked until frothy
Juice from 2–3 lemons
½ cup sugar
1 teaspoon corn starch
3 tablespoons unsalted butter, soft or melted and slightly cooled
1 tablespoon lemon zest, very finely shredded
1 tablespoon ground pistachio nuts

1. In a medium saucepan, combine the whisked eggs and lemon juice and blend well. Heat the mixture and when warm add the sugar bit by bit and stir until fully dissolved.

2. Add cornstarch and butter and whisk in until dissolved and lump-free. Keep on stirring until the mixture begins to thicken. Turn down heat to avoid boiling and work over medium or low heat as needed.

3. Pour and spoon into a serving bowl or into individual dishes and let cool in the refrigerator until cold. Serve cold or chilled. Before serving, garnish with chopped pistachio nuts and a hint of lemon zest.

Mango Lassi

For me, this is the ultimate dessert or cool-me-down on a hot day. Mangoes mixed with milk, yogurt, and sugar combine to make the ultimate subcontinental mango smoothie. For a delicious option, sprinkle with a bit of cinnamon or ground cardamom for a wonderful sweet treat.

3 cups milk
2 cups water
I cup yogurt
I cup mango pulp
¼–½ cup sugar

In a blender, mix milk, water, and yogurt together and blend. Then add mango pulp and blend until smooth. Lastly add sugar to taste, chill, and serve. Perfect every time!

Appetizers and Condiments

Two wonderful appetizers or snacks can be found in the following recipes for **Subcontinental Potato Pancakes**, which blend a whole host of Asian spices like cumin, turmeric, cinnamon, and ginger, and a classic **Samosa,** in which meat or potatoes are stuffed into a pastry and then fried, both with delicious results. Also offered are two quintessentially Bangladeshi chutneys that pair sweet fruits like pineapple and kiwi with sour spices and juice, which complement a host of subcontinental dishes wonderfully.

Subcontinental Potato Pancakes

Potato pancakes with ginger, chili peppers, and a host of Asian spices will be a delicious addition to your globalized table. These pancakes are delicious with a selection of pickles and chutneys or complemented with a mildly spiced yogurt dish like an Indian *riata*.

5–6 medium potatoes, peeled, boiled, and mashed
½ teaspoon ground turmeric
I teaspoon *garam masala*
I teaspoon ground black pepper
I teaspoon sugar
½ teaspoon salt
½ teaspoon ground cumin
3 cloves
Seeds from 3 green cardamom pods
I stick cinnamon, broken (2–3 inches)
2 tablespoons butter
I tablespoon ginger, peeled and grated
2 green chili peppers, diced
Chickpea flour as needed
¼ cup peanut or corn oil for frying (more as needed)

1. In a large mixing bowl, combine the mashed potatoes with the ground turmeric, *garam masala*, black pepper, sugar, cumin, and salt and mix well.

2. On the stovetop, dry roast the cloves, cardamom seeds, and cinnamon stick over low heat until they become aromatic and begin to smoke, about 3–4 minutes. Let cool and then grind.

3. In a small saucepan, heat butter and add the ginger, chili peppers, and ground spices and sauté for a few minutes until the ginger is cooked. Add to potato mixture and mix well.

4. With your hands, form the mashed potatoes into pancakes, or first make a ball and then flatten it to form the pancake. Coat both sides of the pancake lightly in chickpea flour and set aside. Heat oil in a heavy sauté pan and fry each pancake until golden. Drain on paper and serve.

Samosa

These familiar pastries stuffed with spiced meat, potatoes, or a mix are eaten all across the subcontinent and are a wonderful addition to a multicourse meal, or serve just as well as snacks or even as a light meal. Though they are easy to make, they are a little complex to wrap correctly—but delicious enough to make the effort well worthwhile. For a little practice wrapping, cut out an 8-inch circle of paper and try to fold it before trying it with pastry dough. I have also described an alternate folding method that will produce a more dumpling-like pastry similar to Georgia's *hinkali* for those baffled by the complex method of folding a samosa.

Pastry
3 ½ cups flour
2 teaspoons salt
1 cup water (more as needed)

Filling
3 tablespoons butter
1 large onion, peeled and diced
2 tablespoons ginger, peeled and grated
1 tablespoon garlic, peeled and chopped
1 teaspoon chili powder (less if you prefer a milder samosa)
2 bay leaves, crumbled
1 teaspoon ground turmeric
2 teaspoons ground cumin
1 teaspoon ground coriander
½ teaspoon ground cinnamon
1 small bunch fresh cilantro leaves, chopped (15–20 sprigs)
1 pound ground lamb or beef (or parboiled potatoes)
¼–½ cup oil for frying (more if desired)

1. In a large mixing bowl, combine flour, salt, and water and mix well until you have a dough of good consistency (that doesn't stick to your hands). Knead for 3–5 minutes and let rest as you prepare the filling.

2. In a sauté pan, melt butter and sauté the onions until they become translucent and start to color. Add ginger, garlic, and bay leaves and sauté until the garlic swells and starts to color as well.

3. Add ½ cup of beef broth and then add the chili powder, turmeric, cumin, coriander, cinnamon, and cilantro and stir well. When broth is hot, add the ground beef and mix well. Cover and cook for 8–10 minutes or until beef is cooked and coloring nicely. (If using potatoes, feel free to substitute vegetable broth or water instead of beef broth to keep the recipe vegetarian.) When done, set aside.

4. Divide dough into 6–8 balls and roll each ball out into a circle about 8 inches in diameter. Divide evenly in half by cutting down the middle with a sharp knife and turn one of those two pieces so the straight side is horizontal in front of you. Fold right edge of dough. Take the right side of the dough and fold it over about ½ of the length of the dough to form a cone that is narrow on the bottom and wide on the top. Press the seam of this fold together with your fingers to form a stuffable pocket in the dough. Stuff with several tablespoons of stuffing, allowing room to seal the top edge of the dough (don't overstuff). Bring the bottom flap of dough up and seal it. Now, roll the stuffed pastry over to the left and seal. Lastly seal the top edge, making sure all of the seams are sealed well. Or use this alternate method to produce a more dumpling-like pastry: Place 2-3 tablespoons of filling in the center and bring 1 set of opposing edges together and seal by pinching them. Bring a third side in and pinch it closed at the top. If there is more space, add more filling and close by sealing the last side of dough. Make sure top seal is very good or the samosa may burst when you fry it.

5. Heat oil in a heavy cast-iron pan. Deep fry or fry in hot oil, turning each side as it becomes done. Drain on paper towels. Serve with a selection of sauces and pickles.

Kiwi Chutney

This is a delightfully sweet and tart chutney that mixes the naturally bright sourness of the kiwi with mustard and a bit of turmeric. The flavors pull a bit at each other without really balancing, but it is an authentic taste to add to a Bangladeshi meal.

2 firm kiwi fruits, peeled and each cut into 6–8 wedges
1 tablespoon corn, vegetable, or light sesame oil
½ teaspoon mustard seeds
1/2 cup water
3 teaspoons sugar
¼ teaspoon turmeric

Heat oil in a saucepan and add the mustard seeds. Once the seeds start to sputter, add the kiwi fruits and stir for a minute. Add half a cup of water, sugar, and turmeric. Cover and cook on low to moderate heat until the kiwis are done. Serve at room temperature.

Pineapple Chutney

Once again this is a sweet and sour chutney that uses the natural sweetness of the pineapple and accents this with the sour *panchforan* spices, ginger, and apricots or dates. The chutney is given a bright blast of sourness from the addition of raw lime meat and juice at the very end of preparation. I think that this is one of the chutneys that ages very well, and I often make it days or weeks ahead of serving.

1 medium pineapple, peeled, chopped, and eyes removed
2 tablespoons vegetable or light sesame oil
¼–½ teaspoon **Panchforan** (see Bangladeshi Sauces and Spice Mixtures)
2 red or green chili peppers, diced
2 tablespoons ginger, peeled and grated
¼ cup sugar (more or less to taste)
2 teaspoons salt
½ cup dried apricots or dates finely chopped
Juice and meat from 1 lime

1. Heat oil in a large sauté pan and add *panchforan* and chili peppers. Cook for 2–3 minutes over low or medium heat to infuse their flavors into the oil. Add ginger, salt, and sugar and stir well.

2. Add the pineapple and any accumulated juices and cook for 3–5 minutes or until pineapple begins to soften. Add chopped dates or apricots and cook another 3–5 minutes or until the pineapple is soft.

3. Remove from heat and add finely chopped lime meat and juice and mix well. Let cool and serve at room temperature or spoon into a sealable jar and refrigerate until needed.

Sauces and Spice Mixtures

Two sauces that reveal Bangladesh's cultural links to Pakistan and the West can be found in **Cilantro-Mint Sauce** and the **Bangladeshi Tamarind Sauce**, and a third, **Sweet and Sour Olive Sauce**, which reveal connections to Portuguese traders in centuries past. Despite the link to other cuisines, each sauce is uniquely Bangladeshi and provides or sometimes favors sweet flavors over sour and spicy ones. Last up is Bangladesh's ubiquitous five-spice mixture, ***Panchforan***. If cooking lots of Bangladeshi food, don't be without it. It is used widely in recipes, sometimes more like a *garam masala* as an afterthought of flavor added at the end of preparation.

Cilantro-Mint Sauce

Sweeter and lighter than its West Pakistani cousin, **Spicy Cilantro Sauce**, this Bangladeshi sauce illustrates the Bangladeshi love of sweeter flavors more so than other cuisines on the subcontinent.

I medium bunch fresh cilantro leaves (20–25 sprigs)
I medium bunch mint leaves
Water as needed to blend
3 teaspoons garlic
¼ teaspoon tamarind concentrate
I teaspoon salt
2 teaspoons sugar

In a blender, combine all of the ingredients and mix well until you have a sauce. Adjust the consistency as desired by adding more water a bit at a time. Serve after blending or warm on a stove and cook for 5–8 minutes to thicken before serving.

Bangladeshi Tamarind Sauce

This dark sauce complements meat and vegetables alike and is found in one form or another all across the subcontinent and westward into Afghanistan. I like it best used on vegetables such as potatoes, zucchini, and other squashes and mixed vegetables, but it's also great for breads and kebabs or just an extra flavor on a well-appointed table.

1 tablespoon tamarind concentrate
3 teaspoons garlic, peeled and diced
2 teaspoons cumin seeds, roasted and ground
2–3 green chili peppers, minced
Water as needed to blend
1 teaspoon salt
2 tablespoons sugar

In a blender, combine all of the ingredients and mix well until you have a sauce. Adjust the consistency as desired by adding more water. Serve after blending or warm on a stove and cook for 5–8 minutes to thicken before serving.

Sweet and Sour Olive Sauce

This is an unusual Bangladeshi sauce that I believe probably entered Bangladeshi cuisine in the days of trade with the Portuguese. Utilizing vinegar and olives as a flavor base, the Bangladeshis add turmeric, coriander, a host of other spices, and sugar to the mix for a unique flavor combination. Great with kebabs and roast meat dishes as a dip or condiment for a touch of flavor.

2 cups seedless green olives
2 teaspoons salt
1 teaspoon ground turmeric
½ cup water
2 teaspoons ground coriander
½ teaspoon chili powder
½ teaspoon ground mustard
3 tablespoons peanut oil or light sesame oil
½ teaspoon **panchforan**
1 teaspoon ginger, peeled and grated
1 teaspoon garlic, peeled and diced
⅓ cup white vinegar
2–3 tablespoons sugar (or to taste)

1. In a sealable jar, combine the olives, salt, and turmeric. Cover and shake well until all is evenly coated. Let sit for a few hours in the sun or overnight. When done, remove from jar and dice olives.

2. Combine coriander with chili powder, mustard, and water and mix well. In a sauté pan, heat oil and add *panchforan* and sauté for a few minutes. Add ginger and garlic and cook until the garlic starts to swell and color. Add dissolved spices and cook to warm. When warm or hot, add olives and vinegar, cover, and cook over low heat for 15–20 minutes, stirring occasionally.

3. When olives are softened, add the sugar and stir constantly until the sugar is dissolved. When done, remove from heat and pour into a clean bottle or jar and let cool.

Panchforan

This is Bangladesh's five-spice powder that shares the cumin and star anise of many other five-spice mixtures and adds to them fenugreek, mustard, and the delicately flavored black cumin. Some mixtures add black cardamom instead of black cumin, and others change the relative proportions of the spices, but generally, this is Bangladesh's often-used, necessary ingredient.

1 teaspoon cumin seeds
2 star anise
1 teaspoon fenugreek seeds
1 teaspoon mustard seeds
½ teaspoon black cumin seeds

Place all of the spices in a grinder and grind together until you have a well-mixed, fine powder. Store in an airtight container until needed.

Taj Mahal at Sunrise, Agra

India

Main spices and flavors: mustard, ginger, garlic, chili peppers, cumin, coriander, turmeric, cilantro, onions, cashews, cloves, cinnamon, cardamom, peppercorns, mint, saffron, cayenne pepper, tomato, fennel, tamarind, poppy, fenugreek, asafetida, paprika, nutmeg, curry leaves, coconut, peanuts, black cumin, bay leaves, black salt, mango powder

Souring agents: lemons, limes, white vinegar

Mother India. She is a land so large and varied that it is difficult to understand how she came together as a single country. Each state has its own culture and cuisine and within each state the ethnic groups and classes vary so widely that to "know" them is to say one comprehends an endlessly faceted gem. It is a land where famine and malnutrition remain real problems into the twenty-first century, but also a land in which food is so important to culture that basil is placed in the hands of the deceased to try to release them from the cycle of rebirth and gain admittance to heaven. I love India and have traveled there for both business and pleasure several times. Coming into India, usually from a very rural area elsewhere on the subcontinent, always felt like coming home to me.

The history of India and its many cuisines go back over five thousand years to the Indus Valley civilization that flourished in the northern part of the country. The archaeological evidence from this time period shows

263

consumption of beef, eggplant, and sesame as major portions of the diet of most people. As the Indus civilization grew, northern cuisines and southern cuisines began to evolve separately as the tribes that originally inhabited the area migrated south, taking with them the basic concepts of their Aurvedic dietary practices, which divide foods into six tastes: sweet, sour, salty, pungent, bitter, and astringent. As the Indus Valley gave way to later cultures such as the Harappan and Vedic, increasing evidence of the use and later cultivation of turmeric, cardamom, black pepper, and mustard become more common.

During the Vedic period, major differences in the diet between the classes or castes also appeared, with vegetarianism popular amongst the Brahmin. Vegetarianism was further augmented by the rise of Buddhism in India around 600 BCE, and the spread of the religion across Asia over the next several hundred years also brought cultural contacts with foreigners and opened trade routes to the east and west that flourished for the better part of one thousand years. Frequent contacts with Muslim traders Began around 1000 CE and a long period of Muslim rule began by 1300 that lasted until the mid-nineteenth century.

Ibn Battuta, the great Moroccan explorer of this period, describes a meal served to him by in the court of Mohammed Bin Tughluk—one of the northern Sultans—that included the use of clarified butter (ghee), yogurt, pickles, and a milk-based dessert.

Europeans arrived as early as 1498, leaving elements of their cuisines all along the western and southern coasts of the country and introducing New World produce such as tomatoes, potatoes, and chili peppers. During the Mughal dynasty (1526–1857), we see Persian elements—such as the addition of nuts like almonds and cashews, and fruits such as raisins, apricots, and dried plums—to Indian food, as well as the rise of kebabs and a much wider use of saffron. The British took more than they gave to India and were largely responsible for introducing Indian cuisine to Europe, leaving high-tea and the combination of spices called curry powder in their wake. So you see, what we so blithely call "Indian food" today is really the product of thousands of years of cultural evolution, foreign contact, and trade from faraway shores.

Modern Indian cuisine is evolving rapidly once again as more and more Indians rise into the country's middle classes and the information and telecommunications revolution brings knowledge of other ways of life into rural areas. The slow trickle-down of change from the upper classes into the lower classes and from the cities to the countryside is rapidly becoming more of a free-for-all moveable feast. Rapid urbanization and the rise of service sector jobs over agricultural ones is also changing the speed of life, and increasingly women are becoming employed in the formal economy, leaving less time for them to prepare complex multicourse meals.

Still, as those of us who are interested watch to see what sort of cuisine will emerge from this crucible of cultural change, we know that although new foods and ways of preparing them will be adopted, the core of the cuisine will remain Indian. Food is too deeply woven into the regional and national identities to allow too fundamental a change in basic elements. The recipes offered in this section are largely "traditional" Indian fare with some variation by region. As with other countries explored, the recipes are meant to provide only a taste, a toe in the water, of a deep and varied culinary tradition.

Meat Dishes

Although most Hindus practice some level of vegetarianism, a wide variety of meats are consumed by Indian Christians and Muslims who together amount to over 15 percent of the population, or almost 200 million people. These dishes are more widely known in the meat-eating West than many of India's varied vegetarian recipes and include **Lamb or Pork Vindaloo** and **Lamb or Beef with Onions (Do Piaz)**. Both recipes show strong Portuguese influence in the use of vinegar as the major souring agent and in the use of copious amounts of onions. Chicken or hen is probably the most widely consumed meat with lamb following a close second. All meats are usually found in bits and pieces along with vegetables in a stew or curry such as **Cilantro Chicken** instead of as roasted whole meats—luxuries that until the modern age were known only to the privileged few who could afford them. Another way that Indians love to prepare land-based meats is as part of a complex rice dish, as in **Chicken Biryani**, which shows heavy Persian and Arab influence in the use of fruits, nuts, and saffron-laden milk as ingredients and in the complex layered construction of the dish so common in ancient Persian and modern Iranian cuisine.

Oceangoing fish and shellfish are regularly eaten by people inhabiting India's vast coastline, and when available, freshwater fish and prawns are eaten inland. Fish is often consumed seasoned, baked, and whole but can also be prepared as baked steaks or filets. **Spiced Fish with Lemon and Cilantro** is adapted from a whole-fish recipe to make it a bit easier for Western cooks and diners to enjoy. Shellfish is most often eaten as part of a curry, as in **Shrimp or Scallops in a Spicy Tomato Sauce**, but can also be prepared seasoned and grilled, especially in the north. I hope you enjoy the Indian meat dishes offered here, and I hope that they inspire you to continue exploring the wonderful world of Indian cuisine.

Cilantro Chicken

This is a standard dish on our home table—everyone just loves it so much! The cumin and coriander blend nicely with the lemon juice and chili peppers to make this a real treat. It's based on a dish I was once served on the train from Agra to Delhi. Another dinner that I took notes over! The yogurt and fresh cilantro top it off and make it smooth and creamy with just a hint of sourness. It's moderately fiery as offered, but you can adjust it to your own taste—milder or sweat-inducing, as desired.

2 large chicken breasts, cut into bite-size pieces
1 tablespoon mustard oil
2 tablespoons vegetable or light sesame oil
2 tablespoons grated ginger
1 teaspoon garlic, peeled and diced
4 hot, dried, red chili peppers, diced

1 ¼ cups water
3 teaspoons ground cumin
1 ½ teaspoons ground coriander
1 teaspoon ground turmeric
3 tablespoons lemon juice
1 medium bunch fresh cilantro leaves, chopped (25–30 sprigs)
1 teaspoon salt
¾ cup plain yogurt

1. Cut chicken breasts into bite-size pieces. Heat the oil in a sauté pan and when very hot, add the chicken pieces and sear them until the meat firms and starts to color. Take pan off of the heat and then remove meat with a slotted spoon and set aside in a bowl.

2. In a blender or food processor, grind ginger, garlic, and 4–6 tablespoons of the water into a thick paste.

3. Reheat sauté pan over medium heat, add chili peppers, ginger, and garlic paste and stir. After paste starts to cook and swell, add ground spices and continue stirring. After 2–3 minutes, add 1 cup of water and stir to distribute paste evenly throughout liquid. Scrape bottom of sauté pan to loosen cooked bits of paste that cling to the bottom. Add lemon juice.

4. Return chicken along with any accumulated juices to the curry and, if necessary, add more water to barely cover chicken. Bring to a boil and lower heat to medium. Add chopped coriander, cover, and lower heat, if necessary, to just simmer. Cook 15–20 minutes or until chicken has softened. Uncover, stir well, and allow some of the liquid to evaporate while chicken thoroughly cooks. When chicken is done, add yogurt, stir, and cook 5 minutes over low-medium heat to heat yogurt. Serve with rice.

Chicken Biryani

Biryani is the queen of Indian pilafs and is a fine example of Mughal cuisine that persists to the modern day. Mixing meat, nuts, and sometimes fruits such as raisins or currants with spiced rice, a *biryani* is really a well-balanced meal unto itself. It is a delicately flavored dish (despite all the chili peppers in the recipe) because the rice and milk extinguish some of the chili's fire.

Unlike modern Persian and central Asian pilafs, however, the *biryani* has a slightly complex preparation, but it is well worth the effort.

2 chicken breasts, cut into bite-size pieces*
1 cup plain yogurt
1 tablespoon grated ginger
1 teaspoon garlic, peeled and diced
2 teaspoons **Indian *Garam Masala***
4 tablespoons butter or ghee
2 large yellow onions, peeled, sliced, and separated into crescents
6 hot, dried, red chili peppers, diced
⅓ cup cashew nuts, chopped
½ teaspoon ground cloves
1 teaspoon ground cinnamon
Seeds from 1 black cardamom, crushed
1 teaspoon black peppercorns, roughly ground or cracked
2 teaspoons salt (or more to taste)
3 cups water
1 cup basmati rice
¼ cup chopped cilantro leaves, chopped (25–30 sprigs)
2 tablespoons fresh mint, chopped
¼ teaspoon saffron dissolved in 1 cup hot milk

1. Marinate the chicken with 1 cup of the yogurt, *garam masala*, ginger, and garlic for at least 2 hours at room temperature.

2. Heat 3 tablespoons of butter or ghee in a large sauté pan and sauté the sliced onions until they begin to wilt. Remove from the pan and set aside. Add the chili peppers and cashew nuts for 2–3 minutes. Add the chicken along with its marinade and cook for 5 minutes, then add the cloves, cinnamon, black cardamom, 1 teaspoon salt, and pepper and stir well. Cook for 3–5 minutes and add 1 cup water and cook until meat is tender; cover and set aside.

3. Rinse pan clean and in it heat remaining butter and add 2 cups of water and bring to a boil. Add rice and reduce heat to medium-low and cook covered for 20–30 minutes or until done. While waiting, chop the coriander and mint and set aside.

4. Butter, oil, or spray a deep, covered baking dish. Spread a layer of rice and cover it with half of the meat mixture. Sprinkle half of the coriander and onions. Cover with another layer of rice.

5. Add another layer of meat, then coriander, then onions. Finish with a final layer of rice. Sprinkle the rice with saffron milk, cover tightly, and place in oven at 350° for 20–30 minutes. Uncover and cook for five minutes more. Serve.

*To adapt the recipe for the vegetarian table, use ghee, omit the meat, and in its place add 2 cups of cauliflower florets or eggplant, 1 cup of peas, and 2 cups of julienned carrots.

Lamb with Onions, Cardamom, and Cloves (Do Piaz)

This and the *vindaloo* recipe that follows are two of the greatest hits of Indian cuisine. This dish gets its name and the base of its flavor from the abundance of caramelized onions that adorn the meat. Plentiful spices such as cardamom, cloves, cinnamon, cumin, and coriander along with *garam masala* broaden and deepen the flavor and complement the lamb or beef beautifully. Yogurt smoothes out the curry nicely and adds just a bit of sourness to tame the sweet spices.

1 heaping tablespoon garlic, coarsely chopped
2 tablespoons fresh ginger, coarsely chopped
2 cups water
4 medium yellow onions, peeled
½ teaspoon sugar
2 tablespoons mustard or other seed oil
1 cinnamon stick
Seeds from 10 cardamom pods
10 whole cloves
1 pound stew lamb cut into bite-size cubes
1 tablespoon ground coriander
2 teaspoons ground cumin
¾ cup plain yogurt
4 hot, dried, red chili peppers, diced
1 teaspoon salt
¼ teaspoon **Indian *Garam Masala***

1. Put the garlic and ginger into the container of a blender or food processor. Dice 1 of the onions and add it to the ginger and garlic

mix. Add ¼ cup of water (or more as needed) and blend until you have a thick paste.

2. Slice the remaining three onions lengthwise and separate into fine crescents.

3. Put half of the oil into a large sauté pan and heat. Add finely sliced onions and stir to coat them in the oil. Add a pinch of sugar and reduce heat to low, stirring only to stop them from burning. Cook slowly to caramelize and sweeten onions about 20–30 minutes. Remove onions from the oil with a slotted spoon and set aside.

4. Grind cinnamon, cardamom, and cloves into a fine powder. Add powder to the hot oil and stir for a few seconds to cook. Add chopped chili peppers and stir. Add meat to the oil and stir frequently until meat darkens just a bit. When done, remove meat cubes from oil and set aside.

5. If necessary, add another tablespoon of oil to the pan and heat. Put the ginger-garlic-onion paste into the pan and cook for 5 minutes, stirring constantly. Turn the heat down a bit and add the coriander and cumin. Stir for a minute and add the yogurt.

6. Return meat to the pan along with any juices that accumulated in the meat bowl with enough of the remaining water to almost cover. Stir to mix and bring to a simmer. Cover and cook for about 45 minutes or until the lamb is tender. Add the caramelized onions and the *garam masala*. Stir to mix and heat for a few minutes. Remove from heat and serve.

Lamb or Pork with Vinegar and Spices (Vindaloo)

This dish shows a mixture of Mughal and European influences on Indian cuisine. The Mughal elements include the easy use of fiery chili peppers and a complex base of cardamom, cinnamon, and fenugreek as well as in the stepped preparation, and the European element is the abundant use of white vinegar from which the dish derives its name. The paste needs to be made well ahead of cooking—I recommend at least a week for the vinegar to mellow and blend with the other spices.

2 tablespoons grated ginger
3 tablespoons garlic, peeled and diced (1 medium head)
1 ½ cups water (more if needed)
2 tablespoons mustard or other seed oil
1 pound lamb or pork stew meat, cut into bite-size pieces
1 tablespoon ground coriander
½ teaspoon ground turmeric
1 teaspoon salt
3-4 hot, dried red chili peppers
½ cup **Vindaloo Paste**
1 cup water
2 medium yellow onions, peeled and sliced into thin crescents
½ cup plain yogurt
½ teaspoon cayenne pepper (adjust to taste)

1. Put the ginger and garlic into the container of an electric blender or food processor. Add ½ cup water and blend until you have a smooth paste.

2. Heat the oil in a sauté pan and when very hot, put in the lamb or pork cubes to seal in the meat juices. When done, remove meat from the oil and set aside. Add the ginger-garlic paste to the hot oil, lower heat, and stir paste for a few minutes until cooked. Add the coriander, turmeric, salt, and chili peppers. Stir for another minute or two.

3. Add the meat, along with any juices that may have accumulated, and the *Vindaloo* Paste and 1 cup of water. Add more water if it is needed to thin the paste to a stewlike consistency. Bring to a boil. Cover and simmer gently, stirring often, for 30 minutes.

4. Add onions and cook another 15 minutes or so until the meat is cooked. Add yogurt and cayenne and reheat. Serve with rice.

Spiced Fish with Lemon and Cilantro

This fish recipe is a wonderful mix of spicy, hot, and a little bit sour. I find it an interesting dish, because before the addition of the tomatoes, the sauce is reminiscent of the Georgian **Garlic and Walnut Sauce (Garo).** Whether the sauce is indirect evidence of a common Persian ancestor that (to my knowledge at least) no longer exists, or whether it is evidence of trade and cultural contact between the nations is one of the things that makes cooking so exciting.

4 steaks gently flavored white fish, such as carp, cod, rockfish, or roughy
1–1 ½ cups Cilantro Sauce with Lemon and Garlic (see Indian Sauces and Spice Mixtures)
2 tablespoons peanut or light sesame oil
1 large yellow onion, peeled, sliced, and separated into crescents
1 teaspoon sugar (optional)
1 large tomato, diced
1 small bunch fresh cilantro, chopped (15–20 sprigs)

1. Preheat oven to 375°. Wash and pat fish steaks dry and sprinkle with 1 teaspoon of salt; set aside.

2. Heat oil in a sauté pan and sauté onions over medium heat for 3–5 minutes until they begin to soften. Then add the sugar and lower heat to low and cook slowly until the onions caramelize. Add the **Cilantro Sauce with Lemon and Garlic** and cook 8–10 minutes over medium heat until the paste darkens. Add the tomato, sugar (if using) and half the cilantro and cook covered 3–5 minutes more, stirring often, until tomato softens.

3. Butter or spray the inside of a covered baking dish and place the fish, skin side down, in the dish. Spoon the tomato-spice mixture over the fish steaks, taking care to evenly coat all of the steaks. Sprinkle with remaining chopped cilantro. Cover tightly and bake for about 25–30 minutes or until fish is done.

Shrimp or Scallops in a Spicy Tomato Sauce

Tell your taste buds to batten down the hatches and prepare for a spicy, slightly sour surprise that they're going to love! This is a wonderful way to prepare shrimp or scallops that will leave diners looking for more, even after they have devoured heaping plates of this curry. If there's a secret to making this dish well, it's don't overcook the seafood; it really only needs a few minutes to cook before it is done.

1 pound shrimp, peeled, rinsed and deveined, or
1 pound sea or bay scallops

¼ teaspoon cayenne pepper
¼ teaspoon ground turmeric
1 tablespoon mustard or other seed oil
2 tablespoons peanut or light sesame oil
1 teaspoon fennel seeds
1 teaspoon yellow mustard seeds
3–4 hot, dried, red chili peppers, torn or chopped
1 medium onion peeled, sliced, and separated into crescents
1 teaspoon garlic, peeled and chopped
3 teaspoons ground cumin
1 ½ teaspoons ground coriander
1 ½ cups tomato sauce
½ teaspoon tamarind paste dissolved into 2–3 tablespoons lemon juice
1 teaspoon salt
1 small bunch fresh cilantro leaves, chopped (15–20 sprigs)
¼ teaspoon **Indian Garam Masala**

1. Prepare shrimp or scallops and place into a bowl with the cayenne pepper, turmeric, and a pinch of salt. Stir well, cover, and set aside for at least 1 hour.

2. Heat oil in a sauté pan over medium heat and when hot, sauté the fennel and mustard seeds for a minute or two. Add diced chili peppers and remove from the heat and set aside.

3. Warm the sauté pan with the fennel and mustard seeds up again and add the onions and garlic. Stir and fry until the onions turn slightly brown. Now put in the cumin, coriander, and tomato and mix well. Cook 3–5 minutes to fully warm the spices. (If mixture is too dry, add a tablespoon or two of water.)

4. Add tomato sauce, tamarind, lemon juice mixture, salt, and fresh cilantro leaves. Cover and gently simmer for 15 minutes. Add *garam masala* and shrimp and mix well. Cook for 3–5 minutes or until shrimp are fully cooked.

An Indian Vegetable Market

Vegetable Dishes and Salads

Potatoes and gourds and other squashes are the most commonly consumed vegetables in India, followed by long beans or string beans and spinach or other leafy green vegetable. Vegetables are prepared as part of a flavorful stew or curry with a rich sauce or are cooked "dry," as with **Sweet and Sour Okra** or **Ginger Potatoes**.

Sweet and Sour Okra

This really is a nice way to prepare okra that is sweet, sour, spicy, and a bit hot all at the same time—everything that a good Asian dish should be! The secrets to preparing a delicious dish—if there are secrets—are to select fresh young okra and not to overcook them or they may become slippery. This dish goes well with a wide variety of Asian roast meats or kebabs and even works well with Western meats.

1 pound fresh okra, tips and tops removed and sliced in ¼–½-inch slices
2 tablespoons mustard or other nut or seed oil
2 hot, dried, red chili peppers, chopped
1 heaping tablespoon garlic, peeled and diced
2 teaspoons ground cumin
1 teaspoon ground coriander
½ teaspoon ground turmeric
1 teaspoon cumin seeds
½ teaspoon salt
1 teaspoon sugar
2 tablespoons lemon juice
¼ cup water (if desired)

1. Heat the oil and when hot, add the chili peppers and cumin seeds. Sauté for one minute and remove from heat; let sit for 5–10 minutes for the spices to infuse the cooking oil.

2. Reheat oil and add garlic. Lower heat and cook garlic until lightly browned. Add the ground cumin, coriander, and turmeric and mix.

3. Now add the okra, salt, sugar, and lemon juice and stir; bring to a gentle simmer. Add water if needed to cook okra. Cover tightly and gently simmer for about 10 minutes or until the okra is tender.

Ginger Potatoes

This wonderful dish blends turmeric, ginger, and garlic with just a hint of fennel to form a light crust on tender sautéed potatoes. It is a regular visitor to our home table, and my husband's colleagues often ask him to bring it to potluck parties at work. We enjoy them regularly with grilled steaks, but they will grace a table laden with kebabs or other Asian meats just as well.

2–3 medium to large potatoes, parboiled, cooled, and chopped
1 tablespoon mustard oil
2 tablespoons peanut or light sesame oil
1 teaspoon fennel seeds
2–3 hot, dried, red chili peppers, chopped or torn
2 tablespoons fresh ginger, peeled and coarsely chopped
1 teaspoon garlic, peeled and chopped
½ cup water (more if needed)
½ teaspoon ground turmeric
1 teaspoon salt

1. Heat oil in a sauté pan. When warm, add the fennel seeds and the chopped chili peppers. Stir for about 1 minute and remove from heat; set aside.

2. Put the ginger, garlic, 3 tablespoons water, and turmeric into the container of a food processor or blender. Blend until you have a paste. Return sauté pan to the heat and when fully warm, add the ginger-garlic paste; stir and cook for 5 minutes. Add salt.

3. Put in the potatoes. Cook, stirring often, for 5–7 minutes or until the potatoes have a nice, golden-brown crust on them. Scrape the bottom of the pan to loosen the cooked-on bits of spices. Serve immediately.

Fire Pumpkin

Say yes to the sweetest and sourest squash you've ever had! This recipe is a delicious way to prepare pumpkin or squash! It's flavorful and spicy, sweet and sour, all at the same time. Match it with one of the kebab dishes offered for the foundation of a great meal. Serve with rice.

1 small kabocha pumpkin or other squash
5 hot, dried, red chili peppers
1 teaspoon nigella (onion) seeds
1 teaspoon cumin seeds
½ teaspoon mustard seeds
1 teaspoon poppy seeds, lightly roasted
1 teaspoon fennel seeds
½ teaspoon fenugreek seeds
3 tablespoons lemon juice
½ cup water
1 teaspoon asafetida
1 teaspoon salt
4 tablespoons palm sugar, grated or dissolved into above water or lemon juice
1 small bunch fresh cilantro leaves, chopped (15–20 sprigs)

1. In a spice grinder, combine all of the seed spices and grind until you have a fine powder. Heat butter or ghee in a large sauté pan and when it is warm, add spice powder and sauté until it is warm. Add the lemon juice, asafetida, salt, and palm sugar and sauté for another minute or two.

2. Add the pumpkin cubes and cook covered about 15–20 minutes over low heat until vegetable is done. Add cilantro and stir until wilted.

Spinach with Coriander and Nutmeg

This spinach really hits the spot! It takes all of 10 minutes to make, and it is a delicious snack, a light lunch all by itself, or it goes well with other complementary spiced curries such as **Lamb or Beef with Onions (*Do Piaz*)** or **Lamb or Pork with Vinegar and Spices (*Vindaloo*)**.

2 large bunches spinach or 1 12-ounce bag
3 tablespoons butter or ghee
1 teaspoon grated ginger
½ teaspoon asafetida
2 tablespoons ground coriander
½ teaspoon turmeric

¼ teaspoon chili powder (more to taste)
½ teaspoon sweet paprika
1 corm nutmeg grated
1 teaspoon sugar
1 teaspoon salt
½ teaspoon ground black pepper
1 cup plain yogurt

1. Wash well, spin dry, and set the spinach aside. Heat 3 tablespoons of butter or ghee; add ginger, asafetida, ground coriander, turmeric, chili powder, sweet paprika, and nutmeg and stir well. Cook over medium-low heat to warm the spices and then add the sugar, salt, and pepper. Cook full complement of spices for another 2–3 minutes, stirring constantly so it won't burn.

2. Add yogurt and stir well to blend it into the spices. When yogurt warms, add spinach and stir into the yogurt and spices. Cover and cook 2–3 minutes, stirring occasionally. Uncover and cook another minute or two or until spinach is done and serve.

Green Beans with Mustard and Lemon

1 pound green beans, trimmed and cut in half (if using long beans, cut them into 3–4-inch lengths)
2 tablespoons grated ginger
1 tablespoon garlic, peeled and diced
1 ½ cups water
1 tablespoon mustard or other seed oil
2 tablespoons peanut or light sesame oil
3 teaspoons cumin seeds
2 teaspoons ground coriander
2 medium tomatoes, diced
2 tablespoons tomato paste
1 teaspoon salt
1 teaspoon ground black pepper
3 tablespoons lemon juice

1. In a blender combine ginger, garlic, and ½ cup water and mix until you have a smooth paste.

2. Heat the oil in a wide, heavy sauté pan over a medium flame. When hot, put in the cumin seeds. Stir for 2–3 minutes and then pour in the

ginger-garlic paste. Stir and cook for about 5 minutes, stirring often. Then add the ground coriander. Stir well.

3. Add the diced tomatoes and the tomato paste and cook 3–5 minutes, stirring often. Add the beans, salt, pepper, and 1 cup of water and simmer covered. Turn heat to low and cook 15–20 minutes, stirring often, or until the beans are tender.

4. Remove the cover. Add the lemon juice and cook another 2–3 minutes and serve.

Rice and Grain Dishes, Breads

Three great rice dishes and three authentic, wonderful breads await you in this section. Beginning with the **Rice with Curry and Lime**—one of my favorite rice dishes ever—which is a dish that mixes flavors from western and southern Asia. Also included is **Rice with Eggplants**, which combines the earthy flavor of eggplant with the familiar triad of Indian spices: turmeric, cumin, and coriander, sprinkles it with lemon juice, and bakes it into a rice casserole. Also here is a recipe for that wonderful Indian bread that comes to the table full of air like an inflated balloon—**Puri**. A delicious, spicy cracker bread, **Pakora**, is also here, as is the bread stuffed with spiced potatoes.

Rice with Curry and Lime

In this dish, the western Asian flavors of fenugreek and lime blend with southern Asian flavors of mustard, curry leaves, and cashews with a hint of coastal coconut to unite the two. This southwestern Indian dish bears the imprints of the many cultures that traded along the maritime Silk Road with its delicious golden grains. Choosing peanuts instead of the milder cashews gives this dish a decidedly Eastern feel as well.

1 cup uncooked basmati rice
2 ½ cups water
1 teaspoon salt
¼ teaspoon ground turmeric

3 tablespoons butter or ghee
2 red or green chili peppers, diced
½ teaspoon mustard seeds, ground
I teaspoon fenugreek seeds, ground
I tablespoon *dal* (split pea) of your choice, cracked or crushed
2 tablespoons fresh lime juice
5 curry leaves, chopped or crumbled
¼ cup cashews or peanuts, diced
I tablespoon fresh or dried coconut, grated or chopped (optional)

1. In a medium saucepan, combine the water, salt, turmeric, and rice and bring water to a boil. When boiling, cover and reduce heat to a steady simmer. Cook rice for 20–30 minutes or until all of the water is absorbed and the rice is no longer tough. When rice is done, remove from heat, uncover, and cool.

2. In a sauté pan, heat the butter or ghee over low flame. Grind together the chili peppers, mustard seeds, and fenugreek seeds and add to the sauté pan. Also, partially grind the uncooked *dal* and add to the pan as well. Cook over low flame for 8–10 minutes until the seeds and legumes soften and impart their flavors to the butter.

3. Then add the lime juice and stir well. When the lime juice heats, add the curry leaves, cashews or peanuts, and grated or chopped coconut, if desired. Stir well, and then with a fork add the cooled rice into the pan. Mix well, lifting rather than stirring so as not to break down the rice.

Rice with Eggplants

This dish is almost like a simplified eggplant *biryani* with the flavorful eggplant and spice mixture layered in between two layers of plain basmati rice and baked to blend the flavors. Makes a great side dish in a large, multicourse meal or can even be had all by itself for a light meal.

I cup uncooked basmati rice
2 ½ cups water
I ½ teaspoons salt
I teaspoon ground turmeric
I teaspoon ground cumin
I tablespoon ground coriander

½ teaspoon cayenne pepper

½ teaspoon sugar

2 tablespoons lemon juice (more as needed)

I teaspoons chickpea or rice flour

¼ cup unsalted butter

I large Western eggplant, diced

¼ cup vegetable broth or water (more as needed to moisten the eggplant)

1. In a medium saucepan, combine the water, half the salt, and the rice and bring to a boil over high heat. Then cover and reduce heat so that the mixture enters a steady simmer. Cook rice for 20–30 minutes until all the water has been absorbed and rice is no longer tough. Remove the pan from the heat and set aside to cool.

2. Meanwhile, in a small mixing bowl, combine the turmeric, cumin, coriander, cayenne, sugar, lemon juice, chickpea flour, and the remaining salt to form a paste (adding more lemon juice if necessary).

3. In a large frying pan, melt the butter over low heat. Add the spice paste made in step two and sauté, stirring occasionally, for 8–10 minutes. Add the diced eggplant and sauté for 5 minutes. Add the vegetable broth or water and mix well. Cover pan, reduce the heat to low, and cook the eggplant for 15–20 minutes or until the cubes are tender when pierced with the point of a sharp knife. Remove the pan from the heat and set aside.

4. Spread half the rice over the bottom of a sprayed or buttered ovenproof dish. Spread the eggplant over the rice and cover with the remaining rice. Cover and place in the oven. Cook for 20–25 minutes or until the rice is very hot.

Spiced Saffron Rice

This rice is simple to make, delicious, and undeniably South Asian with the flavors of cardamom, cinnamon, and cloves infusing the bright yellow grains. A great anytime rice, this dish complements almost any kebab, chop, or roast and most curries wonderfully. A really versatile recipe you'll want to serve again and again.

¼ cup unsalted butter
Seeds from 6 cardamom pods, crushed
4 cloves, crushed
1 cinnamon stick, about 3 inches long
1 medium onion, finely diced
1 cup basmati or other long-grain rice
2 ½ cups chicken or other meat or vegetable broth
1 teaspoon salt
¾ teaspoon crushed saffron threads, soaked in 2 tablespoons boiling water for 20 minutes

1. Dissolve the crushed saffron in the boiling water, mix well, and set aside. Then, in a medium-sized saucepan, melt the butter over moderate heat. Add the cardamom seeds, cloves, and cinnamon stick to the pan and fry, stirring constantly, for 2 minutes. Add the onion and sauté, stirring occasionally, for 8–10 minutes or until it is golden brown. Add the rice, reduce the heat to medium, and sauté for 5 minutes.

2. Add the broth or water, add the salt, and stir in the saffron mixture. Cover the pan, reduce the heat to low, and cook for 20–30 minutes or until the rice is tender and all the liquid has been absorbed.

3. Remove the pan from the heat. Remove and discard the cinnamon stick. Serve.

Puri

This delicious bread will amaze your guests with its lightness and airiness, especially if they are children or just young at heart. My kids make a habit of ceremoniously popping the puris to deflate them before they tuck into them. Some of the secrets for getting the *puris* to inflate properly include using enough oil to really deep fry, and letting the oil get good and hot before frying the rolled-out dough.

2 cups all-purpose flour
1 cup lukewarm water
1 pinch salt
¼ teaspoon chili powder
½ teaspoon ground turmeric or ground cumin
Oil for deep frying

1. In a large mixing bowl, combine the flour and the water with the spices and mix until you have a firm but slightly sticky dough. Knead for 5 minutes and then set aside in a warm, quiet place for 15 minutes.

2. Divide the dough into golf-ball-sized pieces, dip into flour, and roll out as a *roti* or *chapati*.

3. Heat the oil in a large sauté pan or a wok. Deep fry *puri* until golden. To puff *puri*, press them down lightly when frying. Drain on paper and serve.

Pakora

This is another deep-fried Indian bread, but it is more like a fritter or a *lavash* than a soft bread like a *chapati*, or a puffy bread like a *puri*. It is tasty and can be eaten along with a selection of pickles and chutneys as an appetizer or snack as well.

1 cup chickpea flour
1 small onion, peeled and diced
1 teaspoon salt
1 green chili, diced
¼ teaspoon baking powder
½ teaspoon ground cumin
1 teaspoon *garam masala*
1 teaspoon chopped cilantro
½ cup water
Oil for deep frying

1. In a medium mixing bowl, mix together the flour, salt, onion, chili pepper, baking powder, cumin, and *garam masala*. Add the chopped cilantro and mix again. Slowly add water, mixing as you do, until you have thick paste.

2. Heat oil for deep frying on medium. With a small ladle or a large spoon, place batter in the hot oil until you have rounds of about 4–5 inches in diameter. Turn and cook both sides until golden. Drain and serve.

Flat Bread Stuffed with Potatoes

A different take on the samosa concept, this bread places a spiced mash of potatoes between two bread rounds and lightly fries them in butter or ghee to cook. Often very spicy, this is another bread that makes a great appetizer or snack when served with a selection of pickles and chutneys.

Dough
2 cups whole wheat flour
½ cup warm water
I teaspoon salt
2 tablespoons unsalted butter, melted

3 large potatoes, parboiled and mashed
3 hot red or green chili peppers, diced
I teaspoon salt
I medium bunch fresh cilantro leaves, finely diced
4 tablespoon butter, ghee, or vegetable oil for frying (optional)

1. In a medium bowl, combine, flour, water, salt, and butter and mix well. Turn out onto a floured surface and knead flour for about 5 minutes or until you get soft dough. Set aside in a warm place for at least I hour.

2. In a separate bowl, combine salt, chili peppers, cilantro, and potatoes and mix well.

3. Divide dough into about eight portions and roll out in circles about 6–8 inches in diameter. Place the potato mix between the two rolled-out pieces of dough. Roll again to evenly apply potato mix inside the bread, and cook in butter or ghee or oil.

Rajasthani Men around a Cooking Fire

Desserts and Beverages

A broad sampling of Indian desserts is to be found in the next few pages. Beginning with **"Vanilla" Rice Pudding**, a rice pudding made with the essence of pandanus flowers that gives the dish a vanilla-like flavor, we progress to one of India's many sweet dessert squares, **Semolina Squares with Cardamom and Saffron**. Last up in the dessert category is an Indian **Sautéed Apple**, which is a familiar dish with a twist of Indian spices to turn an old favorite into something brand new. A sweet and delicious **Cardamom-Rose Lassi** recipe follows the cooling **Almond Milkshake** recipe, and the section ends with a delicious and healthful **Ginger Tea** that is delicious hot or cold over ice.

"Vanilla" Rice Pudding

Here is a rice pudding that is richer and more complex than some of the other desserts we've encountered. Here, heavy cream is added to the pudding, which is flavored with both cardamom and kewar essence, which lends a spicy vanilla-like flavor to the dish. Then it is topped off with a bit of raisins and almonds for a delicious treat.

½ cup cooked basmati rice
½ cup water
I cup whole milk
½ cup heavy cream
½ cup sugar
¼ teaspoon ground cardamom
I tablespoon essence of pandanus flowers (kewar)
I tablespoon butter or ghee
I tablespoon dark raisins
10 almonds, soaked for I hour in warm water, sliced or chopped

1. In a medium saucepan, combine water and cooked rice and heat. Add the milk, cream, and sugar and bring to a boil, stirring often. Reduce heat to medium-low and simmer. Add the cardamom and the kewar and cook until the pudding thickens, at least 15–20 minutes. Remove from heat and spoon into a serving bowl or individual dishes. Let cool until surface starts to firm.

2. Melt the butter or ghee and add the almonds and raisins. Stir and cook for about 5 minutes until the raisins soften and plump up. Pour over the pudding. Serve or let cool.

Semolina Squares with Saffron and Cardamom

This sort of sweet dessert is enjoyed all across the subcontinent. Small, usually very sweet dessert squares or diamonds are made from different types of flour, condensed milk, semolina, or even grated vegetables like carrots. Usually some form of nuts and raisins are added, and a gentle flavor like rose, cardamom, or pandanus essence (a vanilla-like flavor) is used. Served room temperature or chilled. Store in the refrigerator until needed.

¾ cup butter or ghee
¼ cup cashews, finely diced
¼ cup raisins
I cup semolina

2 cups hot water
¼ teaspoon saffron
Seeds from 6 cardamom pods, crushed or ground
I can sweetened condensed milk

1. Dissolve the saffron in the hot water and set aside. In a medium saucepan, heat butter or ghee and sauté cashews and raisins over low to medium heat until the raisins plump and the cashews start to color. Remove raisins and nuts from the butter with a slotted spoon and set aside.

2. Add semolina to the butter or ghee and sauté until golden. Add saffron and water and stir in over low heat until all the water has been absorbed.

3. Add sweetened condensed milk and stir well until evenly integrated into the mix. Spoon and press into a buttered or sprayed baking pan or onto a greased plate. Top with nuts and raisins and let set for at least 30 minutes. Cut into diamond-shaped pieces and serve.

Sautéed Apple

Here is a delicious alternative to other apple desserts that blends cinnamon and cloves—traditional spices for apple-based desserts—and revs them up a bit with ginger, ground cardamom, black pepper, and lemon juice. Can be sweetened with sugar or left with a lemony tang as desired.

I apple, red delicious, Rome, or any sweet or sweet and tart variety
2 tablespoons butter or ghee
I teaspoon ginger, peeled and grated
2 cloves, ground
I I-inch cinnamon stick, ground
¼ teaspoon ground cardamom
¼ teaspoon ground black pepper
½ teaspoon lemon juice
I teaspoon sugar or honey (optional)

1. Core apple and cut into thin slices. In a medium sauté pan, heat butter and add the ginger and cook for 2–3 minutes until the ginger starts to color. Add spices and stir well. Cook for 3–5 minutes until the spices infuse their flavors into the butter.

2. Add apple and sauté briskly for 3–5 minutes. Add lemon juice and sugar or honey if desired and serve.

Almond Milkshake

A great, gently flavored milkshake for a delicious dessert or a sweet treat to relax with on a hot day.

¼ cup skinned almonds, soaked in water overnight
3 cups milk
Seeds from 6 cardamom pods, finely crushed or ground
¼ cup sugar
I cup crushed ice

Combine the soaked almonds, sugar, cardamom, and I cup of milk in a blender and mix until the almonds are well mixed with the milk. Add the rest of the milk and blend again for 2–3 minutes until the milkshake is frothy. Add the cardamom and sugar and some crushed ice and serve.

Cardamom-Rose Lassi

A delicious, fragrant, and light drink to cool you down after a spicy meal or to have on a hot afternoon.

I ½ cups yogurt
2 cups milk
I cup water
¼–½ teaspoon ground cardamom
2 tablespoons rosewater
2–4 tablespoons sugar

Combine all ingredients in a blender and blend for 2–3 minutes until frothy. Pour into glasses and serve.

Ginger Tea

A delicious pick-me-up beverage, enjoyed any time of day, but especially in the morning to raise your energy level. Wonderful cold over ice as well.

cups water
3 teaspoons ginger, peeled and grated
¼ teaspoon ground cardamom
¼ teaspoon ground turmeric
¼ teaspoon ground black pepper
Sugar or honey to taste (optional)

In a medium saucepan, bring the water to a boil. Remove from heat and add ginger, cardamom, turmeric, and black pepper. Cover and steep for 5 minutes. Strain, pour into a pot or cups, and serve.

Appetizers and Condiments

Three appetizers and four condiments can be found in the forthcoming pages that will introduce you to the broad range of Indian foods in these categories. First up is a spiced and breaded prawn dish to whet your guests' appetites. **Spicy Prawns** can be followed by the light **Spicy Cucumber Wedges** with overtones of lemon and cumin or served with India's baba ghanoush—**Eggplant and Yogurt Dip** and plenty of fresh, delicious flatbread. Next up are two dals and two chutneys to round out a full Indian table. The **Spicy Tomato Dal** tempers the legumes and vegetables with a delicious, buttery mix of garlic, mustard, cumin, and curry leaves with delicious results, and the **Pumpkin Dal** offsets the natural mild sweetness of the pumpkin with a host of spices.

Spicy Prawns

This is a delicious, spicy, crunchy, shrimp appetizer that can be served with **Tomato and Garlic Sauce** or other Indian sauces for a different start to a meal or as a snack at a cocktail party.

2 dozen large shrimp or prawns, peeled, rinsed, and deveined
1 ½ teaspoons chili powder
1 teaspoon salt
1 teaspoon ground black pepper
2 eggs, beaten
1 cup plain bread crumbs
¼ cup peanut or light sesame oil for frying

1. In a large mixing bowl combine *half each* of the chili powder, salt, and pepper with shrimp or prawns and mix well. Marinate for at least an hour.

2. Combine remaining spices with the bread crumbs and mix well. When done, dip the shrimp or prawns in the beaten egg and then roll in the bread crumbs.

3. Heat oil in a medium or large sauté pan and sauté prawns until golden, then turn and cook on the other side until golden as well. Drain on paper and serve with sauces, condiments, pickles, or chutneys.

Spicy Cucumber Wedges

This is a great, light starter salad that can serve to whet appetites for a great meal. Lemon juice, salt, pepper, and cumin combine with the natural watery brightness of cucumbers for a great treat.

1 large cucumber, peeled, seeded, and cut lengthwise into 1-inch chunks
1 tablespoon lemon juice
½ teaspoon salt
¼ teaspoon ground black pepper
1 teaspoon ground cumin
¼ teaspoon cayenne pepper (if spiciness is desired)

Add lemon juice and spices to a bowl and mix well. Place cucumbers into a bowl and mix with the dressing. Refrigerate at least ½ hour then arrange on a serving plate and serve.

Eggplant and Yogurt Dip

This is a great Indian dip for breads and appetizers that harkens back to the Levant's baba ghanoush. Also good if you bake the eggplants whole or roast them over an open flame for some extra smokiness in the dip's flavor.

3 medium Indian eggplants or one medium Western one
½ teaspoon chili powder
½ teaspoon ground turmeric
½ teaspoon ground black cumin
4 cloves garlic, peeled and crushed
1 cup yogurt
1 teaspoon salt
1 small bunch fresh cilantro leaves, chopped (15–20 sprigs)

1. Slice the eggplant(s) lengthwise and place flesh side down on a sprayed baking sheet and bake in a preheated 350° oven until soft and tender. Baking time will be different for small and large eggplants: about 15 minutes for small eggplants and at least 30 minutes for larger ones.

2. Let cook and then scoop the flesh of the eggplants out of their skins and mash. Add chili powder, turmeric, and black cumin and mix well. Set aside.

3. Mix yogurt with crushed garlic, cilantro, and salt and set aside for at least 1 hour. When ready, combine the yogurt mixture with the eggplants and mix well. Serve with bread or rice.

Tomato and Onion Salad

This is another one of those recipes that every Indian cook makes just a little bit different from her sister. There are many variations out there, but I think I might have invented the use of *garam masala* all by myself and quite by accident. Now, I use the cumin when I feel like a bit of sharp spice and the *garam masala* when I want a little sweetness.

2 medium tomatoes, cut and separated into crescents
1 small to medium onion, peel and diced
2 tablespoons lemon juice
½ teaspoon ground cumin or Indian *garam masala*
1 small bunch fresh cilantro, finely chopped (15–20 sprigs)
½ teaspoon salt (more or less if desired)
⅛ teaspoon ground chili powder or black pepper

Add the lemon juice, cumin or *garam masala*, fresh cilantro, salt, and pepper to a bowl of sliced tomatoes and onions. Mix well and refrigerate for at least 30 minutes before serving.

Spicy Tomato Dal

A wonderful tomato *dal* mix that builds on the tomatoes' natural acidity to create a condiment that is spicy and hot but very flavorful all the same.

2 cups water
1 teaspoon ground turmeric
1 teaspoon chili powder
3–4 red or green chili peppers, diced
2–3 large tomatoes, chopped
1 onion, peeled and diced
1 cup *toor dal*, washed and soaked in water for 1 hour

Tempering
2 tablespoons butter or ghee
¾ teaspoon mustard seeds
1 teaspoon cumin seeds
2 tablespoons garlic, peeled and diced
4 hot, dried, red chili peppers, diced
6 curry leaves

1. In a medium saucepan, heat water and spices until they come to a boil. Add diced chili peppers, tomatoes, and onions and stir well. Cook to heat and add the soaked *toor dal* and mix well. Cook about 20–30 minutes or until the *dal* begins to soften.

2. To prepare tempering spices, heat the butter or ghee in a medium saucepan and add mustard and cumin seeds. Cover until they stop popping and then stir in garlic, diced chili peppers, and curry leaves.

3. When *dal* and vegetables are cooked, turn them into a serving bowl and then pour tempering spices over them. Garnish with chopped cilantro leaves and serve.

Pumpkin Dal

A very complex *dal* with a myriad of spices to bring added flavor to the natural sweetness of the pumpkin or squash.

1 cup *toor dal*, cooked

1 cup kabocha pumpkin or other squash, peeled and chopped
2 tablespoon butter or ghee
1 medium onion, diced
2 teaspoons ginger, peeled and grated
2 teaspoons garlic, peeled and diced
2 hot, dried, red chili peppers, diced
1 cup beef or vegetable broth or water
1 teaspoon tamarind concentrate
Seeds from 2 cardamom pods, crushed
2 cloves, crushed
1 1-inch piece of cinnamon
½ teaspoon black cumin
½ teaspoon ground cumin
½ teaspoon ground mustard
4 curry leaves, diced
½ teaspoon chili powder
½ teaspoon ground turmeric powder
2 bay leaves
½ teaspoon *garam masala* powder
1 teaspoon salt

1. In a medium saucepan, heat butter or ghee and add onion and sauté until it becomes translucent. Then add the ginger and garlic and sauté for 3–5 minutes until the garlic swells and colors. Add the chili peppers and mix well. Add broth or water and stir. Then add tamarind and mix well. Cook for 5 minutes, stirring occasionally.

2. Add cardamom, cloves, and cinnamon and cook for 5 minutes. Add black cumin, ground cumin, ground mustard, and curry leaves and mix well. Add chili powder, turmeric, and bay leaves and mix. Then add *garam masala* and salt and mix again. Cook for 8–10 minutes.

3. Add chopped pumpkin and cook 5 minutes then add cooked *dal* and cook another 5–8 minutes, lifting rather than stirring so as not to mash the vegetables and legumes. Serve.

Tomato Chutney II

This is a great, simple-to-make chutney that is not often encountered in the West. It is sort of like Indian salsa and can be used to impart a bit of extra flavor to dishes, as a dip for breads and crackers, or as a side to broaden the meal.

2 tablespoons butter, ghee, or vegetable oil
1 large red onion, finely diced
1 teaspoon garlic, peeled and chopped
2 medium tomatoes, chopped
¼ cup water, beef, or vegetable broth
½ cup tomato paste
½ teaspoon salt
½ teaspoon sugar
1 teaspoon paprika
½ teaspoon cumin powder
1 small bunch fresh cilantro leaves, chopped (10–15 sprigs)

1. In a medium saucepan or sauté pan, heat the butter or oil and sauté the onions for 2–3 minutes, then add the garlic and cook until garlic swells and starts to color. Add tomatoes and mix well. Cook until the tomatoes start to soften.

2. Add the water or broth and when it warms, add the tomato paste, salt, sugar, paprika, and cumin and stir well. Cook for 3–5 minutes and add the chopped cilantro. Mix well and cook another minute or two. Spoon into serving dishes or into a sealable jar for storage.

Cilantro and Mint Chutney

One of the classic chutneys found on almost every Indian table adds a sweet and sour blast of flavor to any dish. Best if made ahead of time and allowed to sit and blend its flavors. Store in the refrigerator.

1 medium bunch mint leaves
1 medium bunch fresh cilantro leaves, chopped (20–25 sprigs)
5 green chili peppers, diced
2 tablespoons lemon juice
2 tablespoons ginger, peeled and grated
2 teaspoons **Chaat Masala** (see Indian Sauces and Spice Mixtures)
1 teaspoon ground black cumin
1 teaspoon salt
2 teaspoons sugar

In a food processor, combine the mint and cilantro leaves and quickly pulse until the leaves are just chopped. Add chili peppers, lemon juice, ginger, *chaat masala*, black cumin, salt, and sugar and pulse until the ingredients are well blended. (Be careful not to overgrind, or the chutney will get too watery.) Serve or place in a sealable jar until needed.

Sauces and Spice Mixtures

Three great sauces await you in this section, beginning with India's delicious **Tomato and Garlic Sauce**, **Chili-Vinegar Sauce**, and **Cilantro Sauce with Lemon and Garlic**. Each can be used to flavor meats and vegetables or as dipping sauces for breads and appetizers. Then there's a great **Vindaloo Paste** needed to make western India's hot and spicy, vinegary curry. Up last are a couple of spice blends used in everyday Indian cooking. You'll never want to be without a *Garam Masala* and a *Chaat Masala* is a great rub for meats and can be mixed with yogurt for a marinade or sweeter alternative to tandoori.

Tomato and Garlic Sauce

This is a great sauce for kebabs or roasted meats and chops, or it can be used to flavor vegetables like potatoes, zucchini, or other squash. Also great as a dip for breads and appetizers.

1 large onion, peeled, sliced, and divided into crescents
2 tablespoons peanut or light sesame oil
1 tablespoon garlic, peeled and diced
4 large tomatoes, diced
1 tablespoon tomato paste
1 teaspoon salt
½ teaspoon ground black pepper
1 teaspoon ground cumin
1 teaspoon ground coriander
½ teaspoon ground turmeric
¼ teaspoon ground cardamom
1 teaspoon lemon juice

1. Heat oil in a medium sauté pan or sauce pan and cook the onion until it becomes translucent and starts to color around the edges. Add the diced garlic and cook until the garlic swells and starts to color.

2. Add the tomatoes, tomato paste, salt, and ground black pepper and stir well. Cook covered for 10–15 minutes, stirring often, until the tomatoes soften. Add cumin, coriander, turmeric, cardamom and lemon juice and stir well. Uncover and continue to cook over low heat for about 15 minutes, stirring occasionally, until it reduces a bit. Serve warm as a dipping sauce for kebabs or meats, or allow to cool a bit and serve with breads or other appetizers.

Chili-Vinegar Sauce

This is a great hot and sour sauce that can be used as a condiment to add just a bit of flavor to a kebab or roast meat meal. Alternatively, it can be served as a dipping sauce for breads or appetizers.

6 chili peppers
2 tablespoons unsalted butter
1 tablespoon garlic, peeled and diced
1 cup white vinegar
½ cup tomato paste
1 teaspoon black peppercorns, crushed or ground
1 teaspoon lemon juice
1 small bunch fresh cilantro leaves, chopped (15–20 sprigs)

Heat butter in a sauté pan and sauté garlic until it swells and starts to color around the edges. Stir in the white vinegar and tomato paste and stir well. Bring to a boil and then reduce heat to a simmer. Add crushed pepper, lemon juice, and chopped cilantro and cook for 3–5 minutes. Remove from heat and let cool until needed.

Cilantro Sauce with Lemon and Garlic

This is another sauce that links back to Georgia's **Walnut and Cilantro Sauce (*Garo*)** and has links to Pakistan's **Spicy Cilantro Sauce** as well as Afghanistan's analogous sauce. Like Pakistan's more complex sauce, this one has mustard and fenugreek, but unlike that sauce, this one lacks cumin, yogurt, onions, and *garam masala*, giving this sauce a simpler more elegant flavor. Great with fish and chicken or as a dipping sauce with bread.

8 cloves garlic, peeled
5 hot, dried, red chili peppers
1 tablespoon grated ginger
1 medium bunch fresh cilantro leaves, chopped (25–30 sprigs)
1 tablespoon ground coriander
½ teaspoon turmeric
1 teaspoon black mustard seeds
1 teaspoon fenugreek seeds
1 teaspoon salt
½ cup lemon juice (2–3 lemons)
Water as needed to blend into a smooth paste

In a blender, combine all of the ingredients and blend until you have smooth paste. Pour into a medium saucepan and cook over low to medium heat for 10–12 minutes until garlic and chili peppers are cooked and flavors infused throughout the sauce. Serve hot or at room temperature.

Vindaloo Paste

This is the paste needed to make the wonderful Indian dish of vinegared meat called *vindaloo* after the vinegar that Portuguese traders introduced to western India as they traded along maritime Silk Road routes. Prepare ahead of time and allow to sit for days or weeks before using—it improves with age.

2 teaspoons cumin seeds
6 hot, dried, red chili peppers
1 teaspoon black peppercorns
Seeds from 10 cardamom pods
1 cinnamon stick
1 ½ teaspoons mustard seeds
1 ½ teaspoons fenugreek seeds
5 tablespoons white vinegar
1 teaspoon salt
1 teaspoon brown sugar
3 tablespoons butter

2 medium to large yellow onions
½ teaspoon sugar
4 tablespoons water (more if needed)

1. Grind the cumin seeds, red chili peppers, peppercorns, cardamom seeds, cinnamon, mustard seeds, and fenugreek seeds into a fine powder. Put the ground spices in a bowl. Add the vinegar, salt, and sugar; mix and set aside.

2. Heat the butter in a sauté pan. Add onions and stir to coat with butter. Add sugar and reduce heat to low, stirring only to stop them from burning. Cook slowly to caramelize and sweeten onions, about 15–20 minutes. Remove onions from the oil with a slotted spoon and set aside.

3. When the onions have cooled a bit, put them into a blender or food processor. Add water and puree the onions. Add ground spices and vinegar and blend. This is the *vindaloo* paste. It is best when made a few days to a week ahead of time and allowed to sit in the refrigerator allowing the flavors to combine.

Indian Garam Masala

This is a wonderful pungent mixture of spices that smells both sweet and spicy at the same time. It is used in complex curries to balance the more traditional elements and also as a final garnish to sprinkle over dishes. Quite by accident I once used it on a salad of tomatoes and onions and found the taste to be a delicate alternative to the spicier cumin I thought I was using. My family agreed, and that salad has become a regular visitor to our table.

It is always best to grind closest to the time of use for the best aroma and flavor, but I keep a small amount ground and on hand for ease of use. There are many different recipes for *garam masala*, so feel free try others or experiment around with one of your own.

2 tablespoons cardamom seeds
2 2-inch cinnamon sticks
2 teaspoons cumin seeds
2 teaspoons black peppercorns

2 teaspoons cloves
½ average nutmeg corm

Grind all ingredients in a clean food grinder. Store mixture in a jar with a tight-fitting lid.

Chaat Masala

This is another great subcontinental spice blend that can be used to add flavor to meat or vegetable curries and bhajis or can be used to flavor rice. It can also be mixed with yogurt for a lighter, sourer alternative to a tandoori marinade, is also found on many street food carts in India, and is used as a spice for meats and vegetables. The interesting difference between this and other masalas is the addition of black salt, a garnet-colored mineral that has a sulfurish aftertaste like asafetida, and mango powder to lend a bit of tartness to the mixture.

1 teaspoon ground cumin
1 teaspoon ground coriander
1 teaspoon ground black salt
1 teaspoon ground ginger
½ teaspoon ground black peppercorns
½ teaspoon salt
½ teaspoon red peppers
2 tablespoons dried mango powder

Combine all ingredients. If necessary, use a mortar and pestle to grind out any lumps. Store airtight until ready to use.

Kosgoda beach, Sri Lanka

Sri Lanka

Main spices and flavors: garlic, ginger, black pepper, chili powder, sesame, pandanus, lemongrass, cinnamon, cardamom, cloves, tomato, coconut, turmeric, tamarind, curry leaves, paprika, Maldives fish, mustard, cumin, coriander, asafetida, nutmeg, rosewater, rice wine, white vinegar, fenugreek, fennel

Souring agents: lemons, limes, white vinegar, cider vinegar

The mixed Hindu, Buddhist, Islamic, and Christian society that we know as Sri Lanka today has complex roots as a major trading and merchant center—a link between the Eastern and the Western worlds. As early as 1400 BCE, the Sri Lankans had an active trade with Egypt with the island's precious cinnamon nearly fetching its weight in gold. This trade provided large sums of money for the country's rulers, which was translated into fantastic public works projects including water storage systems, aqueducts, palaces, and even a dedicated hospital. Although the country had rulers from the stable Sinha dynasty at the helm for over two thousand years, they remained receptive to foreign ideas and cultural elements. They adopted Buddhism from India in the third century BCE and became an important part of spreading the doctrine along trade routes to Southeast Asia.

Ships from Persia, Arabia, the Malay Peninsula, and Indonesian archipelago regularly visited Sri Lanka as a trading stop along the sea routes of the

Great Silk Road, and eventually many of these merchants established settlements on the island. These settlements brought these foreign cultures into regular contact with that of the native Sri Lankans, who adopted many of their practices.

European domination of the island began slowly at first in the sixteenth century with the arrival of the Portuguese colonial mission in 1505. In the seventeenth century, the Dutch arrived and were soon followed by the British East India Company, which established control over the island and pushed the indigenous civilization into the interior of the country. British control was achieved in the early nineteenth century and persisted until the mid-twentieth century, when the country gained its independence.

All of these foreign contacts have influenced what we now know as Sri Lankan cuisine. Although it shares a great deal of its cuisine with India, it has adopted a large number of Southeast Asian elements that are not commonly used outside of the predominantly Tamil areas of the mainland, including lemongrass, roasted rice, pandanus, and curry leaves. Interestingly, the herb cilantro is not as widely used as in the subcontinent, although coriander seeds from the same plant have been adopted. Western additions to the Sri Lankan tradition include beets, European roasted meats, sweets, and the liberal use of white vinegar.

Sri Lankan curry powder, roasted or unroasted, is a complex mixture that differs significantly from most subcontinental curry powders with the addition of cinnamon, cloves, pandanus leaf, and ground rice as part of the blend. This curry powder along with the use of the island's plentiful coconuts help give Sri Lankan curries their distinct taste.

Meat Dishes

Meat in Sri Lanka is usually served as a curry, as are most of the dishes offered here. If they are not curried, they are baked with a thick sauce of curried vegetables, as in the recipe for **Fish with Tamarind and Oranges**. Although the curries are spiced very differently from each other, shared elements in most dishes include: garlic; black pepper; coconut milk, cream, or flakes; and lime juice. Along with the island's distinct curry powder, these ingredients create the Sri Lankan taste.

Curried Beef with Cinnamon and Lemongrass

Prepare yourself for a truly unusual curried treat! This is a remarkable blend of spicy, sour, and hot seasonings that is moderated by sweeter flavors such as pandanus, cinnamon, cloves, and cardamom. Then, this combination is blanketed in a delicious coconut sauce. A word of warning: it is a fiery dish as written. If you have a more sensitive palate, decrease the chili powder and ground black pepper for a more moderate dish. Excellent with **Sri Lankan Coconut Rice**.

1 pound stew beef cut into bite-size pieces

Marinade
¼ cup white vinegar
3 teaspoons garlic, peeled and diced
1 tablespoon grated ginger
2 teaspoons salt
1 tablespoon ground black pepper
1 tablespoon **Sri Lankan Roasted Curry Powder**
1 teaspoon chili powder (heaping for a hot curry and level or less for a more moderate one)

Stir Fry
3 tablespoons light sesame oil
5 curry leaves, finely diced
2 pandanus leaves, very finely diced
2 lemongrass stalks, very finely diced
1 medium onion, peeled, sliced, and separated into crescents
1 teaspoon ground cinnamon
Seeds from 10 cardamom pods, crushed
3 whole cloves, crushed
2 tablespoons tomato paste
1 ½ cups coconut milk

1. In a large bowl, combine vinegar, crushed garlic, ginger, salt, black pepper, roasted curry powder, and red chili powder and mix well. Add the beef cubes and marinate for 2–3 hours at room temperature.

2. Heat the oil in a wok and stir fry curry, pandanus leaves, and lemongrass for 1 minute. Then add onions and stir fry 2–3 minutes until they start to soften and color. Add the beef and its marinade and stir fry until the meat starts to become firm and opaque, about 3–5 minutes. Then cover and cook for 3–5 minutes, stirring occasionally.

3. Uncover and add cinnamon, cardamom, and cloves and stir until well mixed. Add coconut milk and tomato paste and bring to a boil. Then cover and cook over low heat for 10–15 minutes until beef is done.

Fish with Tamarind and Oranges

Like many Sri Lankan fish recipes, this one calls on cooks to use *goraka* as a souring agent. As a whole fruit (or even in pieces), this is all but unavailable in the West, so I've substituted tamarind concentrate and orange zest instead. Indian tamarind is similar to *goraka* (which is also known as Malabar tamarind), but it is stronger and more robust in flavor and lacks the citrus nip that the *goraka* has—hence the orange zest. Regardless of the substitution, this is a delicious recipe with a range of flavors from sour to spicy that I hope you enjoy.

1 pound meaty white fish, such as sea bass (or rockfish), trout, or cod, cut into pieces or filets
1 ½ teaspoons salt
1 ½ teaspoons ground black pepper
½ teaspoon chili powder
¼ teaspoon ground turmeric
½ teaspoon **Roasted Sri Lankan Curry Powder**
2 tablespoons light sesame oil
1 ½ teaspoons tamarind concentrate
1 sprig curry leaves, diced
1–2 leaves pandanus, very finely diced
2 teaspoons ground cinnamon
1 teaspoon garlic, peeled and diced
½ cup water or chicken stock
2 teaspoons sugar
Zest from 1 orange, finely diced

1. Season both sides of the fish with salt, pepper, chili powder, turmeric, and Roasted Sri Lankan Curry Powder until all the pieces are well coated. Set aside in a greased or sprayed baking pan for 1 hour.

2. Heat oil in a small sauté pan and when hot, add the tamarind concentrate and mix well until dissolved. Add the curry leaves, pandanus, cinnamon, and garlic and cook to warm the spices, 2–3 minutes. Add water, chicken stock, sugar, and orange zest and stir well to blend.

3. When sauce is warm, pour over the fish in the casserole; cover and bake in preheated oven for 15–20 minutes. Uncover and bake another 15–20 minutes or until sauce has evaporated and fish is tender and well cooked.

Curried Scallops with Coconut and Lime

In this lovely dish, the sweetness of the red pepper along with the coconut milk and the sugar offset the crushed red peppers, lemongrass, and lime to bring out the very best in the scallops. If you like the sauce, you can also use it for shrimp, prawns, or even as a sauce for whole baked fish.

1 pound sea or bay scallops, rinsed and left whole
2 tablespoons light sesame oil
1 medium onion, peeled and diced
1 teaspoon garlic, peeled and diced
1 red bell pepper, cored and thinly sliced
2 cups coconut milk
1 teaspoon ground turmeric
1 teaspoon salt
½ teaspoon ground black pepper
2 teaspoons sugar
1 teaspoon **Roasted Sri Lankan Curry Powder**
1 teaspoon crushed red pepper
1 tablespoon lime juice

1. Heat oil in a large sauté pan or wok and when the oil is hot, add the scallops and stir fry over high heat for 2–3 minutes until they start to color. Remove quickly and set aside. Add the onions and sauté them until they start to soften and take on color. Then add the garlic

and sauté it until it swells and begins to color. Add the peppers and sauté them briefly, stirring constantly, for 2–3 minutes. Then add the coconut milk and cook to warm the liquid.

2. When the coconut milk is hot, add the turmeric, salt, and pepper and sugar and stir. Then add the curry powder and crushed red pepper and cook for 5–8 minutes to warm the spices and thicken the sauce a bit. When the curry has reached a good consistency, add the scallops and cook another 2–3 minutes to warm them and serve immediately with rice.

Chicken with Ginger and Peppers

If red means hot, then this is what this chicken is! But it is also light and spicy because of the large amount of ginger it boasts. Another plus is that it is very easy to prepare and takes all of about 15 minutes from slicing the meat to serving over piping hot rice or on warm naan.

3–4 chicken breasts cut into bite-size pieces
1 ½ teaspoons salt
1 ½ teaspoons ground black pepper
1 teaspoon sweet paprika
Juice of 1 lime
3–4 tablespoons light sesame oil
2 medium onions
8 curry leaves, crumbled or diced
3 teaspoons garlic, peeled and diced
2 tablespoons grated ginger
½ cup chicken stock
½ cup water
1–2 teaspoons chili powder
2 teaspoons granulated sugar

1. Sprinkle ½ teaspoon each of salt, pepper, and paprika over the chicken pieces. Add lime juice and stir well to evenly coat all of the pieces with the spices. Set aside for at least 1 hour.

2. Heat oil in a sauté pan or wok and when hot, add the onion and sauté until the onion softens and starts to color. Add the curry leaves, garlic, and ginger and sauté until the garlic swells and starts to color as well. Add chicken stock and water and cook to warm.

3. Add remaining salt, pepper, and paprika along with the chili powder and stir well. Stir marinating chicken pieces and add them as well. Bring back to a near boil and cook uncovered 5–8 minutes or until chicken is done. Just before serving, stir in the sugar and mix well. Cook another minute or two and serve.

Shrimp and Pineapple Curry

Smoky, sweet, sour, and just a bit hot, this dish is a taste sensation! It blends some of the best of Sri Lanka's coastal offerings and blends them to perfection before giving them the bite of Maldives fish, mustard seeds, and chili peppers. This is a dish that starts out sour and turns sweet as the pineapple bursts in your mouth. Great with plain or a simple spiced rice.

1 pound shrimp, peeled, deveined, and rinsed
3 tablespoons light sesame oil (*gingelly*)
1 small onion, peeled, sliced, and separated into crescents
4 curry leaves
2 pandanus leaves, finely diced
2 teaspoons garlic, peeled and diced
2 tablespoons grated ginger
4 hot Thai chili peppers, diced
1 teaspoon Maldives fish, crushed
½ cup water
2 teaspoons unroasted curry powder
¼ teaspoon ground turmeric
1 teaspoon salt
½ teaspoon ground black mustard seeds
1 ½ cups coconut milk
1 teaspoon ground cinnamon
½ teaspoon chili powder (optional)
3 cups pineapple cut into bite-size pieces
1 tablespoon lime juice
2–3 tablespoons sugar

1. In a blender combine the onion, curry leaves, pandanus, garlic, ginger, chili peppers, and Maldives fish with ¼ cup of water (use the rest of the water if needed to make a paste) and blend until you have a smooth paste.

2. Heat oil in a sauté pan or wok and when hot, add the paste from the blender and cook over medium heat for 5–8 minutes, stirring constantly. Add curry powder, turmeric, salt, and mustard seeds and stir well. Cook to warm the spices, 2–3 minutes. Add coconut milk and cinnamon and cook 2–3 minutes.

3. Add pineapple and cook 3–5 minutes to coat the pineapple with the spices and soften the fruit. Add lime juice and sugar and when you have the balance of flavors right, add the shrimp and stir well. Cook 3–5 minutes or until the shrimp have curled and colored, but do not overcook. Serve with rice.

Vegetable Dishes and Salads

Sri Lanka has a rich tradition of curried vegetables and flavorful salads that should satisfy even the most demanding of diners, whether omnivores or vegetarians. Recipes offered here include a **Curried Okra with Sweet Lime and Cinnamon** and a **Butternut Squash in Coconut Cream** on the milder side of taste, and the spicy **Sri Lankan Potato Curry** for the more bold. In addition to currying vegetables, the Sri Lankans sometimes cook them tandoori style, and one such recipe for **Tandoori Cauliflower** is included in these pages. The two salads that I've included are the delicious **Cucumber, Black Pepper, and Lime Salad** and the **Spicy Beet Salad**, which is both spicy and flavorful, as well as simply interesting to see how the Sri Lankans have made that foreign vegetable distinctly their own.

Curried Eggplant in a Ginger-Garlic Sauce

This curry is sour, sweet, and hot due to its curry leaves, vinegar, coconut milk, sugar, and ground chili peppers. Blended together, these flavors make this dish quintessentially Sri Lankan, but it also complements a wide variety of other cuisines as well. Particularly good with **Curried Scallops with Coconut and Lime**.

1 medium western eggplant, sliced crosswise
2 tablespoons oil

I medium onion, finely chopped
½ teaspoon turmeric powder
I teaspoon cumin powder
I teaspoon coriander powder
I teaspoon whole mustard seeds, ground
2 teaspoons garlic, peeled and diced
I tablespoon grated ginger
½ cup coconut milk
I teaspoon chopped chili peppers
10 curry leaves, crushed
I tablespoon cider vinegar
I teaspoon salt
2 teaspoons sugar

1. Preheat oven to 375°. Place sliced eggplant on an oiled or sprayed baking sheet and when the oven is hot, bake for 20–25 minutes. Remove from oven, cool, and slice into quarters or eighths, depending on the size of the slice.

2. Heat oil in a medium sauté pan and sauté onion until it softens and starts to color. Add the turmeric, cumin, coriander, and mustard and stir for a couple of seconds. Add the garlic, ginger, coconut milk, chilies, and curry leaves.

3. Add the vinegar, salt, and sugar and bring slowly to a boil. Add the eggplant pieces, stir, and simmer on a low heat for 5 minutes until the eggplant is warmed.

Tandoori Cauliflower

This is a slightly complex but delicious way to prepare cauliflower that summons up images of a tandoori oven when eaten, even though it is sautéed instead of baked. The marinade is what earns the dish its name, because the spices and yogurt are essentially what is used to flavor tandoori meats that are later slow-roasted in a super-hot clay oven. Here, the lemon and spices blend nicely with the delicate flavor of cauliflower to make this a wonderful dish for any table.

I medium cauliflower
3 cups water
I tablespoon lemon juice
I teaspoon turmeric

Marinade
I cup yogurt
I ½ tablespoons mustard oil
I tablespoon lemon juice
3 teaspoons grated ginger
3 teaspoons garlic, peeled and diced
I teaspoon *garam masala* (use either Indian or Pakistani recipes offered here)
I teaspoon chili powder
½ teaspoon salt
½ teaspoon ground cumin

1. Bring to a boil in a large saucepan water, lemon juice, and turmeric. Break or cut cauliflower into large florets and add to the boiling water. Cook covered for 5 minutes and uncovered for 5 minutes. Then, remove from heat, drain, and set aside. The cauliflower should be parboiled and a lovely shade of yellow.

2. In a large bowl, combine yogurt, mustard oil, lemon juice, garlic, ginger, *garam masala*, chili powder, and salt, and mix well. Add in drained cauliflower and toss gently so cauliflower doesn't break apart too much. Marinate for 2–3 hours at room temperature.

3. Add I tablespoon of light sesame oil to a large sauté pan or wok and turn the cauliflower along with its marinade into the wok. Cook for 2–3 minutes turning occasionally. Finish with a sprinkling of ground cumin and serve.

Cucumber, Black Pepper, and Lime Salad

This cooling salad blends the flavors of cucumbers, green bell peppers, lime, and black pepper with great results! Although the two chili peppers lend a bit of heat, the salad still works to cool and clear the palate after a spicy meal. Refrigerate *all* ingredients before preparing, and then serve immediately for best flavor.

I medium Western cucumber, peeled, seeded, and chopped
I small onion, peeled and diced
I small green bell pepper, very finely diced
2 hot, dried, red chili peppers, diced

1 teaspoon ground black pepper
1 teaspoon salt
¼ teaspoon sugar
1–2 tablespoons lime juice

Combine all ingredients in a serving bowl and stir well. Serve immediately for best flavor.

Butternut Squash in a Coconut Cream Sauce

This wonderful dish may seem similar to the Pakistani coconut-squash dish offered in a previous chapter, but it is more highly spiced and not so sweet as the one enjoyed in Pakistan. Makes an excellent addition to either a vegetarian or an omnivore table.

1 pound pumpkin or butternut squash
2 tablespoons dry coconut flakes
½ medium onion, peeled and roughly chopped
2 teaspoons garlic, peeled and roughly chopped
1 ¼ cups water
2 tablespoons light sesame oil
¼ teaspoon black mustard seeds
5 curry leaves, crumbled or diced
1 teaspoon ground coriander
½ teaspoon ground cumin
¼ teaspoon ground turmeric
¼ cup coconut cream
1 teaspoon salt
¼ teaspoon ground black pepper

1. In a medium sauté pan, dry roast dry coconut until it is golden, stirring constantly. When done, transfer coconut to a blender and combine it with the onion, garlic, and ¼ cup of the water and blend it until you have a smooth paste.

2. In a medium-sized pan, heat the oil, add the mustard seeds, and cook covered on a low heat until the seeds "pop." Add the curry leaves, coriander, cumin, and turmeric and sauté for 1–2 minutes to warm the spices.

3. Add the remaining water and the coconut cream along with the salt and pepper and stir well. When the sauce has heated, add the

pumpkin or squash and cook covered over medium low or low heat for 12–15 minutes, stirring constantly or until pumpkin or squash becomes tender.

Curried Okra with Sweet Lime and Cinnamon

Another wonderful curry that performs a delicate balancing act between hot, sour, and sweet! This time, the main ingredient is okra, a much-loved vegetable all across the subcontinent. The flavor of sweet limes and cinnamon work with the curry powder and mustard to bring out the best in the vegetable. A blast of sugar and a pinch of asafetida just at the end take this dish to new heights that you're sure to love!

1 pound okra, sliced crosswise
4 tablespoons butter or ghee
1 small onion, peeled, sliced, and separated into crescents
2 teaspoons mustard seeds, crushed or ground
2 hot, dried, red chili peppers, diced
¼ cup water or vegetable broth
1 teaspoon **Roasted Sri Lankan Curry Powder**
1 teaspoon turmeric
½ teaspoon cinnamon
1 teaspoon salt
¼ teaspoon ground black pepper
1 tablespoon sugar
1 tablespoon lime juice
¼ teaspoon asafetida

1. Heat butter or ghee in a medium to large sauté pan. When it is hot, add the sliced onion and sauté until the onion softens and starts to color. Then add the mustard seeds and chili peppers and mix well. Add the water or broth and when that is warm, stir in the curry powder, turmeric, cinnamon, salt, and pepper and stir well. Cook 3–5 minutes to warm the spices.

2. Then add the lime juice, sugar, and asafetida and stir well once again. Add the sliced okra and fold in. Cook covered for 10–15 minutes, stirring occasionally, until the okra becomes tender. Serve immediately.

Spicy Beet Salad

This is a nice example of Sri Lankans taking to an introduced foreign food and adopting it and making it their own. The black pepper and lime juice along with the hint of red pepper make them uniquely Sri Lankan. The salad is best served slightly chilled, so you will need to refrigerate *all* ingredients before preparing.

3–4 medium beets, baked until tender, peeled, and chopped
1 medium tomato
1 small onion, peeled and diced
2 red, hot, dried chili peppers
1 ½ teaspoons ground black pepper
1 teaspoon salt
2 tablespoons lime juice

1. Preheat oven to 375°. Wrap the beets in aluminum foil and bake them in the preheated oven for about 1 hour or until they give a bit when pressed with your finger. When cooked, remove from oven, and cool completely.

2. Slice beets into strips about 2 inches long and combine in a bowl with the tomatoes, onion, chili peppers, black pepper, salt, and lime juice. Stir well and serve immediately.

Sri Lankan Potato Curry

This is a unique and wonderful way to curry potatoes that is spicy, hot, and richly delicious and will keep diners coming back for more. The natural spiciness of the mustard, chili peppers, and lemongrass is tempered by the coconut milk, turmeric, and roasted curry powder for delicious results.

4 medium potatoes, parboiled or incompletely cooked in a microwave, cooled and chopped
2 tablespoons mustard oil
1 teaspoon black mustard seeds
1 onion, peeled, sliced, and separated into crescents
1 green bell pepper, cored and diced
1 stalk lemongrass, cut crosswise and then very finely diced
4 hot, dried, red chili peppers

1 cup coconut milk
1 teaspoon salt
½ teaspoon ground black pepper
2 teaspoons **Roasted Sri Lankan Curry Powder**
1 teaspoon ground turmeric

1. Heat oil in a medium sauté pan or wok and when hot, sauté onion and mustard seeds until the onion softens and starts to color. Add the green bell pepper, diced lemongrass, and chili peppers and sauté another 5–8 minutes or until the bell pepper softens and becomes tender.

2. Add coconut milk and cook to warm. When hot, add salt, pepper, curry powder, and turmeric and stir well. When the mixture approaches a boil, add potatoes and stir well. Cook uncovered for 5 minutes or until the potatoes are hot and tender.

Rice and Grain Dishes, Breads

Three great rice dishes and a wonderful flatbread are included in the next section to introduce you to the grains and breads of Sri Lanka. The rice dishes use a lot of coconut, and pandanus leaves, and are often flavored with a combination of black pepper and cardamom—sometimes accented by other spices, and sometimes not. One of the rice dishes, **Fried Rice with Carrots and Leeks**, skips the coconut and adds a lot of vegetables instead. The bread offered is one of the most versatile on all of the subcontinent—a moist flatbread that goes with everything, called *roti*.

Sri Lankan Coconut Rice

This rice is a sweet coconut treat that works well as a base for so many hot and spicy curries and stews from the Indian subcontinent. Try with **Curried Beef with Cinnamon and Lemongrass** or **Fish with Tamarind and Oranges** for a wonderful meal.

2 tablespoons butter
1 medium onion, finely chopped

1 cup basmati rice, washed and drained
1 cup water
1 ½ cups coconut milk
1 teaspoon salt
½ cup coconut flakes, dry roasted

1. Heat a sauté pan over medium heat and dry fry the coconut flakes until they become golden. When done, remove from the heat and set aside. Then in the same pan, heat the butter over moderate heat and sauté the onion until it becomes translucent.

2. Add the washed and drained rice and the coconut flakes and cook for 2–3 minutes. Add the water, coconut milk, and salt and bring to a boil. Then cook covered for 15–20 minutes over low heat or until the rice has absorbed the liquid and has become tender.

Rice with Cardamom and Coconut

This flavorful rice is so delicious all by itself that it's almost a shame to cover it all up with curries as wonderful as they may be. Getting its spice from a mixture of cracked black pepper, cardamom, cloves, and coconut, this rice goes well with other South Asian dishes but is also an excellent dish to serve with a western Asian kebab or a European cutlet for a deliciously globalized plate.

1 cup uncooked basmati rice
4 tablespoons ghee or butter
2 medium onions, peeled, sliced, and separated into crescents
2 pandanus leaves, diced very finely
6 cloves, crushed
20 black peppercorns, crushed or cracked
Seeds from 12 cardamom pods, crushed or cracked
1 ½ teaspoons ground turmeric
1 teaspoon salt
2 ½ cups coconut milk

1. Heat butter in a sauté pan and sauté onions until they soften and start to color. Add the diced pandanus leaves and sauté another 3–5 minutes, stirring occasionally, or until the pandanus starts to become tender instead of fibrous.

2. Crush cloves, peppercorns, and cardamom seeds and add to the onions. Then add turmeric and salt and stir well. Cook 5–8 minutes to soften the cracked spices, then add the rice and stir it into the spices. Let cook another 3–5 minutes to steam the rice.

3. Add coconut milk and stir well. Bring back to a near boil and then reduce heat and cook covered for about 20 minutes or until the rice has become tender and tasty. Let sit covered for 5–10 minutes before serving.

Fried Rice with Carrots and Leeks

Carrots, leeks, green pepper, and peas lend their flavors to this fried rice that also has cardamom, curry leaves, and cumin and lots of black pepper. It's a great rice that goes with almost any dish or it can even be a light meal all on its own.

2 cups cooked basmati rice
2 tablespoons butter or ghee
1 medium onion, peeled and finely diced
6 curry leaves, diced
3 inches pandanus, very finely diced
1 teaspoon salt
1 teaspoon ground black pepper
Seeds from 10 cardamom pods, crushed
½ teaspoon ground cumin
⅓ cup water or broth
2 carrots, peeled and grated
2 leeks, shredded
1 green pepper, cored, cleaned, and diced
¼ cup peas

1. In a large pan, heat the ghee. Add the onions, the curry leaves, and the pandanus and fry until the onions are lightly browned. Add salt, pepper, cardamom, and cumin and mix well. Add the water or broth and cook until warm.

2. Add the carrots, leeks, pepper, and peas. Stir until well mixed. Cover and cook over low heat for 10 minutes, stirring often.

3. Fluff up the rice with a fork and put a little at a time into the vegetables,

stirring after each addition to ensure that the dish is well mixed. Remove from heat, put on a platter, and serve hot.

Roti

This is another great subcontinental flatbread to serve with meals or to have as a snack with dips. Unlike a lot of flatbreads, it tends to stay moist and fluffy, largely because of all the vegetable oil in the dough. Its moistness means that it can be prepared well before meals and be reheated just before dinner and still taste fresh.

2 cups all-purpose flour
1 teaspoon salt
1–2 cups warm water
4 tablespoons vegetable oil, plus 2 tablespoons for frying

1. In a mixing bowl, sift together the flour and salt. Add vegetable oil and warm water ½ cup at a time and mix well. Add water and mix until the dough does not stick to your hands. Knead for 3–5 minutes and separate dough into four balls.

2. Cover the bowl and let it stand for 2–3 hours. Then, take each ball of flour and flatten it to a thin circle about 6–8 inches across. Add oil to griddle or pan and heat. Place dough into pan and fry for a minute or two on each side, turning the bread to ensure even cooking on both sides.

Cinnamon Sticks

Desserts and Beverages

A couple of tropical puddings and custards await you in this section along with a wonderful cake recipe and some Sri Lankan takes on subcontinental sweets.

Sweet Coconut-Nutmeg Custard (Watalappan)

This delicious custard is a standard amongst Sri Lankan desserts – its delicate flavors combining in new ways to conjure up a glimpse of the island paradise.

1 cup *jaggery* or sugar
¼ cup water
⅓ cup creamed coconut
5 eggs, beaten
1 teaspoon grated fresh nutmeg
Seeds from 3 green cardamom pods, crushed
¼ cup slivered almonds or cashews*

1. Heat water in a medium saucepan and when hot, add *jaggery* or sugar and stir until dissolved. Add the creamed coconut and mix well as you bring it to a boil. When the mixture boils, remove from heat and let cool.

2. When the *jaggery* mixture cools, stir well and add to the beaten eggs. Add the grated nutmeg and crushed cardamom. Pour into ovenproof bowls or dishes and steam in a covered pan of simmering water for 20 minutes.

3. About three-quarters of the way through the steaming process, add the slivered nuts and continue steaming until done.

*For a variation, add raisins with or without the nuts.

Cashew-Cardamom Sweets

Here is a subcontinental sweet made with a potato base and flavored with rosewater and cardamom.

1 ½ cups sugar
1 ½ cups milk
1 can sweetened condensed milk
½ cup butter
1 cup potato, peeled, parboiled, and mashed
1 cup finely diced cashew nuts
2 tablespoons rosewater
1 teaspoon ground cardamom

1. In a medium or large saucepan, combine sugar, milk, condensed milk, and butter and cook over medium heat until the mixture evaporates a bit and begins to harden. It will be done when it is almost doughy.

2. Remove from heat, add mashed potato, and mix until well integrated. Return to the heat and cook until the mixture begins to harden once again.

3. Remove from heat, stir in nuts, rosewater, and cardamom and mix well. Pour or spoon into a greased or sprayed dish or baking pan and press to smooth the surface. Let cool and cut into diamonds or squares.

Spiced Coconut Cake

In Sri Lanka, the moist, rich flesh of coconuts fresh from the tree is grated and then ground finely on a stone slab. Mixed with sugar and flour and flavored with a mix of cardamom, cloves, and cinnamon with a touch of rosewater, this cake makes a great dessert after a varied, multicourse subcontinental meal.

3 cups dried, grated coconut[*]
3 cups water
4 eggs, separated
1 ¾ cups sugar
2 cups rice flour
1 cup white flour
2 teaspoons baking powder
½ teaspoon ground cardamom
¼ teaspoon ground cloves
¼ teaspoon ground cinnamon
1 tablespoon rosewater
½–⅔ cup cashew nuts, chopped

1. Preheat oven to 325°. In a blender, combine dried coconut and water and blend until coconut is finely ground. If it is easier, grind the coconut in two batches. Beat egg yolks until they froth and become lighter in color. Then add the coconut mixture and 1 ½ cups sugar until light and creamy.

2. Sift the flours with baking powder and ground spices and in parts, stir into the mixture with the rosewater and nuts. Mix until well blended.

3. Beat egg whites until stiff peaks form, add remaining ¼ cup sugar, and beat again until thick. Fold into coconut mixture and blend well. Grease or spray 2 loaf pans and pour cake mix into prepared pans and bake for 1 ¼–1 ½ hours or until the cake becomes golden on top and a toothpick inserted in the center comes out clean.

4. When done, cool for a while and turn the cake out of the pan and let cool completely before serving.

[*]Can also be made with fresh coconut if you omit the water and the blender stage.

Sweet Split-Pea Pudding

Puddings on the subcontinent are made from many ingredients other than rice, such as beans, peas, carrots, and noodles. Here's one made from split peas that is sweet and delicious with the light flavors of pandanus flower essence—which offers a vanilla-like flavor—coconut, and cashews.

½ cup *Bengal gram*
¾ cup *mung dal*
3 cups milk
I cup water
I tablespoons butter or ghee
I tablespoon chopped cashews
I tablespoon brown or golden raisins
½ cup *jaggery*, soaked, drained, and broken up
2 tablespoons sugar
3 tablespoons coconut, grated

1. Soak *dal* for at least I hour then cook them in a medium covered saucepan with 2 cups of the milk and water for at least 30 minutes, or until the two are tender and well cooked.

2. In a medium sauté pan, heat the butter or ghee and sauté the cashews and raisins until the cashews are golden brown. Mix in the *jaggery* along with fried cashews, raisins, sugar, and remaining milk and bring to a boil then reduce heat and stir into the cooked *dal*. Bring back to a boil and then reduce heat and simmer the mixture to thicken it.

3. When done, remove from the heat and pour into a serving bowl or individual dishes to cool. Just before serving, top with the grated coconut and serve.

Sweet Coconut-Cardamom Balls

After tasting these sweet and spicy treats, you'll want more and more of their coconut-cardamom flavor – so make several batches.

I cup rice flour
½ cup dairy milk
I ½ cups water

2 tablespoons butter or ghee
¼ teaspoon salt
2 tablespoons light sesame or vegetable oil
2 cups fresh coconut, grated*
½ cup *jaggery*, dissolved and drained
½ teaspoon ground cardamom

Coating (optional)
½ cup ground almonds
¼ cup dissolved *jaggery* or sugar

1. In a saucepan over low heat, combine the rice flour with the milk, water, butter or ghee, and salt and stir well until completely blended. Keep cooking over low heat until all of the lumps are removed and the mixture forms a doughy consistency. When done, remove from heat and set aside to cool. When cooled, add half of the oil and blend until the dough softens. Roll into balls about the size of golf balls and set aside.

2. To make the filling, combine in a separate saucepan the grated coconut with the other half of the oil, the *jiggery*, and the ground cardamom. Heat over low heat for 6–8 minutes, mixing often to ensure the mixture doesn't burn. After this time, the oil from the coconut should start to hold the mixture together and it should hold together when pinched. Remove from heat and let cool. When the coconut mixture is cool enough to handle, roll it into balls between half and three-quarters the size of the dough balls.

3. With your fingers, flatten the dough balls until they are between ⅛ inch and ¼ inch thick, then form them into small bowls. Place a filling ball inside each of the dough bowls and bring the sides of the dough bowl up and seal them to completely conceal the filling.

4. Steam the balls in a double boiler fitted with a steamer or in a bamboo steamer for about 10-15 minutes or until firm. When done, remove from steamer and, if desired, roll lightly in ground almond and *jaggery* mixture. Cool to room temperature and serve.

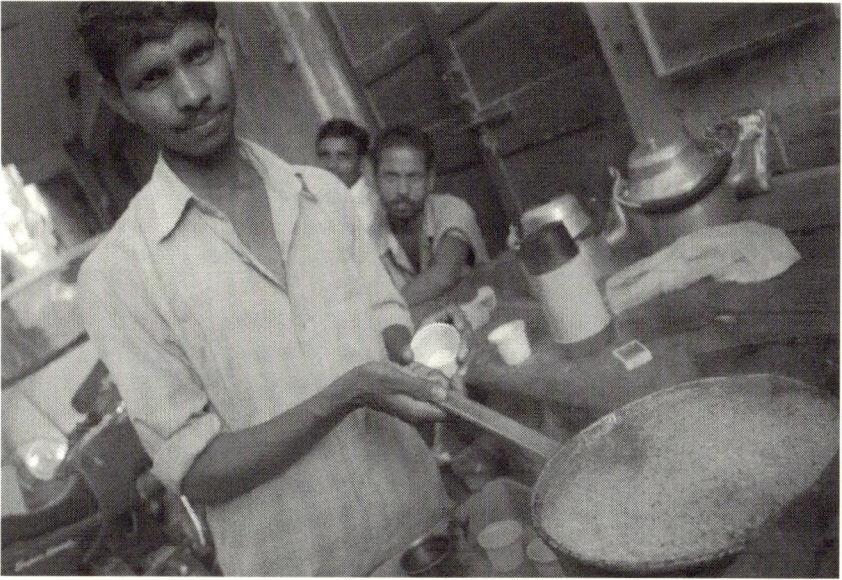

Man Serving Tea

Appetizers and Condiments

"Whether you prepare these recipes as part of a large, multicourse meal, a light meal or as just a snack, these appetizers will bring an authentic taste of Sri Lanka to your table."

Pancakes Stuffed with Chicken or Fish

These little pancakes are a cross between a stuffed crepe and a samosa. Visually, they resemble crepes, but one bite reveals the samosa-like, spicy potato-and-meat stuffing. Serve as an appetizer, snack, or have several as part of a light meal.

Pancakes
1 cup flour
2 cups milk (coconut or dairy)
1 egg
1 teaspoon salt
Oil for frying

323

Filling
¼ cup butter
2 medium onions, peeled and diced
2–3 tablespoons roasted curry powder
1–2 teaspoons chili powder
1 teaspoon salt
1 ½ cups boneless chicken or fish, chopped
2 medium-large potatoes, peeled, parboiled, and chopped

Frying (optional)
⅓ cup oil
2 eggs, beaten

1. Prepare the batter for the pancakes by blending the ingredients in a mixing bowl and whisking until the batter is smooth. When done, set aside and prepare pancake stuffing.

2. Melt butter in a medium to large sauté pan and when hot, add the onions and cook over low to medium heat until they become translucent and start to color. Add the curry powder, chili powder, and salt and mix well. Add the fish or chicken and stir in until well blended. Cook until the meat becomes opaque and firm.

3. Add chopped potatoes and stir, lifting rather than stirring so you won't crush the potatoes too much. If necessary, add just a bit of chicken or vegetable broth to moisten the mix. Bear in mind, however, that it should be kind of dry to avoid making soggy pancakes. When done, remove from the heat and set aside.

4. Heat oil in a sauté pan and pour in a thin layer of batter to cover the bottom of the pan. Cook on low heat for a minute or two and turn out onto a plate. Add a few tablespoons of filling in the middle of the pancake, tuck in the sides of the pancake to make parallel edges and roll the pancake up to form a roll. Continue making the pancakes and the rolls from them. Do not allow the pancakes to cool or stand before adding the stuffing as this makes the pancake less malleable.

5. Finally, if desired, dip each roll into beaten egg and fry lightly until a medium brown color.

Spiced Chickpeas in Coconut Milk

This is a great spicy appetizer that makes diners want more to eat. It's a flavorful blend of earthy chickpeas, cumin, mustard, and garlic all wrapped up in a wisp of a coconut-turmeric sauce. Served with bread and a selection of chutneys or sambals, it's a great way to start a meal.

3 tablespoons unsalted butter
1 medium onion, peeled and finely diced
2 teaspoons garlic, peeled and diced
3 Thai chili peppers, finely diced
1 teaspoon mustard seeds
½ teaspoon turmeric
1 teaspoon salt
1 teaspoon ground black pepper
1 teaspoon chili powder
2 cups chickpeas, cooked and drained
2 small potatoes, cooked, cooled, and cubed
1 cup coconut milk
1 teaspoon cumin seeds, dry roasted

1. In a medium saucepan, heat the butter and sauté the onions until they start to become translucent and color. Add garlic and cook 3–5 minutes until it starts to swell and color. Add chili peppers, mustard seeds, turmeric, salt, pepper, and chili powder and mix well to blend the ingredients.

2. Add the chickpeas and potatoes to the pan and mix well, lifting instead of stirring so as not to mash the potatoes. Cook for a few minutes to warm the peas and potatoes and then add the coconut milk. Bring to a boil, then reduce heat, add the cumin seeds, and cook for 6–8 minutes. When done, remove from the heat and serve with bread and rice.

Coconut Sambal

The title of the recipe alone reveals the importance of Sri Lanka in the maritime Silk Road trade. Yes, the Sri Lankans enjoy sambals just as much as their Malay and Indonesian trading partners who introduced them do. This is a tasty sambal that tastes best fresh out of the mortar and pestle.

2 cups fresh coconut, scraped and chopped*
2 medium shallots, peeled and sliced
2 green or red Thai chili peppers, sliced
1 teaspoon garlic, peeled and diced
1 teaspoon red chili powder
1 teaspoon salt
1 teaspoon Maldives fish, chopped
Juice from 1 lime and chopped pulp

1. In a food processor or mortar and pestle, combine all of the ingredients except the coconut. Grind or chop until all ingredients are blended but still have their form.

2. Add the coconut and continue to grind until the coconut turns evenly red and all ingredients are well mixed. (If using a food processor, however, don't overblend; sambal is best a bit chunky.)

*This sambal can be made with dried coconut if it is soaked in warm water for at least ½ hour before preparation. It's better fresh, though, so try to get a fresh coconut if you can.

Spicy Onion Sambal

"This delicious sambal is easy to make and uses African tamarind combined with South Asian cardamom and cinnamon along with generous amounts of ginger and garlic. A flavorful Silk Road treat to offer your guests!"

2 large onions peeled and finely diced
3 tablespoons light sesame or vegetable oil
1 teaspoon tamarind concentrate
1 tablespoon sugar
2 tablespoons ginger, peeled and grated
1 tablespoon garlic, peeled and crushed
1 tablespoon crushed red chili peppers
3 teaspoons Maldives fish, soaked and chopped
Seeds from 5–6 cardamom pods, crushed
3–4 cloves, crushed
6 curry leaves, diced
2 3-inch pieces of pandanus, very finely diced
1 1-inch piece of cinnamon, crushed
1–2 teaspoons salt

1. Heat the oil in a medium sauté pan and sauté the onions until they start to become translucent and color. Add the tamarind concentrate and stir until mixed into the onions. Add sugar and mix well until dissolved. Continue to cook for 3–5 minutes. Then, remove from heat and set aside.

2. In a food processor, combine the rest of the ingredients and pulse until all ingredients are well blended but still have their form. Add the onion mixture and pulse just one or two more times, or mix together in a bowl and serve.

Eggplant Dip with Garlic and Chilies

This is Sri Lanka's baba ghanoush and clearly shows the western Asian/ Levant legacy in their cuisine. It is a great dip for breads as an appetizer to a main meal. This is a very flexible recipe and varies widely between cooks and families and even from meal to meal, depending on the mood of the chef. Without the yogurt, this recipe makes a fine sambal as well.

1 medium Western eggplant, halved and baked until soft
1 medium onion, peeled and finely diced
2 tablespoons garlic, peeled and diced
2 teaspoons salt
½ teaspoon ground black pepper
2 Thai green chili peppers, diced
1 tablespoon lime juice
¼ cup yogurt (or more if desired)

After the baked eggplant has cooled enough to handle, scoop the pulp out of the skin and mix with the onions, garlic, and other ingredients. Add the yogurt and adjust the consistency to make a dip. Serve at room temperature with some *roti* or other bread.

Shredded Greens with Coconut (Mallung)

Mallung is a common condiment on the Sri Lankan table and is eaten at almost every meal. Many different plants are used to make it, including cassia, passion fruit leaves, and watercress or water spinach leaves. In the West, spinach or beet greens or even parsley can be used without interfering with the flavors of the other ingredients. Serve with rice or with any curry as a side flavor in between bites.

2 cups greens, finely shredded
2 tablespoons water
I medium onion, peeled and finely diced
2 Thai green chili peppers, diced
½ teaspoon ground turmeric
2 teaspoons Maldives fish, soaked and crushed
2 tablespoons lemon juice
I teaspoon salt
I tablespoon coconut, fresh or dried and flaked

In a saucepan, combine all of the ingredients except the coconut. Cook over medium heat for about 8–10 minutes. Add coconut and stir over low heat until the excess liquid is absorbed. Remove from heat and serve or set aside until needed.

Sauces and Spice Mixtures

This section introduces two great Sri Lankan sauces – **Tomato Sauce with Ginger and Garlic and Coconut-Fenugreek Sauce** – to flavor meat and vegetable dishes. Also ahead are three spice mixtures – **Roasted and Unroasted Sri Lankan Curry Powder** and **Sri Lankan Masala Powder** – commonly used in the cuisine of this island nation."

Tomato Sauce with Ginger and Garlic

Here is another great subcontinental tomato sauce—this one using the white vinegar introduced by the Portuguese or the rice wine brought west by the Southeast Asian or Pacific Silk Road traders as souring agents instead of the more western or southern Asian lemon or lime juice. This sauce works well with a lot of different things, but it is particularly good with vegetables such as eggplant, zucchini or other squash, and potatoes, or fish and shellfish.

I ½ cups tomato sauce
2 tablespoons grated ginger

2 teaspoons garlic, peeled and diced
1–2 teaspoons chili powder
⅓ cup granulated sugar
⅛ cup rice wine or white vinegar
1 teaspoon salt

In a medium saucepan, combine all of the ingredients and bring to a boil over medium heat. Lower heat and simmer for 10 minutes. Remove from heat and serve or set aside until needed.

Coconut-Fenugreek Sauce

This is a thinnish sauce that can serve as an accompaniment to be spooned over rice or be enjoyed more like a soup to be sipped between mouthfuls of rice and curry.

2 cups coconut milk
1 tablespoon fenugreek seeds, crushed or ground
1 large onion, finely diced
8 curry leaves
1 1-inch stick cinnamon, crushed
3 green chili peppers, diced
¼ teaspoon ground turmeric
½ teaspoon salt
2 teaspoons dried shrimps, soaked, drained, and crushed
½ cup coconut cream
2–3 tablespoons lemon or lime juice

1. In a medium saucepan, combine over low heat all ingredients except the coconut cream and the lemon or lime juice. Simmer over low to medium heat for 15–20 minutes or until the onions are cooked and softened and the mixture is thickening.

2. Stir in the coconut cream and cook to evenly heat. Then stir in lemon juice and cook for another 10 minutes until thick. Serve warm or hot.

Roasted and Unroasted Sri Lankan Curry Powders

Each ingredient of this uniquely Sri Lankan blend of spices is individually roasted before being ground into this delectable, flavorful, and indispensable spice blend. Used widely in meat and vegetable curries, this blend is a must-have for those wishing to explore the wonderful world of Sri Lankan foods. Unroasted curry powder is made from the same ingredients. Both taste best when made fresh, so make them only in small amounts.

¼ cup coriander seeds
⅛ cup cumin seeds
1 teaspoon fennel seeds
½ teaspoon cinnamon
¼ teaspoon whole cloves
¼ teaspoon cardamom seeds
3 dried curry leaves
3 dried red chilies
1 pandanus leaf, diced
1 teaspoon black peppercorns
2 teaspoons raw basmati rice

In a dry pan over low heat, roast each ingredient separately—stirring constantly. Mix all the roasted ingredients, put into a grinder, and grind to a fine powder. Store in a jar until needed.

Sri Lankan Masala Powder

This would be Sri Lanka's five-spice powder—only it has six spices—but these six form the backbone of the cuisine and show its links to Bangladeshi cuisine by its use of fennel as dominant flavor. For unroasted curry powder, simply grind and combine the ingredients without roasting

2 tablespoons cumin seeds
Seeds from 6 cardamom pods

4 coriander seeds
2 tablespoons fennel seeds
1 clove
1 1-inch stick cinnamon

Crush all ingredients separately to a fine powder and thoroughly mix them together.

Glossary of Unusual Ingredients

Most of the ingredients used in the recipes of *The Silk Road Gourmet* are available in most large, commercial grocery stores. For some of the more unusual herbs, spices, and vegetables, cooks might have to shop at a Persian, Indian, or Oriental market. For ingredients that are difficult to come by, the Internet has a host of food shopping options that range from the gourmet market at Amazon.com to specialty ethnic markets like ThaiFoods.com. I suggest making sure that you have all of the ingredients you need on hand before attempting the recipes and finding that you are short of a crucial part of the dish.

If you are going to be cooking a lot of recipes from *The Silk Road Gourmet*, I suggest starting a windowsill or backyard garden with some of the hardest to find herbs and vegetables, because nothing beats the taste of fresh. This can be done by rooting purchased herbs or by drying and planting seeds.

Sweet Basil	The dried leaves of the herb *Ocimum basilicum*, which is a member of the mint family. Imparts a sweet but spicy flavor to foods. Trade and use began in India and spread from there.
Fennel	Fennel seeds are the dried, ripened fruit of the perennial *Foeniculum vulgare*. Oval seeds form in clusters after the flowers have died and are harvested when they harden. Tall and hardy, this plant has finely divided, feathery, green foliage and golden yellow flowers. Use and trade began in the Mediterranean and spread from there.
Fenugreek	The dried leaves of this plant impart a rich, expansive but bright flavor to stews, curries, and dishes, like a cross between savory and tarragon. Used in the Caucasus, Caspian, and southwestern Asia.
Lemongrass	A fibrous light green stalk of grass 2–3 feet long that has a sweet lemon-lime flavor. Very forgiving and can be frozen until needed. Before use, I pop them in the microwave for 20 seconds and then peel the hardest fibers off, chop off the tops and bottoms, and chop or dice for the recipe. Available at Oriental markets and online at import food retailers. Use and trade originated in Malaysia and spread across Southeast Asia.
Marigold Petals	These flower petals add a soft blanket of flavor to dishes that is not unlike turmeric or saffron, without the added coloring. Used widely in Caucasian, Caspian, and central Asian dishes. Also called calendula, it is available in good tea shops or online from herb and tea ingredient retailers.
Pandanus	A long, fibrous dark green leaf that is sometimes called fragrant screwpine; chopped or ground it is used to add a mild flavor to foods that is reminiscent of vanilla. Available frozen at oriental markets. Sometimes called *Rampe* in Sri Lanka.

Hot, dried, red chili peppers	Although most cultures have their own chili peppers, many of these varieties are difficult to impossible to acquire in the West, unless you grow your own. To help remedy this, I have often called for "hot, dried, red chili peppers" to add heat to dishes. You can use any type of peppers you choose, but I used Japone peppers, because they are only moderately hot and thus easy to control when balancing flavors. Easy-to-acquire peppers such as Indian and Thai chili peppers and the "finger hots" used in Bhutan are called for by name.

SPICES

Asafetida	Asafetida is a species of *Ferula* native to Iran. It has a pungent sulfurous smell when raw, but in cooked dishes, it delivers a complex flavor, reminiscent of a mix between garlic and leeks.
Black Cardamom	The gentler cousin to standard "green" cardamom, black cardamom comes from dried fruit pods of *Amomum subulatum*. Pods are 1 inch long and brown to black. Remove seeds from pods before use and crack, crush, or grind. Trade and use began in Nepal but spread widely to India and all the way to China's Sichuan Province.
Black Cumin	Seed with a nutty, earthier flavor compared to regular cumin. Seeds are thinner and scimitar-shaped and are usually dark brown to black.
Curry Leaves	The leaves of the *Helichrysum italicum* plant lend a smoky, tangy flavor to foods. Trade and use originated in India and spread from there. Widely used in Sri Lankan cuisine.
Fenugreek	The seeds of this plant impart a slightly sour, tangy flavor to dishes when ground. Used throughout the Caucasus, Caspian, central Asia, and down into Nepal, Tibet, and Bhutan. Trade is so old it is difficult to tell where it began, although most people think that it was probably in southwestern Asia or the western Mediterranean. See also Fenugreek entry under the "Herbs" category.

Green Cardamom	Green Cardamom is the dried, unripened fruit of the plant *Elettaria cardamomum*. Enclosed in the fruit pods are tiny, brown, aromatic seeds that bring a powerful, tangy flavor to dishes. Pods are straw colored or greenish and about ¼ inch long. Before use, remove seeds from pod and crack, crush, or grind. Trade and use began in India or Sri Lanka and spread throughout Asia from there.
Nigella	These tiny black seeds are from a member of the onion family. They impart a sharp, oniony flavor to foods they are added to.
Saffron	Saffron is the dried yellow stigmas of the violet flowers of *Crocus sativus*, a member of the Iris family and is used to impart a gentle but slightly sour flavor to food along with a vibrant yellow color. Generally dissolved in a hot liquid before use and added towards the end of cooking Asian dishes. Use and trade of saffron began in southwestern Asia and spread to the rest of the world from there.
Sour Grapes	The dried powder of these grapes is used in Iranian and central Asian cooking as a souring agent and will really make one pucker. More common in the Caspian region than elsewhere, it is available at Persian markets.
Sumac	Dark red powder used widely throughout the Islamic world for flavoring and teas. It is difficult to identify the origin of its use, but it lay somewhere between the Arabian peninsula, the eastern Mediterranean, and western Asia.
Turmeric	Turmeric is the dried root of the plant *Curcuma longa* and is an essential spice used throughout Asia to add a gentle blanket of flavor to dishes that blunts the sharp edges of complex curries, stews, and pilafs. It is also used in place of saffron or to simply add a vibrant yellowy-orange color to food. It is most commonly sold as a brightly colored ground powder and is widely available in Indian and Persian markets. Roots are also available, and if you wish to grind them fresh, feel free to do so. Use and trade of turmeric is so old, it is difficult to tell exactly where it began.

Fruits

Dried Lemons and Limes	Used in Persian and modern Iranian food as souring agents, these are simply desiccated lemons and limes that are used whole with a hole poked in their side as a souring agent for stews and casseroles. Dried limes are easy to find in Persian markets, but dried lemons are not. Dried lemons can be made by simply allowing lemons to dry out over the course of several weeks in a cool dry place. Sometimes available as dried powder.
Dried Sour Plums	These are a special type of red sour plums eaten throughout the Caucasus, Caspian, and central Asia that are available in most Persian groceries and some Indian ones as well. Also available from Internet food retailers. Do not substitute; soaking regular dried plums in cider vinegar as some cooks suggest ruins the delicate balance of sweet and sour found only in the genuine fruit.
Pomegranate	Fruit of the *Punica granatum* tree used widely from the Caucasus through China. Unsweetened juice is used as a souring agent and seeds are used for both flavor and texture in dishes. Available fresh, as sweetened or unsweetened juice, paste, and syrup. Most recipes offered here use unsweetened juice. Use and trade began in Iran or central Asia and spread from there.
Sour Cherries	*Prunus acida* are cherries grown around the Caspian and Black Seas that have a distinctly acidic flavor and are used extensively as accompaniments for meats in stews and as ingredients for sauces. Available in Persian markets.

Gingelly Oil	A light sesame oil sweetened with jaggery used throughout the Indian subcontinent in addition to mustard oil.
Jaggery	Indian cane sugar formed into blocks and sold in chunks at Indian markets. Used widely throughout the Indian subcontinent.
Light Sesame Oil	See gingelly.
Maldives Fish	A type of salted and dried fish used in Sri Lankan cooking to add a mildly fishy flavor to vegetable or rice dishes. If unavailable in your area, the small, dried shrimps or prawns easily available at Oriental markets can be substituted.
Palm Sugar	Juice extracted from the coconut palm flower or aren palm is boiled and packed into molds to make sugar with a faint caramel taste. Available at Oriental markets or from online food retailers. If palm sugar is not available, substitute with jaggery or soft brown sugar.
Paneer	A southern Asian "cheese" that is crumbly and can be made sweet or sour and used as a base for kebab stuffings or as a main ingredient of a curry, in the way that tofu would be used in an eastern Asian stir fry. Available in South Asian markets.
Tamarind	The dark brown pod of the tamarind tree (*Tamarindus indica*) contains a sour fleshy pulp, which is dissolved into hot liquid to add sour flavor to dishes from Iran to Indonesia. There are many different forms of it available, from fresh pods to dried pulp and concentrate. Recipes in this book are written with tamarind concentrate in mind because it is easily available in Indian and Persian markets or from online retailers. Tamarind is African in origin, but its use in Asia centers around India. Probably brought to India by early Arab traders.

Photo Credits

Front Cover: Pomegranates and Nuts, © Gaffer | Dreamstime.com; Georgia chapter: Metekhi Monastery, © Flyergeorge | Dreamstime.com; Georgian Musician, © Maigi | Dreamstime.com; Georgian Clay Wine Bottle, © Kondor83 | Dreamstime.com; Hinkali, © Revinol | Dreamstime. com; Armenia chapter: Mountains of Armenia, © Mikle15 | Dreamstime. com"; Armenian Woman in the Field, © Avatavat | Dreamstime.com; A Dish of Matsoon Yogurt, © Haikik | Dreamstime.com; Azerbaijan chapter: Two Minaret Mosque, © Elnur | Dreamstime.com; Antique Azeri Tableware, © Marcviln | Dreamstime.com; Samovars in Baku, © Marcviln | Dreamstime.com; Iran chapter: "A Mountain Road in Western Iran, © Shanin | Dreamstime.com; Stuffed Peppers, © Dreambigphotos | Dreamstime.com; Iranian Girl Smiling, © Allein | Dreamstime.com; Iranian Girls Touring Persepolis, © Cascoly | Dreamstime.com; Afghanistan chapter: Kabul by Air, © Funnybear | Dreamstime.com; Afghan Kebabs, © Nashekrashe | Dreamstime.com; Traditional Way to Cook Samsas, © Monsteranimal | Dreamstime.com; Antique Afghan Pitchers, © Lori Martin | Dreamstime.com; Pakistan chapter: Kutwal Lake in northwest Pakistan, © Paxi | Dreamstime.com; Henna Decorations on a Girl's Hand, © Chubbywubby | Dreamstime.com; Samosas and Rice, © Thisboy | Dreamstime.com; Bangladesh chapter: A Crowd on the River, © Ryuivst | Dreamstime.com; Bangladeshi Family in a Houseboat, © Ryuivst | Dreamstime.com; Bangladeshi Boys Fishing, © Ryuivst | Dreamstime. com; India chapter: Taj Mahal, © Lieverehan... | Dreamstime.com; An Indian Vegetable Market, © Satyas | Dreamstime.com; Rajasthani Men around a Cooking Fire, © Jeremyrichards | Dreamstime.com; Sri Lanka chapter: Kosgoda Beach,© Priyanthab | Dreamstime.com beach - Sri Lanka ; Cinnamon Sticks, © Viktorfischer | Dreamstime.com; Man Serving Tea, © Paulprescott | Dreamstime.com

Index

341

345

9163729R00218

Printed in Great Britain
by Amazon.co.uk, Ltd.,
Marston Gate.